FLK2 PRACTICE ASSESSMENTS

MOCK EXAM No.1

For 2027 exams

Editor: Mark Thomas

Series editors: Amy Sixsmith and David Sixsmith

REVISE SQE

First published in 2023 by Fink Publishing Ltd
This edition published in 2026

Impression number 10 9 8 7 6 5 4 3 2 1

British Library Cataloguing in Publication Data
A catalogue record for this book is available from the British Library
ISBN: 9781807730277

This book is also available in various ebook formats.
Ebook ISBN: 9781807730291

Cover and text design by BMLD (bmld.uk)
Production and typesetting by Westchester Publishing Services UK

Fink Publishing Ltd
E-mail: hello@revise4law.co.uk
www.revise4law.co.uk

Notes from the publisher

1. This book reflects the SQE1 assessment specification (updated April 2026) applicable for assessments from 1 September 2026.

2. While Fink Publishing has made every attempt to ensure that advice on the qualification and its assessment is accurate, the official specification and associated assessment guidance materials are the only authoritative source of information and should always be referred to for definitive guidance. See the SRA website at https:// sqe.sra.org.uk. Note that the SRA may amend their assessment guidance (including the contents of the assessment specifications) at any point.

3. Fink Publishing has robust editorial processes to ensure the accuracy of the content in this publication, and every effort is made to ensure this publication is free of errors. We are, however, only human, and occasionally errors do occur. Fink Publishing is not liable for any misunderstandings that arise as a result of errors in this publication, but it is our priority to ensure that the content is accurate. If you spot an error, please do contact us at **revise4law.co.uk** so we can make sure it is corrected.

Contents

Contributors

■ THE EDITOR

Mark Thomas is a practising barrister and has taught law for several years at both undergraduate and postgraduate levels, including the Legal Practice Course. Mark has published academic textbooks in the field of criminal law and evidence and has extensive experience in writing revision-style books for law students. He is the co-author of *Revise SQE: Criminal Law*, *Revise SQE: Criminal Practice* and *Revise SQE: Oral Skills for SQE2: Advocacy* and also the editor of *Revise SQE: Ethics and Professional Conduct*. Mark acts as an MCQ adviser and reviewer for the Revise SQE series.

Mark is the author of MCQs on trusts and wills and the administration of estates, and ethics and professional conduct for this volume.

■ MCQ AUTHORS

Revise SQE would like to thank the following for their contribution of MCQs to this book:

- Criminal law and practice: James J. Ball, practising barrister, 36 Crime
- Land law: Daniel Gough, senior lecturer at Nottingham Law School, Nottingham Trent University
- Property practice: Hayley Mynard-Gates, lecturer in law at Birmingham City University
- Solicitors' accounts: Tina McKee, senior lecturer at Lancaster University.

Revise SQE would also like to thank the following for their assistance in reviewing MCQs for FLK2:

- Jonathan Haines, higher education consultant and visiting professor at Arden University
- Elliot Schatzberger, Schatz Legal Learning

■ SERIES EDITORS

Dr Amy Sixsmith is associate professor in law at the University of Sunderland and a senior fellow of Advance HE.

Dr David Sixsmith is assistant professor in law at Northumbria Law School and a senior fellow of Advance HE.

Introduction

Welcome to *FLK2 Practice Assessments*. We are proud to present this book as a companion to our *Revise SQE* series of revision guides. In this book, we aim to continue our goal of assisting you in preparing for and passing the Solicitors Qualifying Examination (SQE1).

This introductory section will explain how the book is structured, and offers practical advice on preparing for your SQE1 assessment, how to approach multiple-choice questions (MCQs) and what to expect on the day of the assessment. An assessment briefing follows, which is designed to get you into the mindset for sitting these SQE1-style MCQs.

We then present 180 SQE1-style MCQs, written by our expert team of *Revise SQE* authors. The MCQs contained within this book are drafted in the style and structure recommended by the SRA and their provider of the SQE, Kaplan. In July 2025, the Editor of this book and many of the authors of the MCQs contained herein attended a workshop organised by the SRA/Kaplan on drafting effective MCQs. We are pleased to say that the approach adopted by Revise SQE throughout its series is entirely consistent with the structure and approach recommended by the SRA/Kaplan. To the best of our skill and understanding, the MCQs contained within this book reflect the style, content and structure of the MCQs you would expect to face in the SQE1 assessments. The MCQs will be broken down into two sessions, each consisting of 90 MCQs (180 in total).

At the end of each session, we offer you the opportunity to reflect on your progress/performance. By honestly reflecting on your experience, you will be in a better position to consider whether you are ready to sit the SQE1 assessments.

You will then be provided with detailed answers to the MCQs for each session, including a summary sheet for easy cross-reference. You will be able to understand why each option was correct or incorrect. Where appropriate or relevant, the answers will refer to legal authorities assessable in SQE1, and link to our series of *Revise SQE* books and associated chapters.

At the end of this book, you are provided with some final words of advice and a list of Frequently Asked Questions (FAQs) on the SQE1 assessments.

We hope that you find this book to be a useful resource in your preparations for SQE1, and we wish you the very best of luck in your assessments.

■ THE SQE1 ASSESSMENTS

Below is a summary of the SQE1 assessments.

ASSESSMENT BREAKDOWN

The SQE consists of SQE1 and SQE2. The SQE1 assessment is broken down into two components:
- Functioning legal knowledge (FLK) 1, and
- Functioning legal knowledge (FLK) 2.

You must achieve the necessary mark in *both* FLK1 and FLK2 to pass SQE1 as a whole. If you fail either FLK1 or FLK2, you are only required to resit the assessment that you failed.

You must pass both SQE1 and SQE2 in order to apply to become a solicitor.

How the assessments are structured

Each FLK assessment for SQE1 consists of 180 single best answer MCQs (360 in total). Each question will have five possible answers, but only one answer that is considered to be correct. This correct answer will score a mark of 1 if you choose it. All other responses, including where multiple responses are recorded, will be awarded a score of 0. No negative marking is used in the SQE1 assessments (ie no marks are deducted for incorrect responses).

You will be provided with two scores as part of your assessment:
- Raw score: a mark out of 180.
- Scaled score: a mark out of 500.

The pass mark is 300. For further details on how the SQE1 assessment is marked, see 'Your Results' on page 155.

If you are undertaking an SQE-preparation course, you may be used to sitting practice assessments within a particular FLK subject matter (eg property practice). You may have, therefore, had the opportunity to revise and prepare for MCQs on a single FLK subject. However:
- The FLK2 assessment will not identify the topic or subject matter of the MCQ: that is for you to determine.
- The assessment will not group MCQs according to the FLK subject matter: all MCQs will be randomly distributed across the two sessions in FLK2.

This book also adopts this approach, to provide you with a more realistic simulation of the FLK2 assessment.

Assessment sessions

Table 1 provides a breakdown of the SQE1 assessment sessions and timings.

Table 1: SQE1 assessment sessions and timings

Assessment	Timings
FLK1 assessment day	Session 1: Answer 90 MCQs (2 hrs 33 mins) - Break for 1 hour Session 2: Answer 90 MCQs (2 hrs 33 mins)
FLK2 assessment day	Session 1: Answer 90 MCQs (2 hrs 33 mins) - Break for 1 hour Session 2: Answer 90 MCQs (2 hrs 33 mins)

Answering 90 MCQs within 2 hours 33 minutes allows *1 minute, 42 seconds per question*, under exam conditions. Of course, some questions will take more or less time to answer than others.

Please take a moment to think about that: on average, within 1 minute and 42 seconds you will have to:
- read the MCQ, including the various answers
- distil from that MCQ what the question is assessing
- work out which of the five possible answers is the correct (or 'single best') answer.

This will be an intensive assessment. You must ensure that you are properly prepared for it, in terms of your subject knowledge and also your mental resilience and time management.

THE FLK2 ASSESSMENT SPECIFICATION

This practice assessment book will prepare you for FLK2. According to the SQE1 Assessment Specification, the following will be assessed on FLK2:
- Property practice
- Wills and the administration of estates
- Solicitors' accounts

- Land law
- Trusts
- Criminal law and practice.

However, please note:
- Solicitors' accounts will be examined only in the context of conveyancing (property practice) and wills and the administration of estates.
- The principles of taxation will also be examined, but only in the context of property practice, and wills and the administration of estates for FLK2.
- Ethics and professional conduct will be examined pervasively across the assessment.

Law at the time of the assessment

The cut-off date for the law upon which candidates are examined in the SQE will be *four calendar months* prior to the date of the first assessment in an assessment window. For example, in respect of the January 2027 assessment window:
- First day of assessment window: 11 January 2027.
- Examinable law cut-off date (up to and including): 11 September 2026.

You will not be tested on the development of the law.

FLK blueprint

The Solicitors Regulation Authority (SRA) has provided a 'blueprint' for the FLK subjects, which identifies the percentage of each topic within the FLK assessment. Table 2 outlines the SRA's blueprint for **FLK2** and the approach adopted in this book regarding the number of MCQs per FLK subject.

Table 2: Blueprint of FLK2

FLK2	Potential percentage of MCQs in FLK2	Number of MCQs in this book
Property Law and Practice, including Solicitors Accounts in the context of conveyancing	14–20%	27
Land Law	14–20%	27
Wills and the Administration of Estates, including Solicitors Accounts in the context of Wills and the Administration of Estates.	14–20%	27
Trusts Law	14–20%	27
Criminal Liability	14–20%	27
Criminal Law and Practice	14–20%	27
Ethics and Professional Conduct	'pervades'*	18

* In any SQE1 sitting (FLK1 and FLK2), Ethics and Professional Conduct and money laundering questions can make *up to* 20% of the questions assessed (money laundering questions being assessed in FLK1 only).

Readers will see that the team at Revise SQE have distributed the number of MCQs in this book equally amongst each of the practice areas. We believe that allocating this number of MCQs per FLK subject in this book is the best possible approach to assist you in your SQE1 preparation because it allows you to test your knowledge of all of the FLK subject areas examinable on SQE1. However, please be aware that:
- The real FLK2 assessment may not be so balanced. It is possible that one subject area is afforded the minimum 14% of questions (approximately 25 MCQs) whilst another FLK2 subject is afforded the full 20% (36 MCQs). In fact, this imbalance can be very common in the SQE1 assessments.

- Further to this, it is possible that the SQE1 assessments focus on very specific aspects of a particular subject. For example, it is possible that an SQE1 assessment may feature a high proportion of questions simply on one very specific topic, such as taxation of business organisations. You may find that your knowledge is tested on a large number of very specific topics within each of the individual FLK subjects.
- FLK MCQs may also draw on any combination of the subject areas that may be encountered in practice (eg a dispute resolution MCQ may require an understanding of contract law and legal services). Equally, it is possible for an MCQ to combine substantive legal knowledge with an ethics and professional conduct issue (eg in criminal practice, the MCQ may seek to test your knowledge on both disclosure and an ethical issue in the same question).

You therefore cannot compartmentalise your understanding of the FLK2 subject matter; you must have a working knowledge of all FLK subjects and how they interact.

Further help from *Revise SQE*

- Our series of *Revise SQE* books covers each FLK subject.
- A *Revise SQE Checklist* is available for each FLK2 subject, which shows the SQE1 Assessment Specification in full and the corresponding *Revise SQE* books and chapters. This checklist is available at revise4law.co.uk/books/.
- A guide on the legal authorities that candidates must be able to recall or recite as part of the FLK2 assessment (eg *Saunders v Vautier* in trusts) has been produced by the team at Revise SQE and is available at revise4law.co.uk/books/table-of-legal-authorities/.
- Visit revise4law.co.uk/legal-updates/ for regular updates relating to the law assessable in SQE1. These updates identify how the law has been impacted or changed, and the assessment period relating to that update.

■ PREPARING FOR SINGLE BEST ANSWER MCQS

For SQE1 assessment, MCQs are designed to allow you to demonstrate the competence required and expected of a newly qualified solicitor (a 'day one' solicitor).

WHAT IS A SINGLE BEST ANSWER MCQ?

Single best answer MCQs are a specialised form of question, used extensively in other fields such as training medical professionals. The idea behind single best answer MCQs is that each option might look equally attractive, sharing commonalities and correct statements of law or principle, but only one option is absolutely correct (in the sense that it is the 'best' answer). Traditional MCQs usually feature distractors (other possible answers) that are implausible and therefore obviously wrong, but in a well-constructed single best answer MCQ, different options will contain some similarities and also subtle differences. Your skill will be to identify which, out of the options provided, is the single best answer.

HOW ARE SINGLE BEST ANSWER MCQS STRUCTURED?

For SQE1, single best answer MCQs will be structured as follows:

A woman is charged with battery, having thrown a rock towards another person intending to scare them. The rock hits the person in the head, causing no injury. The woman claims that she never intended that the rock hit the person, but the prosecution allege that the woman was reckless as to whether the rock would hit the other person.

The factual scenario
First, you will be provided with a factual scenario that sets the scene for the question to be asked (known as the 'stem').

Which of the following is the most accurate statement regarding the test for recklessness in relation to a battery?

A. There must have been a risk that force would be applied by the rock, and that the reasonable person would have foreseen that risk and unjustifiably taken it.
B. There must have been a risk that force would be applied by the rock, and that the woman should have foreseen that risk and unjustifiably taken it.
C. There must have been a risk that force would be applied by the rock, and that the woman must have foreseen that risk and unjustifiably taken it.
D. There must have been a risk that force would be applied by the rock, and that both the woman and the reasonable person should have foreseen that risk and unjustifiably taken it.
E. There must have been a risk that force would be applied by the rock, but there is no requirement that the risk be foreseen.

The lead in
Next, you will be provided with the question that you must find the single best answer to.

The possible answers
Finally, you will be provided with **five** possible answers. There is only one single best answer that must be chosen. The other answers, known as 'distractors', are not the 'best' answer available.

It will be beneficial to guide you through each aspect of the MCQ to further your understanding of the writing process.

The stem

The stem (ie scenario) will differ according to each MCQ and what it is seeking to test. If the MCQ is seeking simply to test a candidate's basic knowledge of the law, without application, then the stem is likely to be short. Where, however, the MCQ is seeking to have a candidate analyse a factual pattern, and apply it to the options available, the stem will be significantly longer.

In general, however, a stem should be a concise and clear introduction to the issue at hand. A well written stem should contain all material facts relevant to answering the question about to be asked (new facts should not be introduced in the lead in or the distractors). The stem should not be ambiguous or open to interpretation.

The lead in

The lead in will be a short question and can be phrased in a variety of ways. The lead in should provide the candidate with everything they need to answer the question. There should be no ambiguity or double meanings.

The length and nature of the lead in will vary dependent on the type of question being asked. These categories of MCQ are detailed in the table below.

Categories of MCQs	Explanation and example
'Knows' MCQs	To *recall* a specific answer (eg the author of X is Y)
'Shows How' MCQs	To *analyse* a fact pattern and *apply* (eg the application of X in this case is Y)
'Knows How' MCQs	To *know* the answer, and *show* the reason *why* (eg the purpose of X is Y because ...)

Most commonly, a lead in may be phrased as:

- Which of the following statements best describes ...?
- Which of the following statements best summarises ...?
- Which of the following best explains ...?

A lead in will not, however, be phrased as:
- Which of the following is true?
- What is the rule for X?
- Which one of the following is not correct?

The options
You will be provided with five possible answers and only one is correct (whether that be outright correct, or the single best).

The options will not ask a candidate to identify multiple options as being correct (eg 'A, C and D are correct; B and E are wrong'). Nor will the options feature an 'all of the above' option.

A well written MCQ will avoid vague language in the options. Words such as 'rarely', 'usually' etc should be avoided as they present too much ambiguity. On the other hand, absolute words such as 'only', 'always' and 'never' should equally be avoided because they are often obvious distractors (there rarely being a circumstance in English and Welsh law where the legal position is absolute without exception).

If written well, each option should be plausible (meaning that some candidates would choose it). Plausibility can come from drawing on faulty reasoning and common misconceptions. It may be the case that some options share identical wording save for one word (eg a change from 'may' to 'must'). You therefore need to pay close attention to the wording of the options.

To achieve that, all options will be of a fairly equal length to ensure that they are consistent with one another. It is often said that the correct answer is likely to be the longest; so the writers of the MCQs will have that in mind.

In addition, to ensure plausibility, each option is either likely to be a variation of the other, or each option will be entirely different to the others. MCQ drafters will often rely on the rule of 'Three and Two'. The idea behind this rule is that three options will be fairly similar to each other (eg starting with 'Yes'), whilst the remaining two answers will be equally similar to each other (eg starting with 'No'). If you know the answer is definitely 'Yes', that therefore removes the 'No' options immediately. If the MCQ has not adopted the rule of Three and Two, it is likely that you will be able to pick out the 'obvious' distractor.

HOW DO I TACKLE SINGLE BEST ANSWER MCQS?
No exact art exists in terms of answering single best answer MCQs; success depends on your subject knowledge and understanding of how to apply it to the question scenario. Despite this, the following tips and tricks might be helpful.

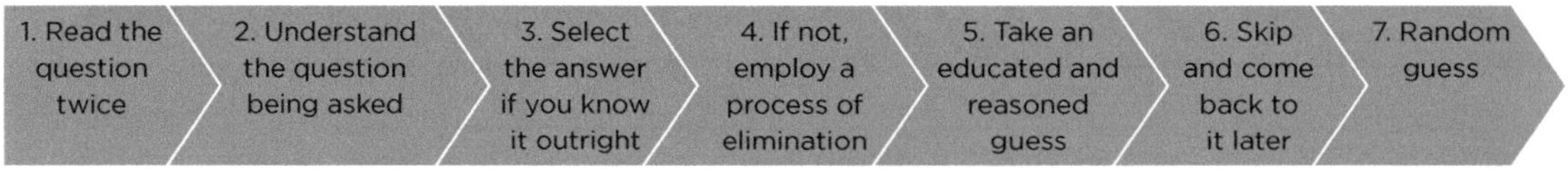

1. Read the entire question at least twice
This sounds obvious but is so often overlooked. You are advised to read the entire question once, taking in all relevant pieces of information, understanding what the question is asking you and being aware of the options available. Once you have done that, read the entire question again and this time pay careful attention to the wording that is used.
- In the factual scenario: Does it use any words that stand out? Do any words used have legal bearing? What are you told, and what are you not told?
- In the lead in: What are you being asked? Are there certain words to look out for (eg 'should', 'must', 'will', 'shall')?
- In the possible answers: What are the differences between each option? Are they substantial or subtle differences? Do any differences turn on a word or a phrase?

You should be prepared to give each question at least two viewings to mitigate any misunderstandings or oversights.

2. Understand the question being asked

It is important first that you understand what the question is asking of you. The SRA assessment specification has identified that the FLK assessments may consist of single best answer MCQs that, for example:

- require you to simply identify a correct legal principle or rule
- require you not only to identify the correct legal principle or rule, but also to apply that principle or rule to the factual scenario
- provide the correct legal principle or rule, but require you to identify how it should be properly applied and/or the outcome of that proper application.

By identifying what the question is asking you to do, you can then understand what it is testing, and how to approach the available answers. Many candidates actually find it beneficial to start with the lead in, before reading the scenario. This gives them the opportunity to understand what the scenario will likely entail. You need to decide what works best for you, so take the opportunity to try both ways.

3. Select the answer if you know it outright

You may feel as though a particular answer 'jumps out' at you, and that you are certain it is correct. It is very likely that the answer is correct. Whilst you should be confident in your answers, do not allow your confidence (and perhaps overconfidence) to rush you into making a decision. Review all of the options one final time before you move on to the next question.

4. Employ a process of elimination if you do not know the answer outright

There may be situations in which the answer is not obvious from the outset. This may be due to the close similarities between different answers. Remember, it is the 'single best answer' that you are looking for. If you keep this in mind, it will be easier to employ a process of elimination. Identify which answers you are sure are *not* correct (or not the 'best') and whittle down your options. Get rid of the distractors. Once you have only two options remaining, carefully scrutinise the wording used in both answers and look back to the question being asked. Identify what you consider to be the best answer, in light of that question. Review your answer and move on to the next question.

5. Take an educated and reasoned guess

There may be circumstances, quite commonly, in which you do not know the answer to the question. If this happens, try as hard as you can to eliminate any distractors that you are positive are incorrect, and then take an educated and reasoned guess based on the other options available. 'Always select C' will not work in this assessment; the correct answers will be randomly distributed amongst the MCQs as options A–E.

6. Skip and come back to it later

If time permits, you might think it appropriate to skip a question that you are unsure of and return to it before the end of the assessment. The assessment portal will highlight any questions that have not been answered, and you are also able to 'flag' questions for your review later on in the assessment (time permitting). If you do so, we would advise that you:

- make a note of what question you have skipped or click 'Flag for review' on your screen, and
- ensure you leave sufficient time for you to go back to that question before the end of the assessment.

The same advice applies to any question that you have answered but for which you remain unsure.

7. Random guess

As a matter of absolute last resort, being unable even to take an educated and reasoned guess, you should simply choose an answer. There is no negative marking in the SQE1 assessments, so it is better for you to select an answer with the possibility, by sheer luck, of answering it correctly than it is to leave the answer blank and have no chance of scoring a point. The advice is simple: answer all of the questions, even if you have to guess at the end.

■ ON THE DAY

The following provides a brief summary of what to expect on the day of the assessment. For further information, see the SQE section of the SRA's website (sqe.sra.org.uk).

A number of FAQs are provided at the end of this book which may assist you with some queries you have about the assessment on the day.

THE TEST CENTRE

The FLK2 assessment will take place in a Pearson VUE test centre. These test centres are located across the country.

After you book your assessments, the SRA will send you an email for each assessment day, confirming the time at which you must report to the assessment centre, the location, and duration of your assessment.

If you are late for the time specified, you will not be permitted entry into the assessment.

SECURITY CHECKS AND THE ASSESSMENT ROOM

When you arrive at the Pearson VUE test centre, you will complete registration, including an ID check (see FAQs on **page 158** for more on ID checks).

Following the security checks, you will then be seated at a computer desk, where you will be required to:

- complete a Fit to Sit declaration
- confirm that you accept the Candidate Confidentiality Policy and the Assessment Regulations.

You must not have any personal belongings with you during the assessment, including food and water. Should you require water, you must leave the assessment room (though see below for further information about unscheduled breaks).

You will be provided with an erasable whiteboard notepad and marker pen to be used only during the assessment. These must be handed in at the end of the assessment.

THE CONDUCT OF THE ASSESSMENT

You will sit the SQE1 assessments on a computer in the Pearson Vue Test Centre. The following will be displayed on each display screen that sets out a question:

- a timer - indicating the time remaining within the session
- a question counter - setting out how many questions are in the session and the number of the question you are answering (eg 8 of 90)
- a calculator icon - this can be selected to bring up the online calculator
- a flag - this can be selected to mark a question for review.

Each MCQ will also feature a tick box, allowing you to choose your answer to that particular question.

SCHEDULED AND UNSCHEDULED BREAKS

Following Session 1, you are provided with a 1-hour break (a 'scheduled break') in which you must leave the assessment room. You may retrieve personal belongings at this time.

You are advised to return after 50 minutes to engage with security checks and be seated at your desk.

You are permitted to leave the assessment room during the assessment (an 'unscheduled break') in order to use the toilet, have a drink of water, eat or obtain medication. However, the assessment timer is not stopped for unscheduled breaks (ie the timer continues to run).

You are not permitted to leave the assessment room for any other reason, or to leave the assessment early.

COMPLETING THE ASSESSMENT

Once you have completed your assessment, you will be escorted from the assessment room and will be permitted to leave the test centre. Please see **page 155** for information relating to your results.

■ HOW BEST TO USE THIS BOOK

FLK2 Practice Assessments have been designed, in so far as is possible, to replicate the assessments you will be faced with for SQE1. In particular, the structure and style of the MCQs in this book attempt to replicate the display screen in the real examination.

ACHIEVING A SIMILAR EXPERIENCE

You should try to sit these MCQs in a timed, closed-book fashion, to replicate the experience of the real SQE1 assessments. To assist with ensuring a similar experience, you are advised to have the following equipment with you:

- Pencil/pen - you could complete the assessment in pencil, so that you can look over your responses should time permit and change your answers.
- Paper - if you do not wish to write in the book.
- Calculator - a mobile phone will be sufficient for this.
- Stopwatch - on a mobile phone will be sufficient; but do not use your mobile for any other purpose. (You are *not* permitted to take a mobile phone or any materials other than those provided to you by the test centre into the real SQE1 assessment.)

We have listed the possible answers to each question A-E in this book, to assist you when it comes to reviewing the answers at the end of the assessment. This approach is also beneficial if you do not wish to write in the book. Note however that the SQE1 MCQs will not feature letters at the start of each answer.

Make use of the 'Flag for review' on each question too: circle the flag if you need to come back to a particular MCQ at a later time.

ANSWERS

Once you have answered all 180 MCQs, you will have the opportunity to review the answers to those MCQs, including an explanation as to why a particular answer was the single best choice.

Please do not be tempted to read ahead and view the answers before or during the assessment. Treat this simulated SQE-style assessment as if you were sitting the real SQE1 assessment.

FURTHER PREPARATION

The SQE website offers candidates the opportunity to experience a simulation of the exam, including sample questions and a realistic user interface. Make sure that you visit the SQE section of the SRA website to try out the exam functionality.

■ FINAL WORDS

We hope that you find this practice assessment book helpful in your preparation for SQE1. Before attempting any MCQs, please read through the Assessment briefing on the opposite page.

Assessment briefing

■ CANDIDATE INSTRUCTIONS

FLK2 Practice Assessments will follow, as far as possible, the format in which the SQE1 MCQs will be presented on a computer screen. On the test day, candidates are given guidance about the test via a tutorial, which is viewed before the test begins. This does not form part of your testing time.

Before you attempt the MCQs that follow, you are strongly advised to do the following:

- Choose a date and time when you are able to dedicate the time required to complete this simulated SQE-style assessment.
- Find a suitably quiet location to complete the practice assessment.

This book has been specifically written to replicate the SQE1 assessment environment that you will face at the test centre. Use this opportunity to prepare for that element of the assessment as well.

■ ASSESSMENT DURATION

Before you sit Session 1, please ensure that you have set a timer for 2 hours, 33 minutes. This is the maximum amount of time you will have to answer the questions.

■ PERMITTED MATERIALS

SQE1 is a closed-book assessment. This means that you are not permitted any materials during the assessment. We advise that you do not use any resources or materials whilst attempting this practice assessment. This will help to give you a more accurate indication of whether you are ready to sit SQE1.

In the SQE1 assessment, your display screen will feature a calculator. You are, therefore, permitted the use of a calculator in this practice assessment.

■ READY TO BEGIN?

Once you are ready to commence Session 1 of *FLK2 Practice Assessments*, click the start button on your timer and begin (questions on the next page).

Session 1 questions

Q1 of 90

Flag for review

A man wishes to create a trust over his holiday cottage during his lifetime for the benefit of his daughter. The man speaks to his intended trustee over the telephone and states, 'I want you to hold my holiday cottage on trust for my daughter'. The intended trustee agrees. The man has only one cottage.

Which of the following most accurately describes the position of the trust?

A. The trust has not been validly declared, and it is not enforceable. ☐

B. The trust has been validly declared, but it is not enforceable. ☐

C. The trust has not been validly declared, but it is still enforceable with the consent of the trustee. ☐

D. The trust has been validly declared, and it is enforceable. ☐

E. The trust has not been validly declared, but it is still enforceable with by order of the court. ☐

Q2 of 90 Flag for review

A solicitor is dealing with the purchase of a property with unregistered title on behalf of a client. Title documentation has identified that the seller originally purchased the property with his wife. The seller and his wife originally held both the legal and equitable title as joint tenants. The seller's wife is now deceased.

Which of the following statements best explains the assumptions on the sale of land by the seller as a survivor of the joint tenancy?

A. The solicitor can assume that the seller and his wife remained joint tenants of the legal and equitable title, and therefore no further investigation is necessary. ☐

B. The solicitor can assume that the seller and his wife severed the joint tenancy before her death and were tenants in common of the legal title at the time of her death, and therefore no further investigation is necessary. ☐

C. The solicitor can assume that the seller and his wife severed the joint tenancy before her death and were tenants in common of the equitable title at the time of her death, and therefore no further investigation is necessary. ☐

D. The solicitor can assume that there was no severance of the equitable title if, following investigation, there is a statement in the transfer to the client that the seller is the sole beneficial owner. ☐

E. The solicitor can assume that there was no severance of the legal title if, following investigation, there is a statement in the transfer to the client that the seller is the sole beneficial owner. ☐

Q3 of 90 Flag for review

A solicitor is acting for a corporate client in the purchase of a commercial property. The corporate client pays £200,000 to the solicitor as a deposit for the purchase.

What are the accounting entries required to record the receipt of the £200,000 deposit?

A. £200,000 credit entry in the client ledger business account and £200,000 debit entry in the cash sheet business account. ☐

B. £200,000 credit entry in the client ledger client account and £200,000 credit entry in the cash sheet client account. ☐

C. £200,000 debit entry in the client ledger client account and £200,000 credit entry in the cash sheet client account. ☐

D. £200,000 debit entry in the client ledger business account and £200,000 credit entry in the cash sheet business account. ☐

E. £200,000 credit entry in the client ledger client account and £200,000 debit entry in the cash sheet client account. ☐

Q4 of 90 Flag for review

A client has recently completed the purchase of a property. Following completion, they realised that the previous owner had removed a free-standing kitchen island from the property. The island was constructed from the same materials as the built-in kitchen with matching doors. The kitchen island was constructed on wheels to allow the item to be moved around the property.

Which of the following best explains how the solicitor should advise the client when considering the kitchen island?

A. Whether the client will be able to claim for the kitchen island will depend solely on the extent to which it was physically annexed to the land. If the island was attached to the land, it would be classed as a fixture and included in the sale of the land. ☐

B. The client will be able to demand the return of the kitchen island if they can show that it was part of the overall design scheme of the property. This would indicate that the purpose of annexation was to provide a permanent benefit to the land and it would therefore be classed as a fixture. ☐

C. The client will only be able to demand the return of the kitchen island if they can show that it was included in the contract of sale. ☐

D. As the kitchen island is on wheels and therefore moveable, it is not capable of being a fixture. The client is therefore not able to make a claim for the kitchen island. ☐

E. Whether the client will be able to claim for the kitchen island will depend on whether the seller has received legal advice on the objects. If the seller was told they could remove the kitchen island, even incorrectly, the client will not be able to claim for the item. ☐

Q5 of 90 Flag for review

A solicitor acts on behalf of a client purchasing a leasehold property in a new build development. There were originally 20 flats in the development when construction began. The landlord then altered 5 of the ground-floor flats, and there are now 25 flats in total. The client is concerned about how the additional costs will be calculated and wants certainty in relation to the service charge apportionments.

Which of the following provisions would be the most appropriate to alleviate the client's concerns?

A. The client's liability for service charge is calculated as a 20th proportion of the landlord's expenditure on maintenance of the building. ☐

B. The client's liability for service charge is calculated as a 'reasonable proportion' of the landlord's expenditure on maintenance of the building. ☐

C. The client's liability for service charge is calculated as a 25th proportion of the landlord's expenditure on maintenance of the building. ☐

D. The client's liability for service charge is calculated as a fixed proportion of the landlord's expenditure on maintenance of the building, dependent upon the square footage of each flat within it. ☐

E. The client's liability for service charge is calculated as a 'fair and reasonable proportion' of the landlord's expenditure on maintenance of the building. ☐

Q6 of 90 Flag for review

A solicitor is prosecuting a case in the magistrates' court. The defendant has pleaded guilty to theft of food from a supermarket and the matter is listed for sentence. The defendant is unrepresented. The police inform the solicitor that the defendant only stole the food as they could not afford to purchase the food, having recently lost their job. The solicitor considers this fact to be mitigation in the defendant's case and also holds the view that it was incorrect to prosecute the defendant.

Which of the following best describes what the solicitor should do in their submissions on sentencing?

A. The solicitor should make no reference to the mitigation or to their personal views on the case. ☐

B. The solicitor should mention the mitigation but should make no mention of their personal views of the case. ☐

C. The solicitor should make no reference to the mitigation but should mention their personal views on the case. ☐

D. The solicitor should make reference to both the mitigation and their personal views on the case. ☐

E. The solicitor should withdraw from the case. ☐

Q7 of 90 Flag for review

A woman is shopping in her local supermarket. As she is queuing at the checkout, an elderly man forcefully pushes past her to pay for his cigarettes. This angers the woman, who confronts the man and tells him to go to the back of the queue. The elderly man is rude to the woman; he takes an item out of her basket and throws it on the floor. The woman pushes the man, who falls back into another person. The elderly man is scared, but not harmed physically.

Which of the following best describes the most appropriate offence that the woman is likely to have committed?

A. The woman has committed a technical assault as she intentionally caused the elderly man to apprehend immediate unlawful violence. As the elderly man was not physically injured, the woman is not guilty of a battery. ☐

B. The woman has committed a battery as she intentionally applied unlawful force to the elderly man through pushing him. The fact that the man was not physically injured is irrelevant for an offence of battery to be made out. ☐

C. The woman has committed a technical assault as she was reckless in causing the elderly man to apprehend immediate unlawful violence. The fact that the man was not physically injured is irrelevant for an offence of battery to be made out. ☐

D. The woman has committed a battery as she recklessly applied unlawful force to the elderly man by pushing him. The fact that the man was not physically injured is irrelevant for an offence of battery to be made out. ☐

E. The woman has committed a battery as she intentionally caused the elderly man to apprehend immediate unlawful violence. The fact that the man was not physically injured is irrelevant for an offence of battery to be made out. ☐

Q8 of 90 Flag for review

A solicitor is advising a client on the enforceability of a lease recently signed on a property for one year. The agreement allows the client to take possession of the property immediately for a market rent of £500 per calendar month. The agreement is headed: 'Deed of Lease', but neither party had their signatures on that agreement witnessed.

Which of the following best describes how the solicitor should explain the agreement that the client has in the property?

A. As the agreement is created by a deed, it will be binding on both of the parties. The client will have a legal lease over the property for one year. ☐

B. As the agreement is signed but not witnessed, the client will only have an equitable lease. This will only be enforceable if the client has complied with their obligations under the agreement. ☐

C. As the agreement is signed but not witnessed, there is not a valid lease agreement. As a result, the agreement will not be binding on either of the parties. ☐

D. As the agreement is for less than three years and takes possession at a market rent, the client will have signed a legal lease even though there was no signature on the deed. ☐

E. As the agreement is signed but not witnessed, it will be a valid contract. As a result, the agreement will be legally binding on both parties. ☐

Q9 of 90 Flag for review

A man executes a valid will prior to his death. Clause 3 in the will reads:
'I GIVE £300,000 to my trustees and executors for the education of the children of my employees.'

The man was the managing director of an independent factory that employed over one thousand people.

Has the man created a valid charitable trust?

A. Yes, as the trust is for the benefit of over one thousand people, it will have a sufficient public benefit. ☐

B. No, as there is a personal nexus between the man and those who will benefit from the trust. ☐

C. Yes, as the trust is for an exclusively charitable purpose. ☐

D. No, as the purpose of the trust is not sufficiently charitable. ☐

E. Yes, as the trust is for the education of the children of employees, and not the employees themselves. ☐

Q10 of 90 Flag for review

A solicitor has drafted a commercial lease for one of her corporate clients. The solicitor has just submitted her bill for £500 + VAT (standard rate) to the client.

What accounting entries are required on the client ledger to record the submission of the bill?

A. There are no entries in the client ledger on submission of the bill. ☐
B. Credit client ledger business account with £600 for profit costs and VAT. ☐
C. Debit client ledger business account with £500 for profit costs and £100 for VAT. ☐
D. Credit client ledger client account with £500 for profit costs. ☐
E. Debit client ledger business account with £500 for profit costs. ☐

Q11 of 90 Flag for review

A client is seeking advice on their rights in a house that she and her partner moved into 10 years ago. Since moving in, the client has paid half of the mortgage payments every month and has shared all household bills with her partner. The legal title is solely in the client's partner's name. The relationship has recently broken down and the client's partner is seeking to sell the house. The client is concerned she will not receive any money from the sale of the house.

Which of the following best explains the rights of the client in respect of the sale of the house?

A. As the client is not listed on the legal title, she will have no interest in the house. Her partner will hold both the legal and equitable title and, if the house is sold, the client will not be entitled to benefit from the sale. ☐
B. The client would only have an interest in the house if she could demonstrate that there were express discussions with her partner that she had an interest in the house. Without this, the client would have no interest in the house and could not benefit from the sale. ☐
C. As the client contributed directly to the purchase price, she would be entitled to an equitable share of the house. As she has contributed equally to the house to be a family home, the client would be entitled to 50% of the equitable title. ☐
D. Although the client is not listed on the legal title, she will still hold 50% of the legal title as she contributed to the purchase price. As a result, if the house were to be sold, the proceeds of sale would be split equally between the client and her partner. ☐
E. As the client is not listed on the legal title, they will not have any legal ownership of the house. However, as the client was in a long-term relationship with the legal owner, she will be entitled to the whole of the equitable ownership. ☐

Q12 of 90 Flag for review

A client is seeking legal advice after being prevented from using an access track across neighbouring land. The previous owner of the neighbouring land granted the client an easement over the property in perpetuity. The agreement was validly executed by both parties, but neither party sought to have the easement registered with HM Land Registry. The new owner of the neighbouring land is claiming he is not bound by the easement.

Which of the following most accurately represents whether the client has a valid easement over the access track?

A. As the agreement has been validly executed, the client could seek to protect their right by registering a restriction against the property. This would ensure that the client has a legal right to use the access track.

B. As the agreement has been validly executed, the client will have created a legal easement. This means that the client has a legal right to use the access track in accordance with the agreement with the previous owner.

C. Although the agreement has been validly executed, as it has not been registered the client will have a binding equitable easement. The client will only have an equitable right to use the access track if they have complied with all of their lease obligations.

D. As the agreement has been validly executed but not registered, the client must show that they used the easement within the previous 12 months to take effect in law. If the client can demonstrate this, they will have a legal right to use the access track.

E. Although the agreement has been validly executed, as it has not been registered it will not take effect in law. The client will not have a valid legal easement and has no legal right to use the access track.

Q13 of 90 Flag for review

A solicitor appears in the Crown Court representing a defendant charged with theft in a contested bail application. The court list identifies that the judge hearing the case will be HHJ Brown KC.

How should the solicitor address HHJ Brown KC in court?

A. Judge.

B. Your worship.

C. My lord / My lady.

D. Your honour.

E. Master.

Q14 of 90 Flag for review

A solicitor acts for a defendant who has been charged with burglary. The defendant pleads not guilty to the charge. In preparation for the trial, the solicitor advises the defendant that he should give evidence in his own defence. The defendant in an interview with the solicitor raises the defence of alibi. The defendant is nervous and does not want to give evidence in the case. The defendant says that he will not give evidence.

Which of the following best describes the advice the solicitor should give to the defendant?

A. The final decision of whether to give evidence must be taken by the defendant himself. ☐

B. If the defendant continues to refuse to give evidence, the solicitor cannot represent him and must withdraw from the case. ☐

C. If the defendant does not give evidence in the case, he must change his plea to guilty. ☐

D. If the defendant does not give evidence in the case, adverse inferences will automatically be drawn against him by the jury. ☐

E. The solicitor will make the decision of whether to give evidence for the defendant. ☐

Q15 of 90 Flag for review

A solicitor is advising a client who is in the process of negotiating a 10-year lease on a commercial property. The client has agreed terms with the landlord and is seeking advice on the formalities required to ensure the lease is fully protected.

Which of the following best explains the steps that the client would need to follow in order to ensure the lease is fully protected?

A. As the lease is for more than seven years, this would be a registrable estate. The client would need to ensure that the lease has been created by a validly executed deed and registered as its own registered title in order to take effect in law. ☐

B. As the lease is for more than three years, this would be automatically overriding. So long as the lease is created by a validly executed deed, the lease will be legally binding. ☐

C. As the lease is for more than three years, the client will only need to be in actual occupation in order for it to take effect in law. The lease will take effect in law once the client takes occupation. ☐

D. As the lease is for more than seven years, it must be registered as a minor interest to be equitable. The client should ensure that the lease is made by a valid contract and registered against the Charges Register of the landlord's title. ☐

E. As the lease is for more than three years, it should be registered as a restriction to be protected. The client should ensure that the lease is made by a valid deed and then protected by a Restriction on the Proprietorship Register of the landlord's title. ☐

Q16 of 90 Flag for review

A man is charged with theft, contrary to s 1 of the Theft Act 1968. The man is alleged to have stolen a watch from a jewellery shop, valued at £250. The man makes his first appearance in the magistrates' court.

Which of the following best describes the legal position of the man's case?

A. Given the value of the watch, the offence is triable only summarily. The court will ask the man to indicate a plea on the charge. The man must be given the option of electing trial in the Crown Court. ☐

B. Given the value of the watch, the offence is triable either way. The court will take the man's plea and, if the man pleads not guilty, proceed to allocation. ☐

C. Given the value of the watch, the offence is triable only summarily. The court will take the man's plea on the charge. The man cannot elect trial in the Crown Court. ☐

D. Given the value of the watch, the offence is triable only on indictment. The court will send the man to the Crown Court forthwith without any indication of plea. ☐

E. Given the value of the watch, the offence is triable either way. The court will ask the man to indicate a plea on the charge and, if the man indicates a not guilty plea, proceed to allocation. ☐

Q17 of 90 Flag for review

A solicitor is instructed by the executors in a probate matter. Once the estate accounts have been approved by the executors, the solicitor pays the £365,000 remainder of the estate to the sole beneficiary.

What accounting entries are required to record the payment to the sole beneficiary?

A. Credit £365,000 cash sheet business account and debit £365,000 profit costs ledger. ☐

B. Debit £365,000 cash sheet client account and credit £365,000 client ledger client account. ☐

C. Debit £365,000 cash sheet business account and credit £365,000 client ledger business account. ☐

D. Credit £365,000 cash sheet client account and debit £365,000 client ledger client account. ☐

E. Credit £365,000 cash sheet client account and debit £365,000 client ledger business account. ☐

Q18 of 90 Flag for review

A solicitor is representing a client in a dispute over the validity of a will. During proceedings, the solicitor discovers that the client has lied about a factual piece of evidence relevant to the dispute.

Which of the following best describes what the solicitor should do in this situation?

A. The solicitor must withdraw from acting for the client immediately.

B. The solicitor must correct the factual position regardless of whether the client consents.

C. The solicitor must keep the information confidential and continue to represent the client.

D. The solicitor must seek the client's consent to correct the factual position. If the client refuses to give consent, the solicitor must withdraw from acting for the client.

E. The solicitor must report the matter to the courts and the police.

Q19 of 90 Flag for review

A man executed a will when he was of sound mind and signed it in the presence of two witnesses, who also signed the will. However, later in life, the man had a disagreement with his son and made a codicil to his will that revoked a gift of his property to his son. The codicil is signed only by the man and not by any witnesses. The man died and the son is contesting the validity of the codicil.

Is the codicil valid?

A. Yes, as the codicil was made by the man when he was of sound mind.

B. No, as the codicil was not signed by any witness.

C. Yes, as the codicil was made by the man himself.

D. No, as the codicil revoked the gift of property made in the original will.

E. Yes, as the codicil was made after the man's argument with his son and consequently reflects his true intention.

Q20 of 90 Flag for review

A solicitor is representing a woman in the sale of commercial property. The woman becomes dissatisfied with the solicitor's performance. The woman has complained to the solicitor's firm, but is also dissatisfied with the outcome of that complaint. The firm's complaint procedure has been exhausted and the woman requests information on how she may escalate her complaint.

Which of the following best describes what the woman should be told by the solicitor?

A. If the woman remains dissatisfied with the outcome of her complaint, she can report the solicitor to the Solicitors Regulation Authority. This information must be provided in writing.

B. If the woman remains dissatisfied with the outcome of her complaint, she can file a complaint with the legal ombudsman. This information must be provided in writing.

C. If the woman remains dissatisfied with the outcome of her complaint, she can file a complaint with a more senior member of the firm. This information may be provided orally or in writing.

D. If the woman remains dissatisfied with the outcome of her complaint, it can be reconsidered by the firm at a cost to the woman. This information may be provided orally or in writing.

E. If the woman remains dissatisfied with the outcome of her complaint, there is no further action that can be taken. This information must be provided in writing.

Q21 of 90 Flag for review

A woman wishes to dispose of her 500 ordinary shares in a limited private company to her son. The woman declares a trust over the shares in favour of her son, with her brother acting as trustee. The woman executes a valid stock transfer form and posts it to her brother, along with the share certificate. A day later, the woman dies in a car accident. The brother had not sent the paperwork to the company before the woman died.

Is the trust over the shares to the woman's son valid?

A. No, as legal title to the shares has not been validly vested in the brother due to the lack of registration prior to the woman's death.

B. Yes, as the woman did everything in her power to effect the transfer of the shares, which will be recognised in equity as a valid transfer.

C. No, as the woman has not done everything necessary to effect the transfer and equity will not perfect an imperfect gift.

D. Yes, as it would be unconscionable for the trust not to be recognised as valid.

E. No, as the son is intended to receive the shares as a volunteer and equity will not assist a volunteer.

Q22 of 90 Flag for review

A client has recently completed the purchase of an unregistered property which she intends to use as both her home and a veterinary surgery, and is seeking advice from a solicitor. The client's new neighbour has recently confronted her and said that there is a restrictive covenant on the property preventing it from being used for anything other than residential purposes. The neighbour shows the client a deed from the previous owner of the land, which is dated 2002, but the signatures are not witnessed.

Which of the following best represents the legal position of the client?

A. The freehold covenant is a legal right as it has been made by deed. However, it is only binding on the client if a land charge has been registered. ☐

B. The freehold covenant is only ever capable of being an equitable right. As the land is unregistered, the client will be bound under the doctrine of notice. ☐

C. The freehold covenant is an equitable right only as the signatures were not witnessed. The freehold covenant is not binding on future purchasers, therefore the client will not be bound by this and can operate their veterinary surgery from the property. ☐

D. The freehold covenant is a legal right as it has been made by deed and so it will be binding on the client. The client will not be able to operate their veterinary surgery from the property. ☐

E. The freehold covenant is only ever capable of being an equitable right. However, it is only binding on the client if a land charge has been registered. ☐

Q23 of 90 Flag for review

A woman is arrested following a fight in a nightclub. The woman is charged with assault occasioning actual bodily harm, contrary to s 47 of the Offences Against the Person Act 1861. The woman is alleged to have attacked another patron, whom she did not previously know. The woman repeatedly tells the police that she was acting in self-defence. The woman has a full-time job and a stable residence. The woman has had several previous convictions in recent years for fights in nightclubs, including the commission of an offence whilst the woman was previously on bail. At her first appearance in the magistrates' court, the prosecution is considering objecting to the grant of bail. The prosecutor forms the view that, if convicted, there is a real prospect of immediate imprisonment due to the woman's previous convictions.

Which of the following is the most likely approach that the prosecution will take when objecting to the grant of bail?

A. That there are substantial grounds for believing that the woman will fail to surrender. ☐

B. That there are substantial grounds for believing that the woman will fail to surrender and commit further offences. ☐

C. That there are substantial grounds for believing that the woman will commit further offences. ☐

D. That there are substantial grounds for believing that the woman will interfere with witnesses. ☐

E. That there are substantial grounds for believing that the woman will fail to surrender and interfere with witnesses. ☐

Q24 of 90 Flag for review

A solicitor has recently completed the assent of a registered leasehold property. The client is the personal representative of the deceased owner, and the stamp duty certificate has been obtained. Registration with HM Land Registry remains outstanding.

Which of the following documents must be sent to HM Land Registry to register the personal representative as the owner of the land?

A. Forms AP1 and TP1, and an SDLT5 certificate.

B. Forms AP1 and AS1, and an SDLT5 certificate.

C. Forms FR1 and TP1, and an SDLT5 certificate.

D. Forms AP1 and AS1, a lease and an SDLT5 certificate.

E. Forms FR1 and AS1, a lease and an SDLT5 certificate.

Q25 of 90 Flag for review

A client has recently approached a solicitor seeking advice about recovering their interest in a property. The client contributed £100,000 towards the purchase of a property with his son and daughter-in-law. The son and daughter-in-law borrowed £200,000 from a bank secured by a mortgage over the property for the remainder of the purchase price, and the property was registered in the name of the son and daughter-in-law only. The son and daughter-in-law have since failed to keep up with the mortgage payments.

Which of the following best explains the client's current interest in the land?

A. As the legal estate was owned by a sole owner, the client's interest must have been registered as a minor interest to be valid. If it has not been registered, then it will not be binding on the mortgage company and the client will have no interest in the land.

B. As the bank has paid the mortgage monies to two trustees, their interest has automatically overreached any unknown third-party interest in the land. The client no longer has any interest in the land.

C. As the client has a right in the land, so long as they were in actual occupation of the property at the time of the mortgage, their interest will be binding on the bank. If the client was not in actual occupation of the property, then it will only be binding if the bank did not make reasonable enquiries.

D. As the bank has paid the mortgage monies to two trustees, although this does not automatically overreach the interest of the client, the bank will not be bound if it can demonstrate that it made reasonable enquiries.

E. As the client's right is a legal right, it continues to bind all future owners regardless of whether it has been registered or whether the bank was aware of the same. The bank will therefore be bound by the third-party interest.

Q26 of 90 Flag for review

A man is in a busy city centre in the early hours in the morning with his friends. The man and his friends have all been out drinking and have just left a nightclub. As the man and his friends are walking down the street, some other men approach them. There is an altercation that results in a brawl between some of the individuals. At this time, the man is standing at the side watching the brawl, before he brandishes a knife and stabs one of the men twice. The man then walks off into the crowd of people watching the commotion. The man is arrested and charged with an offence contrary to s 18 of the Offences Against the Person Act (OAPA) 1861.

Which of the following best describes the statutory elements of an offence under s 18 OAPA 1861 as applied to this case?

A. An offence under s 18 OAPA 1861 is where the man unlawfully and maliciously wounds or causes grievous bodily harm with intent to cause grievous bodily harm. ☐

B. An offence under s 18 OAPA 1861 is where the man intentionally or recklessly wounds or causes grievous bodily harm. ☐

C. An offence under s 18 OAPA 1861 is where the man unlawfully and maliciously wounds or inflicts any grievous bodily harm. ☐

D. An offence under s 18 OAPA 1861 is where the man unlawfully or maliciously wounds or causes grievous bodily harm with intent to wound. ☐

E. An offence under s 18 OAPA 1861 is where the man unlawfully or maliciously wounds or causes grievous bodily harm with intent to resist or prevent the lawful apprehension or detainer of any person. ☐

Q27 of 90 Flag for review

A man is charged with murder, following the death of his wife. The man has no previous convictions and is brought before the magistrates' court.

Which of the following best describes how the man's bail application will be dealt with?

A. The magistrates' court must send the man forthwith to the Crown Court where a Crown Court judge will determine the question of bail, and must be satisfied that there is no significant risk that the man, if released, would commit an offence that would be likely to cause physical or mental injury to another person. ☐

B. The magistrates' court must send the man forthwith to the Crown Court where a Crown Court judge will determine the question of bail in the ordinary way. ☐

C. The magistrates' court may determine the question of bail for themselves, but must be satisfied that there is no significant risk that the man, if released, would commit an offence that would be likely to cause physical or mental injury to another person. ☐

D. The magistrates' court may determine the question of bail for themselves but will only grant bail where there are exceptional circumstances justifying the grant of bail. ☐

E. The magistrates' court must send the man forthwith to the Crown Court where a Crown Court judge will determine the question of bail, and will only grant bail where there are exceptional circumstances justifying the grant of bail. ☐

Q28 of 90 Flag for review

A man owns shares in a private limited company. He owns 500 ordinary shares and 200 preference shares. The man writes a letter to his son where he says: 'I am creating a trust in your favour; your sister will hold 100 of my shares in your favour until you are old enough to be trusted with them.' The man only owns shares in one company. The man dies a few days later. He had executed a will a number of years ago where he disposed of all shares to a charity.

Which of the following is the most likely position?

A. The trust is certain because the man only holds shares in one company. ☐
B. The trust is uncertain because the son had to make a choice as to whether the trust property was 100 ordinary shares or 100 preference shares before the man died. ☐
C. The trust is certain because intangible property does not require segregation. ☐
D. The trust is uncertain because the man did not identify whether the trust property was 100 ordinary shares or 100 preference shares. ☐
E. The trust is certain because the son will be able to choose whether the trust property is 100 ordinary shares or 100 preference shares. ☐

Q29 of 90 Flag for review

A trainee solicitor is tasked with representing a client in a complex property dispute case. As part of the preparation for the case, the trainee solicitor discovers some information that could harm their client's position in the litigation.

Which of the following best describes the action that the solicitor should take?

A. The solicitor should keep the information confidential and not disclose it to the client. ☐
B. The solicitor should disclose the information to the client, having first obtained the consent of the senior partner to do so. ☐
C. The solicitor should disclose the information to the client immediately, and take instructions from the client about how to proceed. ☐
D. The solicitor should keep the information confidential, but should inform their supervisor at the firm of the information. ☐
E. The solicitor should disclose the information to the opposing party immediately as part of pre-trial disclosure. ☐

Q30 of 90

Flag for review

An elderly and physically infirm woman has recently died. Shortly before her death, the woman changed her will to leave the majority of her estate to her neighbour. Prior to her death, the woman relied heavily on the neighbour to manage her daily life. The woman's will previously left the entirety of her estate to her children. The woman's children are unhappy with the provisions of the new will and are concerned that the neighbour exerted pressure on the woman to change her will.

Which of the following best describes whether the woman's children can challenge the new will?

A. The woman's children can challenge the new will if they can prove that they have suffered injustice because of the new will.

B. The woman's children cannot challenge the new will as evidence of undue influence does not affect the validity of the new will.

C. The woman's children can challenge the new will if they can prove that the neighbour exercised undue influence over the woman when she made the new will.

D. The woman's children cannot challenge the new will as there is no evidence to support the fact that the neighbour has exercised undue influence over the woman when she made the new will.

E. The woman's children can challenge the new will if they can prove that the woman did not fully understand the consequences of her actions when she made the new will.

Q31 of 90

Flag for review

A woman creates a trust over her estate for the benefit of a number of family members. The trust is written as follows: 'My estate is to be held on trust for the benefit of my twin sons for their lives, then to my daughter, once she turns 25 years of age, then to my sister absolutely.' The twin sons are 18 years of age, the daughter is 12 years old and the sister is 50 years old.

Which of the following best describes the beneficial interest of each person?

A. The twin sons have concurrent interests vested in possession; the daughter has a contingent interest vested in remainder; the sister has an interest vested in remainder.

B. The twin sons have concurrent contingent interests vested in possession; the daughter has an interest vested in possession; the sister has an absolute interest.

C. The twin sons have consecutive interests vested in possession; the daughter has a contingent interest vested in possession; the sister has an interest vested in remainder.

D. The twin sons have concurrent interests vested in remainder; the daughter has an interest vested in remainder; the sister has a contingent interest vested in remainder.

E. The twin sons have consecutive interests vested in remainder; the daughter has a concurrent contingent interest in possession; the sister has an interest vested in remainder.

Q32 of 90 Flag for review

A client is in the process of purchasing an unregistered house. As part of the process, she has employed a solicitor to conduct a search of the Land Charges Register which reveals a Class D(iii) entry.

What advice should the solicitor provide to the client about this entry?

A. The property is subject to an equitable lease. As the client has knowledge of the charge, she will be subject to the lease and will be unable to use the property. ☐

B. The property is subject to a legal easement. If the client purchases the property, they will be bound by the easement as they will be deemed to have notice of it. ☐

C. The property is subject to a restrictive covenant. As it has been revealed on the Land Charges Register, it will be automatically binding and will be enforceable against the client. ☐

D. The property is subject to Home Rights. The previous owner's spouse has a legal right to occupy the property. ☐

E. The property is subject to an equitable easement. This will be binding as an equitable interest as it is registered on the Land Charges Register. ☐

Q33 of 90 Flag for review

A man is a trustee over a large family trust worth £2 million. The man has recently misappropriated £60,000 from the trust. The man purchases a diamond ring for £50,000 for his wife and presents it to her as a present. The wife regularly receives gifts from her husband and is unsuspecting of the source of the funds. The man is being chased for repayments on a loan to the amount of £10,000. The man forwards the remaining £10,000 misappropriated from the trust to an agent for the loan company, who then forwards the money to the company. The agent is a friend of the man and knows that the money has been misappropriated from the trust. The loans company has no knowledge of the source of the funds. The beneficiaries discover this fact and seek advice on whether they can recover the money from these parties.

Which of the following most accurately describes the liability of each party?

A. The man is personally liable for breach of trust; the wife and agent are both l iable for knowing receipt of trust property; the loans company is not liable for its receipt of money. ☐

B. The man is personally liable for breach of trust; the wife is not liable for her receipt of the diamond ring; the agent and loans company are liable for knowing receipt of trust property. ☐

C. The man is personally liable for breach of trust; the wife is liable for knowing receipt of trust property; the agent is liable for dishonest assistance in the breach of trust; the loans company is not liable for its receipt of money. ☐

D. The man is personally liable for breach of trust; the wife is liable for dishonest assistance in the breach of trust; the agent and loans company are liable for knowing receipt of trust property. ☐

E. The man is personally liable for breach of trust; the wife is not liable for her receipt of the diamond ring; the agent is liable for dishonest assistance in the breach of trust; the loans company is not liable for its receipt of money. ☐

Q34 of 90

Flag for review

A solicitor is acting for a client business in a complex property purchase transaction, and has sent the client an interim bill for £1,000 + VAT (standard rate). The client sends £3,000 by bank transfer to cover payment of the interim bill and to include monies on account of future costs and disbursements.

Into which account(s) should the £3,000 payment be paid or transferred?

A. The payment of £3,000 is client money so it should all be paid into the client account. ☐

B. The payment of £3,000 is business money so it should all be paid into the business account. ☐

C. The payment of £3,000 constitutes £1,200 business money and £1,800 client money. It is best for the £3,000 payment to go into the client account and then for the solicitor to transfer the £1,200 business money into the firm's business account. ☐

D. The payment of £1,000 constitutes £1,200 client money and £1,800 business money. It is best for the £3,000 payment to go into the business account, and then for the solicitor to transfer the £1,200 client money into the general client account. ☐

E. The payment of £3,000 must be paid into the client account initially, and then the solicitor should transfer an estimated £200 for future disbursements into the business account. ☐

Q35 of 90

Flag for review

A woman acts as trustee for a family trust. The trust property consists of shares in a private limited company. The trust owns 25% of all shares in that company. The woman has recently been appointed as director of that company and receives a director's fee for her role. The company's constitution provides for the appointment of directors by way of a simple majority. The woman did not seek the beneficiaries' consent to become a director. The minutes of the meeting show the voting patterns of the remaining shareholders:

- Shareholder A: 10% – Voted in favour of the woman's appointment.
- Shareholder B: 10% – Voted against the woman's appointment.
- Shareholder C: 30% – Voted in favour of the woman's appointment.
- Shareholder D: 15% – Voted in favour of the woman's appointment.
- Shareholder E: 10% – Voted against the woman's appointment.
- Woman: 25% – Voted in favour of her own appointment.

Which of the following best describes the situation regarding the director's fee obtained by the woman?

A. The woman is in breach of her fiduciary duty as she has been appointed as a director by virtue of her position as a trustee. ☐

B. The woman is not in breach of her fiduciary duty as she has not been appointed as a director by virtue of her position as a trustee. ☐

C. The woman is in breach of her fiduciary duty as she has voted in favour of her appointment; the woman should have abstained in the vote. ☐

D. The woman is not in breach of her fiduciary duty as she is entitled to make additional profits by virtue of her position as a trustee. ☐

E. The woman is in breach of her fiduciary duty as she failed to seek the consent of the beneficiaries to her appointment as a director. ☐

Q36 of 90 Flag for review

A solicitor has recently exchanged contracts on behalf of a client selling a registered freehold property. The client has provided an executed transfer which has been witnessed by a family member.

Which of the following statements best represents what the solicitor should do next in accordance with best practice?

A. The solicitor should forward the current executed transfer on completion to the buyer's solicitor. ☐

B. The solicitor should contact the client and advise that they send via email an amended executed transfer with an independent witness present to ensure that completion is not delayed. ☐

C. The solicitor should contact the buyer's solicitor to confirm that they will accept the executed transfer to ensure that completion is not delayed. ☐

D. The solicitor should arrange for the client to attend the firm's office or send the transfer out by post again to be witnessed by an independent witness. ☐

E. The solicitor should sign the transfer as a second witness alongside the family member's details to ensure that completion is not delayed. ☐

Q37 of 90 Flag for review

A client has recently completed the process of purchasing an unregistered house. The previous owner's brother is now claiming to have a beneficial interest in the property under a trust.

Which of the following best explains the circumstances in which the client will have purchased the house free from any beneficial interests under a trust?

A. The client would need to have been a bona fide volunteer of a legal estate or interest. ☐

B. The client would need to have been a purchaser for value of a legal or equitable estate or interest. ☐

C. The client would need to have been a purchaser for value of a legal estate or interest. ☐

D. The client would need to have been a bona fide purchaser for value of a legal estate. ☐

E. The client would need to have been a bona fide volunteer of a legal or equitable estate or interest. ☐

Q38 of 90 Flag for review

A solicitor acts on behalf of a client purchasing a plot of unregistered freehold land which is part of a much larger plot of land. The client and the seller have exchanged contracts. The contract requires the client to enter into new restrictive covenants, and the solicitor is now required to draft the transfer of part in respect of the plot of land being purchased separately from the remainder of the land.

Which of the following best explains where the solicitor would include restrictive covenants created for the benefit of the land retained by the seller?

A. Box 12, under the heading 'Rights granted for the benefit of the property'. ☐
B. Box 12, under the heading 'Rights reserved for the benefit of other land'. ☐
C. Box 12, under the heading 'Restrictive covenants by the transferee'. ☐
D. Box 12, under the heading 'Restrictive covenants by the transferor'. ☐
E. Box 12, under the heading 'Other'. ☐

Q39 of 90 Flag for review

A client is in the process of purchasing a registered property consisting of a house with an attached field. During visits to the house, the client has noticed a caravan belonging to a neighbouring property owner stored in a corner of the field. The neighbouring property owner produced a deed from 2020 granting them the right to store the caravan for 30 years.

What will the buyer's solicitor look for when examining the title of the property to establish whether there is a legal right of storage?

A. An entry referring to an easement on the Property Register. ☐
B. A registered charge over the property on the Charges Register. ☐
C. An entry referring to an easement on the Charges Register. ☐
D. A restriction against the property on the Proprietorship Register. ☐
E. An entry referring to a restrictive covenant in the Charges Register. ☐

Q40 of 90

Flag for review

A woman is charged with inflicting grievous bodily harm, contrary to s 20 of the Offences Against the Person Act (OAPA) 1861, after throwing a plant pot at a man, who was her ex-partner. The plant pot missed the man's head but caught his index finger on his right hand; an x-ray later showed that his finger was broken as a result. The woman argues that she did not intend for the plant pot to hit him; the prosecution argues that she was reckless in throwing the plant pot.

Which of the following best describes the test for recklessness in relation to an offence contrary to s 20 OAPA 1861?

A. There must have been a risk of causing some harm in throwing the plant pot, and the woman must have appreciated the risk of some harm occurring but continued without justification. ☐

B. There must have been a risk of causing serious harm in throwing the plant pot, and the woman must have appreciated the risk of serious harm occurring but continued without justification. ☐

C. There must have been a risk of causing serious harm in throwing the plant pot, and any reasonable person would have foreseen the risk of serious harm occurring, and that the woman continued without justification. ☐

D. There must have been a risk of causing some harm in throwing the plant pot, and both the woman and the reasonable person would have foreseen the risk of some harm occurring but the woman continued without justification. ☐

E. There must have been a risk of causing some harm in throwing the plant pot, and the woman ought to have appreciated the risk of some harm occurring, but continued without justification. ☐

Q41 of 90

Flag for review

A solicitor acts on behalf of a client purchasing a new build leasehold property. The client is purchasing the property with the assistance of a mortgage and the solicitor has also received instructions to act on behalf of the lender. The developers of the new build have provided the client with an incentive of £2,500 reduction in the purchase price. A few weeks later the solicitor receives the client's mortgage offer, which does not make any reference to the reduction.

Which of the following statements best represents what the solicitor should do next?

A. The solicitor should telephone the lender and report the incentive immediately. ☐

B. The solicitor should firstly advise the client that the lender needs to be informed and secondly obtain the client's consent to do so. ☐

C. The solicitor should send a copy of the incentive disclosure form to the lender immediately. ☐

D. The solicitor should advise the client that they can no longer act for the lender as there is a conflict of interest. ☐

E. The solicitor should advise the client that they cannot accept the incentive. ☐

Q42 of 90 Flag for review

A man is charged and convicted of assault by beating in the magistrates' court. The man wishes to appeal against his conviction on the basis that he disagrees with the factual findings of the magistrates' court. The man makes no complaint regarding the law.

Which of the following represents the best course of action the man should take?

A. The man should appeal from the magistrates' court to the Crown Court by way of case stated. ☐

B. The man should appeal from the magistrates' court to the High Court for a complete rehearing of the case. ☐

C. The man should appeal from the magistrates' court to the High Court by way of case stated. ☐

D. The man should appeal from the magistrates' court to the Crown Court for a complete rehearing of the case. ☐

E. The man should appeal from the magistrates' court to the High Court by way of judicial review. ☐

Q43 of 90 Flag for review

A woman gets into an argument in a pub with a man over a game of football. The argument escalates and becomes violent. More people become involved, and the argument turns into a brawl. The woman, in a hurry, picks up a glass beer bottle and hits the man on the head. The man suffers only a concussion and bruising.

Which of the following statements best describes the likely offence the woman may be charged with?

A. Common assault. ☐

B. Assault by beating. ☐

C. An offence contrary to s 18 of the Offences Against the Person Act 1861. ☐

D. An offence contrary to s 20 of the Offences Against the Person Act 1861. ☐

E. An offence contrary to s 47 of the Offences Against the Person Act 1861. ☐

Q44 of 90 Flag for review

A client has recently completed the purchase of a registered property. The client completed the conveyancing without the use of legal assistance and did not conduct enquiries as to whether anyone else had an interest in the property. The partner of the seller of the property claims that they have an interest in the property under a trust of land. The partner paid half of the purchase price and was living in the property at the time of sale, but admits that they never sought to protect their interest.

Which of the following best explains whether the partner's purported trust of land will be binding on the client?

A. The partner's trust of land cannot be binding as it would need to have been protected by a restriction on the Proprietorship Register. ☐
B. The partner's trust of land is binding - it is automatically overriding as a home right. ☐
C. The partner's trust of land will only be binding if their occupation of the property would have been obvious on a reasonably careful inspection of the land. ☐
D. The partner's trust of land is not binding as it would need to have been protected by a notice on the Charges Register. ☐
E. The partner's trust of land will not be binding if their occupation of the property would have been obvious on a reasonably careful inspection of the land. ☐

Q45 of 90 Flag for review

A solicitor was instructed by a client to set up a discretionary trust. On completion of the matter, the solicitor charges the client £1,500 + VAT (standard rate) in accordance with their original quotation. However, the client has asked that the bill is abated due to delays in drafting the trust documentation. The solicitor agrees to reduce the bill to £1,200 + VAT accordingly.

What accounting entries are required to record the reduction in the bill?

A. Credit client ledger business account with £1,200 and debit cash sheet business account with £1,200. ☐
B. Credit client ledger business account with £300 for profit costs and £60 for VAT, debit profit costs ledger with £300 and debit HMRC-VAT ledger with £60. ☐
C. Credit client ledger business account with £1,200 for profit costs and £240 for VAT, debit profit costs ledger with £1,200 and debit HMRC-VAT ledger with £240. ☐
D. Credit client ledger client account with £1,440 and debit cash sheet client account with £1,440. ☐
E. Credit cash sheet business account with £1,200 profit costs and £240 VAT, debit profit costs ledger with £1,200 and debit HMRC-VAT ledger with £240. ☐

Q46 of 90

Flag for review

A settlor creates a trust in favour of his four children for their life. Each child is under the age of 18. The settlor appoints four trustees to manage the trust fund. The first trustee is a qualified professional hairdresser who has run a successful business for 20 years, the second trustee is a care worker with a degree in nursing, the third trustee is a practising solicitor with experience managing trusts who is not paid for their services, the fourth trustee is an accountant who is paid for their services.

Which of the following best describes the duty of care owed by each trustee?

A. All four trustees are subject to the ordinary duty to act with such care and skill as is reasonable in the circumstances as none of them are professional trustees. ☐

B. The first and second trustee are subject to the ordinary duty to act with such care and skill as is reasonable in the circumstances; the third and fourth trustee will be subject to an elevated standard of care due to their skills and experience relevant to the management of a trust. ☐

C. The first, second, and third trustee are subject to the ordinary duty to act with such care and skill as is reasonable in the circumstances as they are not being paid for their services; the fourth trustee will be subject to an elevated standard of care as they are being paid for their services. ☐

D. The first and second trustee are subject to the ordinary duty to act with such care and skill as is reasonable in the circumstances; the third trustee will be subject to an elevated standard of care due to their skills and experience relevant to the management of a trust; the fourth trustee will be subject to an elevated standard of care as they are being paid for their services. ☐

E. All four trustees are subject to an elevated standard of care due to their professional qualifications. ☐

Q47 of 90

Flag for review

A woman, who is wearing a balaclava, approaches a man as he is leaving his house and demands that the man's car keys are handed over immediately. Initially, the man refuses. The woman then reveals a plastic gun which looks real and points it at the man, demanding that he gives her the keys now. The man, in panic, hands over the keys and the woman takes his car. The man calls the police who later arrest the woman.

Which of the following statements best describes the use of force element for an offence contrary to s 8 of the Theft Act (TA) 1968?

A. For an offence contrary to s 8 TA 1968 to be made out, the defendant must use force in order to steal but before the time of the stealing. ☐

B. For an offence contrary to s 8 TA 1968 to be made out, force or the fear of force must be used in order to steal either before or at the time of stealing. ☐

C. For an offence contrary to s 8 TA 1968 to be made out, force or the fear of force must be used in order to steal either at the time or after the time of stealing. ☐

D. For an offence contrary to s 8 TA 1968 to be made out, fear of force must be used in order to steal either before or at the time of stealing. ☐

E. For an offence contrary to s 8 TA 1968 to be made out, the defendant must use force in order to steal either before or at the time of stealing. ☐

Q48 of 90

Flag for review

A solicitor is visiting a man at court who has been charged with theft, contrary to s 1 of the Theft Act 1968. The man is accused of stealing a silver bracelet that belonged to one of his neighbours after he found it in a bush on his street. Due to a concealed engraving on the back, the bracelet was identified as belonging to the man's neighbour. The man has been previously advised to plead guilty but tells the solicitor that he thought the bracelet was his. The man has brought photographs to show that he had a bracelet that was almost identical and explains that he lost his bracelet several weeks prior. The solicitor is now considering the law and the best advice to give to the man.

Which of the following statements best describes the relevant law and the best course of action the solicitor should take?

A. The man does not have a defence. The fact that the man genuinely thought the bracelet was his is irrelevant as the bracelet was later identified as belonging to the man's neighbour. The solicitor should advise the man to plead guilty. ☐

B. The man does not have a defence. The fact that the man genuinely thought the bracelet was his is insufficient. He needed to take all reasonable steps to ascertain who the true owner was and has failed to do so. The solicitor should advise the man to plead guilty. ☐

C. The man may have a defence. The fact that the man thought the bracelet was his may amount to a defence, providing that the belief was genuinely held. The solicitor should advise the man that on what has been discussed, the man may have a defence and should plead not guilty. ☐

D. The man may have a defence. The fact that the man thought the bracelet was his may amount to a defence, providing that the belief was reasonably held. The solicitor should advise the man that on what has been discussed, the man may have a defence and should plead not guilty. ☐

E. The man does not have a defence. The fact that the man thought the bracelet was his is irrelevant and does not negate the fact that the bracelet belonged to his neighbour. The solicitor should advise that man that there is no defence, but the explanation which the man has given is mitigation. The solicitor should advise the man to plead guilty. ☐

Q49 of 90 Flag for review

During his lifetime, a man intends to create a trust for the benefit of his children. The trust consists of shares in a private company. The man asks his friends, a husband and wife, to act as trustees. The husband and wife agree. Separate to the trust, the man also executes a will where he leaves the entirety of his estate to a local charity. The man chooses the husband to act as executor and trustee of the will. The husband agrees. The man dies before he is able to complete the transfer of the shares to the husband and wife. The man is predeceased by the husband on the previous day. The court appoints the wife as administrator of the man's estate. Both the man's children and the charity are claiming an interest in the private company shares.

Do the man's children or the charity have the better claim to the private company shares?

A. The children have the better claim because the man created a valid express *inter vivos* trust in their favour.

B. The charity has the better claim because the trust was improperly constituted.

C. The children have the better claim because the man did everything in his power to complete the transfer, and the transfer is recognised in equity as complete.

D. The charity has the better claim because the husband died before the man, and the husband was the intended executor and trustee of the man's estate.

E. The children have the better claim because the wife has been appointed as the administrator of the man's estate.

Q50 of 90 Flag for review

A solicitor has been appointed as a deputy by the Court of Protection to look after the finances of a woman who lost the mental capacity to manage her own affairs as a result of serious head injuries arising from a cycling accident. The solicitor will shortly receive £450,000 compensation from the accident to hold on behalf of the woman.

Is the compensation money deemed to be client money, and should the solicitor pay it into a client account?

A. The compensation money is client money and must be paid into a client account.

B. The compensation money is client money but there is an exception in the Solicitors Regulation Authority Accounts Rules that permits the solicitor to withhold it from a client account. This allows the solicitor to pay it into, for example, a separate deputyship bank account, to comply with the requirements of their deputyship role.

C. The compensation money is client money and must be paid into a third-party managed account.

D. The compensation money is not client money and must be paid into the firm's business account.

E. The compensation money is not client money so the solicitor can pay it into a separate account, for example, a deputyship bank account.

Q51 of 90 Flag for review

A man appears in the Crown Court on a charge of assault occasioning actual bodily harm, contrary to s 47 of the Offences Against the Person Act 1861. The prosecution case is that the man punched his wife several times and kicked her when she fell to the floor. The man pleads guilty but claims in mitigation that he only punched his wife once and did not kick her at all.

Which of the following best describes the approach that the judge should take in the sentencing hearing?

A. The judge should either hold a Newton hearing or sentence on the basis of the man's version of events. ☐

B. The judge should sentence on the basis of the man's version of events, unless the judge is satisfied beyond reasonable doubt that the prosecution's version is correct. ☐

C. The judge should sentence on the basis of the prosecution's version of events, unless the judge is satisfied beyond reasonable doubt that the man's version is correct. ☐

D. The judge should advise the man that because the man does not accept the prosecution's version of events, his plea is equivocal. The man should then be given the opportunity to enter a not guilty plea. ☐

E. The judge should either hold a Newton hearing or sentence on the basis of the prosecution's version of events. ☐

Q52 of 90 Flag for review

A testator executed a will where they appointed a man and woman as executors. After the testator's death, the man seeks to renounce his appointment as executor.

Which of the following best describes the effect of the man's renunciation of appointment as executor?

A. The woman automatically becomes the sole executor of the will. ☐

B. The testator's will becomes invalid due to the absence of an executor. ☐

C. The courts will appoint a public trustee as the executor of the will. ☐

D. The will must be rewritten to appoint a new executor. ☐

E. The woman must also renounce her appointment as executor and name alternative executors. ☐

Q53 of 90 Flag for review

A man is charged with theft, contrary to s 1 of the Theft Act 1968. The man consents to trial in the magistrates' court and is convicted following summary trial. The magistrates' court sentences the man to a community order with a 240-hour unpaid work requirement. The man wishes to appeal to the Crown Court against that sentence.

Which of the following best describes the powers of the Crown Court should the appeal against sentence fail?

A. If the appeal fails, the Crown Court cannot increase the sentence imposed by the magistrates' court in any circumstance.

B. If the appeal fails, the Crown Court can increase the sentence, but only by increasing the number of hours of the unpaid work requirement to the maximum of 300 hours.

C. If the appeal fails, the Crown Court can substitute any sentence that it could have passed had the man been convicted following a trial on indictment.

D. If the appeal fails, the Crown Court cannot increase the sentence imposed by the magistrates' court unless satisfied that there are exceptional reasons justifying the increase.

E. If the appeal fails, the Crown Court can substitute any sentence that was available to the magistrates' court at the time of the original sentencing.

Q54 of 90 Flag for review

Two men are carrying out construction work on a jewellery shop whilst it is open and trading. The men are permitted on the shop floor, the back office and, only when accompanied by a member of staff, the secure stock room. Throughout the day, one of the men notices that the secure stock room was open and knowing that a member of staff was not with him, he enters and takes an expensive designer watch. This is captured on CCTV and the man is arrested and charged with burglary contrary to s 9(1)(b) of the Theft Act 1968. In conference at his first hearing in the magistrates' court, the solicitor is advising the man on the law relating to burglary.

Which of the following best describes the advice which the solicitor should give to the man on the relevant law?

A. The man should deny that he committed burglary as he was not a trespasser. The man had permission to be on the site and to go into the secure stock room. The man should offer a plea to a charge of theft.

B. The man should deny that he committed burglary as he was not a trespasser. The man thought that he had permission to enter the secure stock room and entered under such mistake. The man should offer a plea to a charge of theft.

C. The man should accept that he committed burglary as he was a trespasser. The man went beyond the permissions which he was granted as he knew a member of staff needed to accompany him to the secure stock room. The man should plead guilty.

D. The man should accept that he committed burglary as he was a trespasser. The event was captured on CCTV and the evidence of guilt is compelling. The fact that the man had permission to be on the site is irrelevant as the man did not have permission to take the watch. The man should plead guilty.

E. The man should deny that he committed burglary as he was not a trespasser. The man had permission to be on site, and the requirement that he was accompanied by a staff member to the stock room did not preclude him from entering. Permission to enter was therefore implicit. The man should offer a plea to a charge of theft.

Q55 of 90 Flag for review

Four siblings inherited a property as express beneficial joint tenants. The eldest sibling has recently died, and in their validly executed will they have disposed of their share of the property to their wife. The wife is now claiming to have co-ownership of the property.

Which of the following best describes whether the wife will have co-ownership of the property?

A. The wife will not have co-ownership of the property as she did not gain an interest at the same time as the four siblings, and therefore does not have unity of time. ☐

B. The wife will not have co-ownership of the property as the eldest sibling's share of the property was held as a joint tenancy, and the eldest sibling's interest will pass to the remaining joint tenants. ☐

C. The wife will have co-ownership of the property as the eldest sibling's share of the property was severed by the will to a tenancy in common, and therefore passes to the wife as his next of kin. ☐

D. The wife will not have co-ownership of the property as the eldest sibling's share of the property was held as a joint tenancy and could only have been severed by a written contract. ☐

E. The wife will have co-ownership of the property as the eldest sibling held their share as a tenancy in common, and this automatically passes to the wife as their next of kin. ☐

Q56 of 90 Flag for review

A solicitor acts on behalf of a client who is purchasing a residential property. Contracts have been exchanged but time was not made of the essence. Completion was due yesterday, but the seller's solicitors advised that the seller could not complete due to being in hospital. In addition, the client advised the solicitor that they did not have the full completion monies available due to a bank error, had found a cheaper property and wanted to withdraw from the purchase.

Which of the following statements provides the best advice to the client?

A. The client can seek contractual compensation for the total delay to completion. ☐

B. The client will need to send a notice to complete to be entitled to contractual compensation for the total delay to completion. ☐

C. The client can immediately rescind the contract and claim for contractual compensation for the total delay to completion. ☐

D. The client can immediately rescind the contract and proceed with the new purchase but will forfeit any contractual compensation due. ☐

E. The client can rescind the contract but will not be able to claim for contractual compensation unless they have evidence that the seller is well enough to complete. ☐

Q57 of 90

Flag for review

A solicitor takes over a file for a residential sale transaction from a colleague. The solicitor finds that the net proceeds of sale (£210,000) have been held in a separate designated deposit client account for just over 12 months. The file note reveals that the client's instructions are to hold the sale proceeds on deposit so that they can be used to finance future overseas expenses of the client as and when they arise. There has been no contact with the client over this period.

What action, if any, should the solicitor take with respect to the money held in the separate designated deposit client account (SDDCA)?

A. The solicitor should retain the money in the SDDCA and wait until they receive further instructions from the client. ☐

B. The solicitor should contact the client to seek instructions and, in the meantime, retain the money in the SDDCA, including any interest earned on the account. ☐

C. The solicitor should transfer the money from the SDDCA into the firm's business account immediately, including any interest earned, whilst awaiting further instructions from the client. ☐

D. The solicitor should pay the client the balance of all monies in the SDDCA immediately, including any interest earned on the account. ☐

E. The solicitor should transfer the money to the Law Society on the basis that the firm has not heard from the client for a period of over 12 months. ☐

Q58 of 90

Flag for review

Three sisters purchased a house together 10 years ago for the purpose of occupation. The house was conveyed to them as express beneficial joint-tenants in equity. The youngest sister recently vacated the house and declared her intention to sever her share of the house. The youngest sister sent a letter by registered post to the other two sisters stating that she wished to sever immediately. The letter was lost in the mail and never arrived at the property.

Which of the following best describes whether the severance has been effective?

A. The severance will be effective. So long as the letter is sent by registered post, and is not returned to the sender, it will be deemed to have been delivered. ☐

B. The severance will be effective. So long as the letter is sent by registered post and addressed to the last known abode of the sisters, it will be deemed to have been delivered. ☐

C. The severance will not be effective. The letter, sent by registered post, must be shown to have been left at the last known abode of the sisters in order for it to be deemed to have been delivered. ☐

D. The severance will not be effective. The letter, sent by registered post, must be shown to have been read by the sisters in order for it to be deemed to be delivered. ☐

E. The severance will be effective. So long as the letter is addressed to all of the remaining co-owners and contains words of immediate severance, the delivery is inconsequential. ☐

Q59 of 90 Flag for review

A solicitor acts on behalf of a client who is purchasing a property that was converted into a single dwelling house last year. The client is concerned about potential breaches of planning control and the repercussions that could ensue.

Which of the following would be the best advice for the solicitor to provide to the client?

A. As the conversion falls into the category of operational development, the solicitor should advise the client that enforcement action must be taken within 10 years where substantial completion took place on or after 25 April 2024. ☐

B. As the conversion falls into the category of operational development, the solicitor should advise the client that enforcement action must be taken within four years where substantial completion took place on or after 25 April 2024. ☐

C. As the conversion falls into the category of operational development, the solicitor should advise the client that enforcement action must be taken within four years. ☐

D. As the conversion falls into the category of material change of use of a building, the solicitor should advise the client that enforcement action must be taken within 10 years where the change of use took place on or after 25 April 2024. ☐

E. As the conversion falls into the category of material change of use of a building, the solicitor should advise the client that enforcement action must be taken within four years of substantial completion of the development. ☐

Q60 of 90 Flag for review

A woman is preparing to commit burglary of an elderly person's dwelling. The woman takes a bladed article with her in the event that she needs to defend herself. The woman arrives at the dwelling, gains entry as a trespasser and steals some valuable items of jewellery. The elderly person is not at the dwelling, but a neighbour sees the woman enter the dwelling and calls the police. The woman is arrested at the scene and the bladed article is found on the woman after being searched. The woman insists that she did not use the bladed article at all. Prosecutors are now considering a charge of aggravated burglary, contrary to s 10 of the Theft Act 1968.

Which of the following most accurately reflects the legal situation?

A. The woman can be guilty of aggravated burglary as she had a weapon with her at the time of entry to the dwelling. ☐

B. The woman cannot be guilty of aggravated burglary as she did not use the weapon when the alleged burglary was committed. ☐

C. The woman can be guilty of aggravated burglary as she intended to use the weapon during the course of committing the burglary. ☐

D. The woman cannot be guilty of aggravated burglary as she only intended to use the weapon in self-defence. ☐

E. The woman cannot be guilty of aggravated burglary as a bladed article is not a weapon for the purposes of this offence. ☐

Q61 of 90 Flag for review

A trustee holds a lease of the profits of a market for an infant beneficiary, alongside their co-trustee. When the lease was approaching its expiry, the trustee sought to renew the lease for the beneficiary. The landlord refused to renew the lease on the basis that they would not be able to enforce any covenants against the infant beneficiary. The trustee obtains the consent of their co-trustee to take the lease for themselves. Using their own funds, the trustee takes the lease on their own behalf and makes profits from the market. The trustee uses the trust money saved from the attempted renewal for the trust to make other investments, which proves profitable.

Which of the following best describes the legal position of the trustee?

A. The trustee has not breached their fiduciary duty to avoid unauthorised profits as the landlord never intended to renew the lease for the infant beneficiary.

B. The trustee has breached their fiduciary duty to avoid unauthorised profits as they used their position as trustee to renew the lease in their own favour.

C. The trustee has not breached their fiduciary duty to avoid unauthorised profits as the trustee has obtained the consent of their co-trustee to renew the lease for themselves.

D. The trustee has breached their fiduciary duty to avoid unauthorised profits as they have not acted in good faith.

E. The trustee has not breached their fiduciary duty to avoid unauthorised profits as the renewal of the lease is for the benefit of the trust.

Q62 of 90 Flag for review

A client (aged 17) is charged with burglary, contrary to s 9 of the Theft Act 1968. The client is jointly charged with a man (aged 22). At the plea before venue, both the client and the man plead not guilty to the offence. During allocation, the magistrates' court accept jurisdiction and the man consents to summary trial.

Which of the following best describes how the client's case will be dealt with?

A. The client is an adult and must therefore be tried in the adult magistrates' court.

B. The client is a youth and must therefore be tried in the youth court.

C. The client is a youth but, as they are jointly charged with the man, the youth must be tried in the adult magistrates' court.

D. The client is a youth and as they are jointly charged with the man, the youth may be tried in the magistrates' court or be remitted to the youth court.

E. The client is an adult but may be tried in either the adult magistrates' court or the youth court.

Q63 of 90

Flag for review

A solicitor acts for a client in the sale of their home. The buyer's solicitor undertakes to transfer the proceeds of sale on the completion date. Accordingly, the solicitor authorises payment of sufficient funds to redeem the client's mortgage on the same date. Later that day, the solicitor receives an urgent call from the buyer's solicitor to warn them that the transfer of the purchase monies has failed unexpectedly, and that it cannot be processed until the next day at the earliest.

Which of the following best describes what action the solicitor should take immediately?

A. The solicitor should contact the client's mortgage lender to ask for an immediate return of the mortgage redemption monies. ☐

B. There is no need for the solicitor to take any action as the proceeds of sale will be received by the next day. ☐

C. The solicitor should wait until the next day to see whether the proceeds of sale are received. If not, the solicitor must transfer money from the firm's business account into the client account temporarily whilst they await the receipt. ☐

D. The client ledger now has a debit balance in the client account, so the solicitor must transfer sufficient business money into the client account temporarily until proceeds from the sale are received. This must be done immediately. ☐

E. The solicitor should report the buyer's solicitor to the Solicitors Regulation Authority for failing to comply with an undertaking. ☐

Q64 of 90

Flag for review

Two clients have recently purchased a property together for a family home. Client One contributed 75% of the purchase price and Client Two contributed 25%. There was no statement as to how the property was to be held.

Which of the following most accurately explains how the equitable title is held between the two clients?

A. The clients will hold the equitable title as joint tenants. This is because there is clear unity of possession, interest, title and time. ☐

B. The clients will hold the equitable title as tenants in common. This is because they did not contribute equally to the purchase price and must have intended to hold their shares separately. ☐

C. The clients will hold the equitable title as joint tenants. This is because equity always follows the law, and the legal title can only ever be held as a joint tenancy. ☐

D. The clients will hold the equitable title as tenants in common. This is because there must be an express declaration of trust in order for there to be a joint tenancy. ☐

E. The clients will hold the equitable title as joint tenants. This is because unequal contributions are insufficient to rebut the presumption that equity follows the law, and the legal title is always held as a joint tenancy. ☐

Q65 of 90 Flag for review

A solicitor acts on behalf of a client who is purchasing a leasehold flat with the assistance of a mortgage. Upon investigating the lease, the solicitor has identified that two of the covenants are too restrictive of its use and could be problematic for the client.

Which of the following best explains what the solicitor should do next?

A. The solicitor should seek to renegotiate the terms of the lease with the seller of the flat. ☐

B. The solicitor should seek a variation of the lease with the current landlord of the flat. ☐

C. The solicitor should seek an agreement from the original landlord of the flat that the client will not be bound by the two covenants. ☐

D. The solicitor should suggest that the client withdraw from the transaction immediately. ☐

E. The solicitor should suggest that the client seek approval from their lender, and once obtained proceed with the purchase immediately. ☐

Q66 of 90 Flag for review

A client has approached a solicitor for some advice in relation to capital gains tax (CGT). The client has informed the solicitor that they own two investment properties in one part of the UK, but their main residence is in another part of the UK. The client is considering whether they should sell one of their investment properties, which has been rented out since they bought it. The client has asked the solicitor to advise them in relation to the principal private dwelling exemption.

Which of the following statements provides the best advice for the client?

A. The client can elect to use the CGT principal private dwelling exemption on the sale of their investment property. ☐

B. The only residence eligible for CGT principal private dwelling exemption would be the main residence in which the client lives. ☐

C. The client can elect to use the CGT principal private dwelling exemption if their property or surrounding grounds are two hectares or more. ☐

D. The main residence would not be eligible for CGT principal private dwelling exemption because the client owns investment properties. ☐

E. The client can choose to elect either their main residence or investment property on which to use the CGT principal private dwelling exemption. ☐

Q67 of 90 Flag for review

A newly qualified solicitor has been instructed by a woman who has been involved in a legal dispute for a number of years. The dispute relates to a breach of trust allegedly committed by the woman. The woman had previously instructed another solicitor from the same law firm where the newly qualified solicitor is working. The other solicitor recently left the firm, resulting in the woman instructing the newly qualified solicitor. The newly qualified solicitor has access to the previous solicitor's notes, containing confidential information about the woman's case which may be advantageous in her case.

Which of the following best describes the action that the newly qualified solicitor should take?

A. The newly qualified solicitor should use the information without disclosing that they have access to the previous solicitor's notes as it would be advantageous to the woman.

B. The newly qualified solicitor should return the previous solicitor's notes without looking at them and proceed with the woman's case, irrespective of whether the information is advantageous to the woman's case.

C. The newly qualified solicitor should read the previous solicitor's notes and, dependent on the view they take about how advantageous the information is, use the information without first seeking the woman's consent.

D. The newly qualified solicitor should destroy the previous solicitor's notes and proceed with the woman's case.

E. The newly qualified solicitor should inform the woman that they have access to the previous solicitor's notes and seek the woman's consent before using the information.

Q68 of 90 Flag for review

Three clients purchased a property together for use as a holiday home. The sale included an express declaration that the property would be held as beneficial joint tenants in equity. Client One has subsequently mortgaged their share of the property to a bank and has failed to keep up with the repayments. Client Two has recently moved into the property with their newborn baby. Client Three visits the property regularly as a holiday home. The bank has sought an order for possession.

Which of the following is the most likely approach that the court will take when considering s 15 of the Trusts of Land and Appointment of Trustees Act 1996?

A. The court will only consider the welfare of any minors who can be expected to occupy the property. As Client Two has a newborn baby at the property, the court will refuse the possession order.

B. The court will prioritise the interests of the bank as secured creditors. Although other factors will be considered, the courts will seek to ensure any mortgage is repaid and will therefore grant the possession order.

C. The court will consider any of the factors but will not order a sale of the property unless one of the clients is bankrupt.

D. The court will only consider the original intention of the clients. As the property was purchased as a holiday home and is still being used as one by Client Three, the court will refuse the possession order.

E. The court will consider the current purpose of the land and the original intention of the parties. As the original intention was for it to be used as a holiday home, but it is now being used as a permanent residence for Client Two, the court will grant the possession order.

Q69 of 90 Flag for review

A woman correctly executed a will in 2010, leaving her entire estate to her sister. In 2015, the woman decided to change her will and correctly executed a codicil to the 2010 will, bequeathing part of her estate to a friend, but leaving the remainder of the estate to her sister. In 2020, the woman executed a new will containing a revocation clause, leaving her entire estate to her daughter.

What is the effect of the alterations made to the woman's will?

A. The 2015 codicil is valid, and only the 2010 will is revoked. ☐
B. The 2015 codicil and the 2020 will are both valid, but only the 2010 will is revoked. ☐
C. The 2010 and 2020 wills and the 2015 codicil are all valid and will be read concurrently. ☐
D. The 2010 will is still valid as it was not properly revoked. ☐
E. The 2010 and 2020 wills and the 2015 codicil are all valid, but the 2020 will shall revoke the 2010 will and 2015 codicil. ☐

Q70 of 90 Flag for review

A solicitor appears in the magistrates' court representing a man charged with assault occasioning actual bodily harm, contrary to s 47 of the Offences Against the Person Act 1861. At the close of the prosecution's case, the solicitor is considering making a submission of no case to answer. However, the solicitor is unsure whether their submission is properly arguable.

Which of the following best describes whether the solicitor should make the submission of no case to answer?

A. The solicitor should make the submission of no case to answer regardless of whether it is properly arguable. ☐
B. The solicitor should seek the court's view as to whether to make the submission of no case to answer. ☐
C. The solicitor should seek instructions from their client as to whether to make the submission of no case to answer, regardless of whether it is properly arguable. ☐
D. The solicitor should not make the submission of no case to answer if it is not properly arguable. ☐
E. The solicitor should seek the prosecutor's view on whether to make the submission of no case to answer. ☐

Q71 of 90

Flag for review

A woman is charged with an either-way offence. The woman seeks advice from her solicitor as to the rules of disclosure applicable to her case.

Which of the following best describes the rules of disclosure in the woman's case?

A. The woman is obliged to supply a defence statement to the prosecution whether the case is to be tried in the magistrates' court or in the Crown Court.

B. The prosecution, in their continuing duty to disclose, only need to serve material which might reasonably be considered capable of undermining the case for the prosecution against the woman.

C. Adverse inferences may be drawn against the woman if she fails to supply to the prosecution a list of proposed defence witnesses or if the woman, at trial, calls a witness who was not included in the list of proposed defence witnesses.

D. Should the woman make an application for disclosure, the court may require the prosecution to disclose the material sought to the woman without the prosecution being present at the hearing of the application or having an opportunity to make written representations.

E. If the case remains in the magistrates' court, the prosecution's duty of disclosure is limited and the woman is not entitled to the same level of disclosure as would be received if the trial was held in the Crown Court.

Q72 of 90

Flag for review

A man acts as trustee for a large family trust, which includes a beach house in the south of England. The man has invested all trust property in accordance with his duty of care. However, the beach house has performed poorly for the last three years due to its location in comparison with other properties. The man has attempted to rent out the beach house on a number of occasions without success. The beneficiaries do not use the beach house for their own benefit. The man is fond of the beach house and wishes to purchase it for his own use. The man is advised by his fellow trustee to place the beach house on public auction for £120,000 (its market value) and has consented to the man purchasing it. The beach house generates interest from buyers and the man makes the winning bid at £125,000.

Which of the following best describes the legal position?

A. The man is not in breach of his fiduciary duty as he purchased the beach house above market value.

B. The man is in breach of his fiduciary duty as he has only made a £5,000 profit for the trust which is not in line with his duty to act reasonably.

C. The man is not in breach of his fiduciary duty as he purchased the beach house at a public auction.

D. The man is in breach of his fiduciary duty as he was not permitted to purchase the beach house as it is trust property.

E. The man is not in breach of his fiduciary duty as he obtained the consent of his fellow trustee to purchase the beach house.

Q73 of 90 Flag for review

A solicitor acts for a client in a property transaction. The solicitor provided an undertaking to the client's bank that the mortgage would be granted within a specified timescale. However, due to unforeseen delays, the mortgage has not been granted within the agreed timescale and the bank has started to charge interest on the loan.

Which of the following best describes the legal position of the solicitor?

A. The solicitor should offer to compensate the bank for the interest cost and inform the client of the delay. ☐
B. The solicitor should take no action; the delay was unforeseen and out of the control of the solicitor. ☐
C. The solicitor should ignore the undertaking and should not inform either the client or the bank of the delay. ☐
D. The solicitor should inform the client and bank of the delay, but not offer to cover the interest costs. ☐
E. The solicitor should offer to compensate the client for any costs incurred as a result of the delay and inform the bank of the delay. ☐

Q74 of 90 Flag for review

A woman acts as trustee for a family trust. The woman intends to invest money from the trust into a villa outside of the UK. The villa is projected to make a large profit for the trust. The woman seeks advice from a solicitor before proceeding with the investment. The woman's fellow trustee approves of her investment. The trust instrument is silent as to investment.

What advice should the solicitor give to the woman?

A. The woman will be in breach of trust if she invests trust property into the villa as the land is outside the UK. ☐
B. The woman will not be in breach of trust if she invests trust property into the villa as, whilst the land is outside the UK, it is projected to make large profits for the trust. ☐
C. The woman will be in breach of trust if she invests trust property into the villa as she is not permitted by the trust instrument to invest in land. ☐
D. The woman will not be in breach of trust as she has the approval of her fellow trustee. ☐
E. The woman will be in breach of trust if she invests trust property into the villa as such an investment is not suitable. ☐

Q75 of 90 Flag for review

A man is charged with causing criminal damage to a motorcycle belonging to his neighbour. The man wishes to elect trial on indictment. At his first appearance before the magistrates' court, the prosecution adduce evidence showing that the total cost of the damage amounts to £4,000. Receipts for the repairs are produced for the Court's inspection.

Which of the following best describes the legal situation?

A. The offence is triable only summarily, and the man must be tried in the magistrates' court. ☐

B. The offence is triable only on indictment, and the man must be tried in the Crown Court. ☐

C. The offence is triable only summarily, but the man must be offered the opportunity to elect trial in the Crown Court. ☐

D. The offence is triable either way, and the man may be tried in either the magistrates' court or the Crown Court. ☐

E. The offence is triable only on indictment, but the man must be offered the opportunity to elect trial in the magistrates' court. ☐

Q76 of 90 Flag for review

A solicitor is instructed by a client in respect of a property dispute. The client is concerned about the potential costs involved in the case and asks the solicitor to provide a breakdown of any potential expenses. The solicitor is aware of the Solicitors Regulation Authority (SRA) Code of Conduct, but is confused as to the extent of their responsibility.

Which of the following best describes the course of conduct that the solicitor should take?

A. The solicitor should refuse to provide a breakdown, explaining that they are not obliged to do so under the SRA Code of Conduct. ☐

B. The solicitor should provide a general estimate of the potential costs, including hourly rates and expenses, without giving precise details. ☐

C. The solicitor should provide a detailed estimate of the potential costs, including hourly rates and expenses and a statement of all anticipated expenditure. ☐

D. The solicitor should explain to the client that the costs are unpredictable, and as a result no detailed breakdown of costs can be provided. ☐

E. The solicitor should advise the client to seek funding options, but not provide a breakdown of potential costs. ☐

Q77 of 90

Flag for review

A woman died in September 2014, having executed a will in 2013. In that will, the woman leaves an estate of £100,000 to be divided between her five children equally on attainment of the age of 25. The eldest daughter (aged 21) has asked for an advancement of £20,000 to fund her new start-up business. The executors and trustees have approached a solicitor for advice. The will is silent in respect of the power of advancement.

What advice is the solicitor most likely to give in this case?

A. The eldest daughter can be advanced the full £20,000.
B. The eldest daughter cannot be advanced any money.
C. The eldest daughter can be advanced a maximum of £10,000.
D. The eldest daughter can be advanced a maximum of £5,000.
E. The eldest daughter cannot be advanced any money until she has reached the age of 25.

Q78 of 90

Flag for review

A firm acts for the executors of an estate. During the probate period, funds from the estate have at different times been held in both the general client account, and in a separate designated deposit client account (SDDCA).

Which of the following best describes how the firm should account to the executors of the estate for any interest on these funds?

A. The firm should account to the clients for all interest earned on funds held in the SDDCA, but never on funds held in the general client account, in accordance with the firm's interest policy.
B. The firm should account to the clients for all interest attributable to the estate funds from the general client account, but not interest earned on funds held in the SDDCA, in accordance with the firm's interest policy.
C. The firm should account to the clients for all interest earned on the estate funds, whether they have been held in the SDDCA or in the general client account, in accordance with the firm's interest policy.
D. The firm should account to the client for all interest earned on funds held in the SDDCA, and for a sum in lieu of interest for funds held in the general client account, in accordance with the firm's interest policy.
E. The firm has no obligation to pay interest on the estate funds, wherever held, as it is standard practice for executors to sign a written agreement with a firm to this effect at the outset of a probate matter.

Q79 of 90

Flag for review

A man executed a will in 2010 leaving his entire estate to his brother. In 2022, the man got married to a woman and did not make any changes to his will, nor did he execute a new will. The man died last month without any children.

Which of the following best describes the legal position of the man's will?

A. The will was not revoked by the man's marriage to the woman; the estate will pass to the man's brother and the woman may apply to the court for relief under the Inheritance (Provision for Family and Dependants) Act 1975. ☐

B. The will was partly revoked by the man's marriage to the woman; any personal property under the estate will pass under the intestacy rules whilst the real property will pass in accordance with the will. ☐

C. The will was revoked by the man's marriage to the woman; the man's estate will pass under the intestacy rules. ☐

D. The will was not revoked by the man's marriage to the woman; the estate will pass to the man's brother and the woman has no claim for relief under the Inheritance (Provision for Family and Dependants) Act 1975. ☐

E. The will was not revoked by the man's marriage to the woman as the will was made in contemplation of marriage. ☐

Q80 of 90

Flag for review

A man wished to create a trust over his house during his lifetime for the benefit of his son (age 14). The man located the title deeds to the house and wrote on the back of them 'This house is now yours; your uncle will act as trustee until you are old enough to own the house yourself. Take these title deeds as a deed of transfer.' The man then gave the title deeds to the uncle. The man had only one house, which was registered at HM Land Registry, and was the absolute owner at the time.

Has the intended trust been properly constituted?

A. Yes, as by writing on the back of the title deeds, the man has validly disposed of the house. ☐

B. No, as the man should have executed a deed of conveyance over the house which was then registered with HM Land Registry. ☐

C. Yes, as the title deeds represent the title to the house and can stand in the place of a deed of transfer where this is expressly stated. ☐

D. No, as the man should have executed a deed of transfer over the house which was then registered with HM Land Registry. ☐

E. Yes, as the land is registered, the only requirement is that the new legal owner be in possession of the title deeds. ☐

Q81 of 90

Flag for review

A woman is on trial for murder. Part of the prosecution evidence is a confession made by the woman. The woman claims that she only made the confession after the police made threats that if she did not confess, the questioning would continue for a further six hours without food or water, and that her wife would be brought in for questioning. The woman wishes to make an application to exclude the confession pursuant to s 76 of the Police and Criminal Evidence Act (PACE) 1984.

Which of the following best reflects the legal position?

A. Once the issue of admissibility of the confession is raised, the woman must prove so that the judge is sure that the confession was obtained by oppression or by something said or done that was likely in the circumstances to render it unreliable. ☐

B. Once the issue of admissibility of the confession is raised, the woman must prove so that the judge is sure that the confession was obtained by oppression or by something said or done that was likely in the circumstances to render it unfair to rely on. ☐

C. Once the issue of admissibility of the confession is raised, the prosecution must prove so that the judge is sure that the confession was not obtained by oppression or by something said or done that was likely in the circumstances to render it unreliable. ☐

D. Once the issue of admissibility of the confession is raised, the woman must prove on the balance of probabilities that the confession was obtained by oppression or by something said or done that was likely in the circumstances to render it unreliable. ☐

E. Once the issue of admissibility of the confession is raised, the prosecution must prove on the balance of probabilities that the confession was not obtained by oppression or by something said or done that was likely in the circumstances to render it unfair to rely on. ☐

Q82 of 90

Flag for review

A man (aged 31) is convicted in the Crown Court of assault occasioning actual bodily harm, contrary to s 47 of the Offences Against the Person Act 1861. The man is due to be sentenced. The man has a previous conviction for theft, contrary to s 1 of the Theft Act 1968, for which he was sentenced to six months' imprisonment suspended for two years, with an unpaid work requirement of 150 hours. The s 47 offence was committed 19 months into the operational period of the suspended sentence.

Which of the following statements best describes the legal position of the suspended sentence?

A. The trial judge must activate the custodial sentence in full or in part, unless it would be unjust to do so. ☐

B. The trial judge must activate the custodial sentence in full, unless it would be unjust to do so. ☐

C. The trial judge must impose a more onerous community requirement, unless it would be unjust to do so. ☐

D. The trial judge must not activate any part of the suspended sentence because the present offence is not of the same type as the offence for which the suspended sentence was imposed. ☐

E. The trial judge must not activate any part of the suspended sentence because the man was reaching the end of the operational period. ☐

Q83 of 90 Flag for review

A solicitor is advising a client following the renegotiation of a lease on a business property. The property consists of a hotel that the client runs as a nature retreat, surrounded by forests that are owned by the landlord. The client previously sought permission from the landlord to enter the forest to run forest yoga sessions, which the landlord permitted for 10 years. Since the renegotiation, however, the landlord has now told the client they must stop entering the forest.

Which of the following best explains the advice that the solicitor would give as to whether the right to enter the forest is a valid easement?

A. The easement would not be valid. As the easement is for 10 years, it does not fulfil the requirement of being permanent. ☐

B. The easement would not be valid. As the easement is for a right to enter, it is not within a recognised class of easements. ☐

C. The easement would be valid. As the easement is a benefit to the current owner's business, it would therefore be valid. ☐

D. The easement would not be valid. As the easement is only a benefit to the current owner, rather than the land, it would not be valid. ☐

E. The easement would be valid. As the easement is for a right to enter, it is within a recognised class of rights and would therefore be valid. ☐

Q84 of 90 Flag for review

A solicitor acts on behalf of a client purchasing a property that is currently used as a literature museum. The client wants to change its use to a public library and has asked if planning permission will need to be obtained prior to this being done.

Which of the following statements best represents the advice that should be provided to the client?

A. Planning permission will be required as the change of use falls outside the remit of General Permitted Development Order. ☐

B. Planning permission will be required as the change of use falls into a different class use. ☐

C. Planning permission will not be required as although the change of use falls into different classes, there will be no material change. ☐

D. Planning permission will be required as the property will be listed due to it being a museum. ☐

E. Planning permission will not be required as the change of use falls within the same use class. ☐

Q85 of 90 Flag for review

A man dies leaving a validly executed will. The will provides that the man's estate is to be 'held on trust for my husband for life, remainder to my son so long as he attains the age of 21'. A substitution clause is inserted into the will that provides that if the son dies before attaining the age of 21, the estate will pass to the man's brother. The husband and son are considering bringing the trust to an end early. The son is 22 years of age.

Which of the following best describes the requirements to bring the trust to an end early?

A. The consent of the husband, as the life tenant, alone is sufficient to bring the trust to an end early. ☐

B. The consent of the son, as the remainder man, alone is sufficient to bring the trust to an end early. ☐

C. The consent of the husband, the son and the brother is required to bring the trust to an end early. ☐

D. The consent of the husband, the son, the brother and the trustees is required to bring the trust to an end early. ☐

E. The consent of the husband and the son is required to bring the trust to an end early; the consent of the brother is not required to bring the trust to an end early. ☐

Q86 of 90 Flag for review

A client has recently completed the lease of the basement of an office building for 15 years. The property was leased with the intention of being run as a gym. As part of the agreement, the client was given permission to install all the necessary equipment, including converting two small sections to changing rooms with showers. In order to install the showers in the changing rooms, the client needs to run water pipes through the ground floor of the office building.

Which of the following best explains whether the client will be able to run water pipes through the ground floor?

A. The client would be able to run water pipes through the ground floor as there was a common intention between the parties for the showers to be installed, and to do so it is necessary to imply the right. ☐

B. The client would not be able to run water pipes through the ground floor as there was no express agreement made by deed stating this. ☐

C. The client would be able to run water pipes through the ground floor as they will have an easement through prescription. ☐

D. The client would be able to run water pipes through the ground floor as they will be implied through necessity. ☐

E. The client would not be able to run water pipes through the ground floor as the right has not been used for 20 years. ☐

Q87 of 90 Flag for review

A solicitor acts on behalf of a client who is purchasing a freehold registered property. The client is concerned that a two-storey extension appears to have been recently built at the back of the property. The client wants to ensure that they will not be liable for any enforcement action if the relevant permissions were not obtained.

Which of the following documents would a solicitor refer to in order to identify whether planning permission was obtained?

A. The land charges register. ☐

B. The local land charges register. ☐

C. The property information form. ☐

D. The survey. ☐

E. The title deeds. ☐

Q88 of 90 Flag for review

A man has been convicted of burglary, contrary to s 9 of the Theft Act 1968, in the magistrates' court. The man was not legally represented for the trial in the magistrates' court and now wishes to appeal against his conviction to the Crown Court. The man wishes to apply for a representation order. The man earns an adjusted annual income of £24,000.

Which of the following best describes the man's likely position regarding a representation order?

A. The man does not automatically satisfy the interests of justice test, and must prove that it is in the interests of justice that he is represented. However, the man may be passported through the means test. ☐

B. The man automatically satisfies the interests of justice test as he has been convicted of an offence and may lose his liberty should he not appeal. The man also satisfies the initial means test due to his adjusted annual income. ☐

C. The man does not automatically satisfy the interests of justice test, and must prove that it is in the interests of justice that he is represented. The man does not satisfy the initial means test due to his adjusted annual income and must satisfy the full means test. ☐

D. The man automatically satisfies the interests of justice test as he has been convicted of an offence and may lose his liberty should he not appeal. The man may also be passported through the means test. ☐

E. The man does not automatically satisfy the interests of justice test, and must prove that it is in the interests of justice that he is represented. However, the man does satisfy the initial means test due to his adjusted annual income. ☐

Q89 of 90

Flag for review

A man is charged with inflicting grievous bodily harm, contrary to s 20 of the Offences Against the Person Act 1861. The prosecution's case is that the man hit a woman over the head with a beer glass in a brawl in a pub. In conference, the man says that he only struck the woman with the beer glass because the woman was going to attack the man's friend with a chair. The man then asks his solicitor whether self-defence is available.

Which of the following statements best describes the law on self-defence?

A. The force used in self-defence must be necessary and proportionate in the circumstances. Self-defence does not apply when force is used to protect another person. ☐

B. The force used in self-defence need not be necessary, but must be proportionate in the circumstances. Self-defence does not apply when force is used to protect another person. ☐

C. The force used in self-defence must be necessary but it need not be proportionate in the circumstances. The defendant must have a genuinely held belief that force is necessary. Self-defence may apply when force is used to protect another person. ☐

D. The force used in self-defence must be necessary and proportionate in the circumstances. The defendant must have a reasonably held belief that force is necessary. Self-defence may apply when force is used to protect another person. ☐

E. The force used in self-defence must be necessary and proportionate in the circumstances. The defendant must have a genuinely held belief that force is necessary. Self-defence may apply when force is used to protect another person. ☐

Q90 of 90

Flag for review

A man is charged with fraud by failing to disclose information. The man runs an accountancy business and is the sole practitioner. The man is alleged to have misappropriated over £1,000,000 from clients over the past five years. The prosecution alleges that the man was involved in a number of fraudulent schemes, of varying size and complexity. The prosecution expects any trial on the matter to last for a number of months.

Which of the following best describes how the man's case will be dealt with?

A. Fraud is an either-way offence and the normal rules on allocation apply. ☐

B. Whilst fraud is an either-way offence, the prosecution is likely to give notice that the case must be sent to the Crown Court due to the seriousness and complexity of the offence. ☐

C. Whilst fraud is generally an either-way offence, the value of the misappropriated property makes the offence indictable-only. ☐

D. Fraud is an indictable-only offence and the magistrates' court must send the case forthwith to the Crown Court. ☐

E. Whilst fraud is an either-way offence, the magistrates' court must send the case to the Crown Court due to the complexity and seriousness of the case. ☐

■ REFLECTION

CANDIDATE INSTRUCTIONS

Session 1 has now ended. In the real SQE1 assessment, once Session 1 has ended you cannot return to it during the break or during Session 2.

In the SQE1 assessment, you will now be given a break of one hour before Session 2 begins. During this break you may leave the test centre. You are advised to return to the test centre after 50 minutes to ensure that the security checks can be carried out in time for you to commence Session 2 on time.

We advise that you follow the same timings for this simulated SQE-style assessment, and now take a one-hour break.

PAUSE TO REFLECT

You could use the break from your assessment as an opportunity for reflection. Ask yourself the reflective questions in Table 3.

Table 3: Reflecting on FLK2 Session 1 MCQs

How did you find the MCQs in Session 1?	• Did you find them to be easy? • Did you find them to be challenging? Why was this? • Did you flag any for review? If so, what was troubling you about the MCQ?
How confident were you with the MCQs?	• Did you know the answers? • Did you guess any? If so, do you need to revisit your substantive knowledge of the FLK subjects? • Can you identify any particular FLK subjects that you found easier or harder than other subjects?
Did you manage to complete all 90 MCQs in the time permitted?	• Did you manage your time well? • Did you end up with time left over at the end, or did you have to rush? • Did you keep an eye on the clock at regular times during the assessment?
How did you approach the MCQs?	• Did you know some answers straight away? • Did you read the MCQ in full twice before choosing an answer, or did it take you more attempts at reading the MCQ?

In asking yourself these questions, we hope that you will appreciate that there is a skill involved in approaching MCQs as a form of assessment. Refer back to the Introduction to consider whether your approach to MCQs is working for you. Do you need to alter your approach? For example, if you did not manage to complete 90 questions in the allocated time, consider keeping a closer eye on your clock during Session 2.

RETURN FOR SESSION 2

When you return from your scheduled break, remove all distractions and prepare for Session 2.

Once you are ready to commence Session 2 of *FLK2 Practice Assessments*, set a timer for 2 hours, 33 minutes: click the start button and begin (questions overleaf).

Session 2 questions

Q1 of 90 Flag for review

A woman executed a will that included the following clause:

> Clause 3: 'I GIVE my entire book collection to my brother.'

The will also included a remainder clause that the remainder of the woman's estate is to be distributed to the woman's sister.

The woman had only one brother and sister.

Which of the following best describes the legal position?

A. The gift to the brother is a specific gift of a generic kind and the brother is entitled to any books that the woman owned at the time of her death. ☐

B. The gift to the brother is a general gift and the brother is entitled to any books that the woman owned at the time of writing the will. ☐

C. The gift to the brother is invalid for uncertainty as it is unclear which books are included and the books will pass to the sister as part of the residue. ☐

D. The gift to the brother is a general gift and the brother is entitled to any books that the woman owned at the time of her death. ☐

E. The gift to the brother is a specific gift and the brother is entitled to any books that the woman owned at the time of writing the will. ☐

Q2 of 90 Flag for review

A woman is charged with an either-way offence. This is the woman's first alleged offence and she is unsure as to the procedure to be followed. The woman has indicated a not-guilty plea during the plea before venue.

Which of the following best describes the approach that the magistrates' court will take in accordance with s 19 of the Magistrates' Courts Act (MCA) 1980?

A. The court shall first give the prosecution an opportunity to inform the court of the woman's previous convictions (if any). The court shall then give the prosecution and the woman an opportunity to make representations as to whether summary trial or trial on indictment would be more suitable. In making its decision as to allocation, the court must consider the adequacy of its sentencing powers, the representations of the parties and the allocation guidelines issued by the Sentencing Council. ☐

B. The court shall first give the prosecution an opportunity to inform the court of the woman's previous convictions (if any). The court shall then give the prosecution an opportunity to make representations as to whether summary trial or trial on indictment would be more suitable. The woman is not entitled to make such representations. In making its decision as to allocation, the court must consider the adequacy of its sentencing powers, the representations of the prosecution and the allocation guidelines issued by the Sentencing Council. ☐

C. The court shall first give the prosecution and the woman an opportunity to make representations as to whether summary trial or trial on indictment would be more suitable. The court must not consider previous convictions (if any) of the woman in making its decision. In making its decision as to allocation, the court must consider the adequacy of its sentencing powers, the representations of the parties and the allocation guidelines issued by the Sentencing Council. ☐

D. The court shall first give the prosecution an opportunity to inform the court of the woman's previous convictions (if any). The court shall then give the woman an opportunity to make representations as to whether summary trial or trial on indictment would be more suitable. The prosecution is not entitled to make such representations. In making its decision as to allocation, the court must consider the adequacy of its sentencing powers, the representations of the woman and the allocation guidelines issued by the Sentencing Council. ☐

E. The court shall first give the prosecution an opportunity to inform the court of the woman's previous convictions (if any). The court shall then give the prosecution and the woman an opportunity to make representations as to whether summary trial or trial on indictment would be more suitable. In making its decision as to allocation, the court may consider the adequacy of its sentencing powers, the representations of the parties, and the allocation guidelines issued by the Sentencing Council. ☐

Q3 of 90 Flag for review

A solicitor is acting for the administrators of an estate following the death of their relative. During the administration period, the solicitor receives an invoice for £500 + VAT (standard rate) from a surveyor valuing the deceased's home. The invoice is addressed to the personal representatives of the deceased and the solicitor ensures that it is paid promptly.

Which of the following best describes the accounting entries that should be made to record this transaction?

A. Debit £600 client ledger business account and debit £600 cash sheet business account. ☐

B. Debit £500 client ledger business account and credit £500 cash sheet business account. ☐

C. Debit £600 client ledger client account and credit £600 cash sheet client account, providing there is a sufficient credit balance on the client account from which to pay this. ☐

D. Debit £500 client ledger client account and credit £500 cash sheet client account, providing there is a sufficient credit balance on the client account from which to pay this. ☐

E. The firm must not make any accounting entries. As the invoice is addressed to the personal representatives of the deceased, the solicitor should forward it to them so that it can be paid by them instead. ☐

Q4 of 90 Flag for review

On a hot day, a man (who has a visual impairment) walked past a car that was parked in a car park. The man noticed what he thought was a dog in the rear seat. After walking round the car to see that there was no ventilation, the man feared that the dog was in danger of overheating imminently. The man broke the window and removed the dog. However, when the man removed the dog, he discovered that it was a stuffed toy. Prosecutors are considering a charge of criminal damage.

Which of the following statements best describes whether the man is likely to be liable for criminal damage?

A. The man is unlikely to be liable for criminal damage as, objectively, the man broke the window to protect property, and subjectively, the man believed that the property was in need of immediate protection. ☐

B. The man is unlikely to be liable for criminal damage as, subjectively, the man broke the window to protect property, and objectively, the man believed that the property was in need of immediate protection. ☐

C. The man is likely to be liable for criminal damage because even though the window was broken to protect property, the property did not belong to the man. ☐

D. The man is likely to be liable for criminal damage because even though the window was broken to protect property, the man did not think, subjectively, that the property was in need of imminent protection. ☐

E. The man is unlikely to be liable for criminal damage because, objectively, the man broke the window to protect property, and subjectively, the man believed that the property was in need of protection. ☐

Q5 of 90 Flag for review

A man is a trustee for a family trust. The man misappropriates £10,000 from the trust. The man transfers the £10,000 from the trust's bank account into his own personal account, which is £1,000 in credit. The man loses £10,000 gambling one evening. One week later, the man wins £5,000 on the lottery; the man purchased a lottery ticket using a £1 coin he found in his house. The man's bank account now stands at £6,000 in credit. The beneficiaries of the trust discover these facts and seek advice.

What is the maximum amount of money the beneficiaries can recover through equitable tracing?

A. £10,000.
B. £6,000.
C. £5,000.
D. £1,000.
E. Zero.

Q6 of 90 Flag for review

A man invited a woman to his house for a meal and some drinks. After dinner, the man and woman went for a walk. During the walk, the woman started complaining of severe back pain. When the man and woman returned, the woman still had severe back pain. The man forgot that he left a bottle of a prescription-strength painkiller (which was prescribed to the man) on the table in his house. Unbeknown to the man, the woman picked up the bottle and self-administered the painkiller. She later died of an overdose. The man is charged with gross negligence manslaughter.

Which of the following directions to the jury is the most accurate on the law relating to gross negligence manslaughter?

A. Amongst other elements, the risk of death needed to be serious, obvious and reasonably foreseeable. The risk of death also needed to actually exist.
B. Amongst other elements, the risk of death needed to be serious, obvious and sufficiently foreseeable in the circumstances. The risk of death also needed to actually exist.
C. Amongst other elements, the risk of serious injury needed to be serious, obvious and reasonably foreseeable. The risk of death also needed to actually exist.
D. Amongst other elements, the risk of death needed to be grave, apparent and reasonably foreseeable. The risk of death also needed to actually exist.
E. Amongst other elements, the risk of serious injury needed to be serious, apparent and reasonably foreseeable. The risk of death also needed to actually exist.

Q7 of 90 Flag for review

A man is being tried on indictment for theft, contrary to s 1 of the Theft Act 1968. The prosecution wishes to rely on a confession that the man allegedly made during interview at the police station. During conference, the man tells his solicitor that the police delayed access to legal advice, shouted at him before interview and told him that confessing would assist him at court. The solicitor is now considering objecting to the admissibility of the confession.

Which of the following best describes the first argument the solicitor should make to exclude this confession?

A. The confession is inadmissible as the treatment from the police amounts to oppression; it shall not be admitted. ☐

B. The confession is inadmissible as the treatment from the police renders the confession unreliable; it shall not be admitted. ☐

C. The confession is inadmissible as admitting it would have such an adverse effect on the fairness of the proceedings that it ought to be excluded. ☐

D. The confession is inadmissible as there was no sufficient reason to delay access to a solicitor; it may be excluded. ☐

E. The confession is unreliable as delaying access to a solicitor is a breach of the man's fundamental human rights; it must be excluded. ☐

Q8 of 90 Flag for review

A solicitor acts for a client in the sale of a residential property for £300,000. On exchange of contracts, the solicitor receives a deposit of £30,000 from the buyer's solicitor to be held as stakeholder. It is the firm's policy to record receipts of funds held as stakeholder in the client ledgers, rather than in separate stakeholder ledgers.

Which of the following best describes how the receipt of the stakeholder deposit should be recorded in the firm's ledgers?

A. Credit client ledger client account and debit cash sheet client account. The details column of the client ledger must show that the money is held as stakeholder on behalf of both the buyer and the seller. ☐

B. Debit client ledger client account and credit cash sheet client account. The details column of the client ledger must show that the money is held as stakeholder on behalf of both the buyer and the seller. ☐

C. Credit client ledger client account and debit cash sheet client account. There is no need to use the details column of the client ledger to record that the funds are held as stakeholder. ☐

D. Credit client ledger business account and debit cash sheet business account. There is no need to use the details column of the client ledger to record that the funds are held as stakeholder. ☐

E. Credit client ledger client account and debit cash sheet business account. There is no need to use the details column of the client ledger to record that the funds are held as stakeholder. ☐

Q9 of 90 Flag for review

A client is selling their property for £350,000 and buying a new property for £620,000. The client has instructed solicitors to act for them in respect of each transaction. The client has asked how much stamp duty land tax (SDLT) they will be liable to pay to HMRC upon completion.

Which of the following statements best represents the advice that should be provided to the client?

A. The client will need to pay £6,000 in SDLT.
B. The client will need to pay £9,750 in SDLT.
C. The client will need to pay £21,000 in SDLT.
D. The client will need to pay £18,500 in SDLT.
E. The client will need to pay £52,000 in SDLT.

Q10 of 90 Flag for review

A woman is charged on indictment with assault occasioning actual bodily harm, contrary to s 47 of the Offences Against the Person Act 1861. The woman pleads guilty at the earliest opportunity, but she disputes some of the injuries to the victim, saying that they were sustained because the victim was intoxicated and were suffered as a result of his own conduct. A basis of plea is not agreed between the prosecution and defence; therefore, a Newton hearing will take place.

Which of the following statements best describes a Newton hearing?

A. A Newton hearing takes place before a judge and jury, who will hear evidence or submissions to determine the facts of the offence.
B. A Newton hearing takes place before the magistrates, who will hear evidence or submissions to determine the facts of the offence.
C. A Newton hearing takes place before a judge, who will hear evidence or submissions to determine the facts of the offence.
D. A Newton hearing takes place in conference between the prosecution and defence, where parties make submissions to each other on evidence and agree a basis of plea.
E. A Newton hearing takes place as an appeal in the High Court, where a judge will hear evidence or submissions to determine the facts of the offence.

Q11 of 90 Flag for review

A solicitor is in the Crown Court defending a woman accused of unlawful act manslaughter. The prosecution case is that the woman spiked a man's drink with a powerful drug designed to render the man unconscious. However, the man had an unexpected reaction to the drug and died after a cardiac arrest. The judge is about to explain the law relating to unlawful act manslaughter to the jury.

Which of the following is the most accurate explanation of unlawful act manslaughter?

A. There must be a base offence that is unlawful, subjectively dangerous, and caused the death of the man. The prosecution does not need to prove an intention to kill or cause really serious harm; proving the mens rea and actus reus of the base offence in full is sufficient. ☐

B. There must be a base offence that is intrinsically criminal, objectively dangerous, and caused the death of the man. The prosecution does not need to prove an intention to kill or cause really serious harm; proving the mens rea and actus reus of the base offence in full is sufficient. ☐

C. There must be a base offence that is unlawful, objectively dangerous, and caused the death of the man. The prosecution does not need to prove an intention to kill or cause really serious harm; proving the mens rea and actus reus of the base offence in full is sufficient. ☐

D. There must be a base offence that is objectively dangerous and caused the death of the man. The prosecution needs to prove that there was an intention to kill or cause really serious harm as well as the mens rea and actus reus of the base offence. ☐

E. There must be a base offence that is unlawful and objectively dangerous. The prosecution does not need to prove an intention to kill or cause really serious harm; proving the mens rea and actus reus of the base offence in full is sufficient. ☐

Q12 of 90 Flag for review

A trustee improperly draws a cheque for £50,000 against the trust's bank account, payable to himself. The trustee paid the money into his own bank account. The trustee's bank account was overdrawn by £10,000 at the time of this payment, so the resulting credit balance was £40,000. The trustee then received £40,000 from the sale of investments (in his personal capacity), which he paid into the same account, giving him a credit balance of £80,000. The trustee subsequently bought a vintage motorcar for £30,000. The car was mistakenly undervalued by the seller and is now valued at £50,000. The trustee then spent £20,000 on a racehorse, which died when it fell during a race. The trustee subsequently lost the remaining balance of the money in the account from gambling.

Which of the following best describes the claim of the beneficiaries?

A. The beneficiaries can trace into the vintage motorcar and can claim £30,000 of the car as representing the proceeds of the trust money. ☐

B. The beneficiaries have no traceable assets to claim. ☐

C. The beneficiaries can trace into the vintage motorcar and can claim £50,000 of the car as representing the proceeds of the trust money. ☐

D. The beneficiaries can trace into the racehorse and the vintage motorcar, and can claim £30,000 of the car as representing the proceeds of the trust money. ☐

E. The beneficiaries can trace into the racehorse and the vintage motorcar, and can claim £50,000 of the car as representing the proceeds of the trust money. ☐

Q13 of 90 Flag for review

Two solicitors are setting up a law firm in partnership. They intend to specialise in property law.

Which of the following best describes the type of banking arrangements the solicitors should use?

A. The solicitors may choose to set up a joint bank account into which they pay both client money and business money.

B. The solicitors cannot choose to use a third-party managed account.

C. The solicitors must use a third-party managed account.

D. The solicitors do not need to operate a client account as the only client money they will receive is for their own fees and unpaid disbursements prior to delivery of a bill.

E. The solicitors will need to operate a client account unless they choose to use a third-party managed account.

Q14 of 90 Flag for review

A probate solicitor is currently undergoing training to become her firm's Compliance Officer for Finance and Administration (COFA). She is unsure as to what the bank reconciliation process entails.

Which of the following statements most accurately describes the bank reconciliation process?

A. Bank reconciliation involves checking bank statements for the firm's business accounts against the firm's internal accounting records on a weekly basis.

B. Bank reconciliation involves checking bank statements for the firm's client accounts against the firm's internal accounting records on a weekly basis. It is considered good practice to do the same for the firm's business accounts.

C. Bank reconciliation involves checking bank statements for all the firm's client and business accounts against the firm's internal accounting records on a weekly basis.

D. Bank reconciliation involves checking bank statements for the firm's client accounts against the firm's internal accounting records at least every five weeks. It is considered good practice to do the same for the firm's business accounts.

E. Bank reconciliation involves checking bank statements for all the firm's client accounts against the firm's internal accounting records at least every 10 weeks. It is considered good practice to do the same for the firm's business accounts.

Q15 of 90

Flag for review

A man discovers that his wife has been having an affair with his best friend. Enraged, the man gets in his car and drives off aggressively towards his best friend's house. On the way, the man notices a person walking on the footpath wearing a distinctive jacket. The man believes that this is his best friend. The man, who knows what he is doing, accelerates aggressively and drives at the person on the footpath. The man drives over the person with his car. Once the man gets out of his car, he realises that the person is not his best friend. The person dies at the scene, and the man is charged with murder.

Which of the following statements best describes the mens rea for murder in this case?

A. The mens rea for murder is not made out. The man did not intend to kill or cause really serious harm to the person whom he drove over as he thought it was his best friend. Murder is an offence of specific intent and transferred malice does not apply.

B. The mens rea for murder is made out. Whilst the man mistook the identity of the person whom he drove over, there was still an intention to kill or cause really serious harm. Even though murder is an offence of specific intent, mistaken identity is irrelevant.

C. The mens rea for murder is made out. Whilst the man mistook the identity of the person whom he drove over, there was still an intention to kill or cause some harm. Even though murder is an offence of specific intent, mistaken identity is irrelevant.

D. The mens rea for murder is not made out. There was no virtual certainty that driving over the person would have resulted in death or really serious harm, and mistaken identity is relevant. Murder is an offence of specific intent, and to convict, there must be no mistake as to the intended victim.

E. The mens rea for murder is made out. There was a virtual certainty of death or serious injury when the man decided to drive at, and over, the person. As such, a jury must find, as a matter of law, that the requisite intent is satisfied.

Q16 of 90 Flag for review

A man is being tried in the magistrates' court for theft, contrary to s 1 of the Theft Act 1968. The man denies the charge, arguing that he was not there at the scene at the material time. The prosecution relies solely on one witness who places the man at the scene, but when giving evidence, several significant inconsistencies and credibility issues come to light. The prosecution closes its case, and the man's solicitor is considering making a submission of no case to answer.

Which of the following would be the best argument for a submission of no case to answer in this situation, and when should it be made?

A. The prosecution evidence, even taken at its highest, is insufficient for a properly directed bench to convict. A submission should be made to the court after the defendant has given evidence.

B. The prosecution has not offered any evidence on which the man could be convicted, and therefore the trial should cease. A submission should be made to the court following the closure of the prosecution case.

C. The prosecution evidence, even taken at its highest, is insufficient for a properly directed bench to convict. A submission should be made to the court following the closure of the prosecution case.

D. The prosecution has not offered any evidence on which the man could be convicted, and therefore the trial should cease. A submission should be made after the defendant has given evidence.

E. The prosecution evidence, even taken at its highest, is insufficient to support a conviction; therefore, in the interests of justice, the trial should cease. A submission should be made following the closure of the prosecution's case.

Q17 of 90 Flag for review

The trustee of a family trust misappropriates £10,000 from the trust. The trustee uses part of the funds to pay his £5,000 accountancy debt. The trustee transfers the £5,000 to an agent of the accountancy firm. The agent is surprised at the receipt of the money as he knows the trustee struggles financially. The agent chooses not to question the source of the money, forwards the funds to the accountancy firm and treats the trustee's debt as settled.

Which of the following best describes the liability of the agent?

A. The agent is likely to be liable for dishonest assistance in a breach of trust because his assistance is dishonest by the standards of ordinary decent people.

B. The agent is unlikely to be liable for dishonest assistance in a breach of trust because he did not appreciate that he was dishonest by the standards of ordinary decent people.

C. The agent is likely to be liable for dishonest assistance in a breach of trust because his assistance is dishonest by the standards of ordinary decent people, and the agent appreciated that he was dishonest by those standards.

D. The agent is unlikely to be liable for dishonest assistance in a breach of trust because his assistance was not dishonest by the standards of ordinary decent people.

E. The agent is likely to be liable for dishonest assistance in a breach of trust because he appreciated that he was dishonest by the standards of ordinary decent people.

Q18 of 90

Flag for review

A man kills his wife in an act of aggression. The man suffers from a mental condition that causes him to hallucinate. The man's solicitor believes that he may be able to plead voluntary manslaughter.

Which of the following statements best describes voluntary manslaughter?

A. Voluntary manslaughter cases involve the unlawful killing of another where both the actus reus and mens rea for murder are possessed by the defendant. However, for whatever reason, an intoxication defence applies.

B. Voluntary manslaughter cases involve the unlawful killing of another where both the actus reus and mens rea for murder are possessed by the defendant. However, for whatever reason, a special or partial defence applies.

C. Voluntary manslaughter cases involve the unlawful killing of another where the actus reus and mens rea of a base offence are possessed by the defendant, but there is no intention to kill or cause really serious harm.

D. Voluntary manslaughter cases involve the unlawful killing of another where the actus reus, but not the mens rea, for murder is possessed by the defendant. However, for whatever reason, a special or partial defence applies.

E. Voluntary manslaughter cases involve the unlawful killing of another where the mens rea, but not actus reus, for murder is possessed by the defendant. However, for whatever reason, a special or partial defence applies.

Q19 of 90

Flag for review

A solicitor is reviewing the accounting records for the firm's probate department. The firm has used digital accounting software for at least seven years but there is a storage cupboard at the firm's offices that contains lots of paper-based probate accounting records from the preceding 20 years, including client ledgers. The senior probate partner wants to know whether the cupboard can be cleared to use it for other purposes.

Which of the following answers most accurately describes what the solicitor should do?

A. The solicitor can clear the cupboard as all the records are over six years old. The documents should be destroyed as confidential waste.

B. The solicitor can clear the cupboard as all the records are over six years old. The records can be placed in a skip in the firm's car park for disposal.

C. The solicitor must sort through the documentation so that any accounting records less than 10 years old must be retained. Older documents can be destroyed as confidential waste.

D. The solicitor must sort through the documentation so that any accounting records that are less than 10 years old must be retained. Older documents can be placed in a skip in the firm's car park for disposal.

E. The solicitor must ensure that all the records are retained indefinitely, and that the cupboard is locked securely to protect client confidentiality.

Q20 of 90 Flag for review

A woman was charged with unlawful act manslaughter and was tried in the Crown Court. The circumstances of the case were complex, and submissions on points of law were made during the trial where the judge ruled against the woman. After the woman was convicted, the judge adjourned for a pre-sentence report, and the sentencing hearing is due to take place eight weeks later. In consultation with counsel, the solicitor considers that there are grounds for appeal. The woman's solicitor is now considering appealing against the conviction.

Which of the following best describes the process for appealing against conviction?

A. Leave to appeal is not required to appeal against conviction. An appeal notice must be served on the Registrar not more than 28 days following sentence. The appeal will be heard in the Court of Appeal.

B. Leave to appeal is required to appeal against conviction. An appeal notice must be served on the Registrar not more than 28 days following conviction. The appeal will be heard in the High Court.

C. Leave to appeal is not required to appeal against conviction. An appeal notice must be served on the Registrar not more than 28 days following sentence. The appeal will be heard in the High Court.

D. Leave to appeal is required to appeal against conviction. An appeal notice must be served on the Registrar not more than 28 days following sentence. The appeal will be heard in the Court of Appeal.

E. Leave to appeal is required to appeal against conviction. An appeal notice must be served on the Registrar not more than 28 days following conviction. The appeal will be heard in the Court of Appeal.

Q21 of 90 Flag for review

A solicitor specialises in private client law and the drafting of wills. The solicitor has been instructed by a woman to draft her will for her. The woman is deaf and primarily communicates through British Sign Language (BSL). The solicitor has no experience of working with deaf clients and does not know BSL.

Which of the following best describes the course of conduct that the solicitor should take?

A. The solicitor should request that the woman attends all meetings with the solicitor in person, and attends with a BSL/English interpreter at personal cost to the woman.

B. The solicitor should refer the woman to another solicitor who has experience in working with deaf clients.

C. The solicitor should teach themselves BSL in order to communicate with the woman.

D. The solicitor should communicate only by email and written communications.

E. The solicitor should identify any specific equipment or support needed to help communication during the meeting.

Q22 of 90 Flag for review

A man spent time preparing to commit robbery. He obtained an imitation firearm, acquired alarm codes for the property where he intended to commit the offence, organised a get-away car and noted down on paper a false alibi. However, the man's plan was foiled, and the police raided his house before the robbery took place. The prosecution is considering a charge of attempted robbery.

Which of the following statements best applies to this case?

A. It is likely that the man has taken steps that are merely preparatory and intended to commit the offence in full. Therefore, the man is likely to be charged with attempted robbery. ☐

B. It is unlikely that the man has taken steps that are more than merely preparatory but it is likely that he intended to commit the offence in full. Therefore, the man is unlikely to be charged with attempted robbery. ☐

C. It is likely that the man has taken steps that are more than merely preparatory and intended to commit the offence in full. Therefore, the man is likely to be charged with attempted robbery. ☐

D. It is likely that the man has taken steps that are more than merely preparatory and intended to commit the offence in full. Therefore, the man is likely to be charged with robbery and, in the alternative, attempted robbery. ☐

E. It is likely that the man has taken steps that are more than merely preparatory, but it is unlikely that he intended to commit the offence in full. Therefore, the man is unlikely to be charged with attempted robbery. ☐

Q23 of 90 Flag for review

A woman is being tried summarily for assault occasioning actual bodily harm, contrary to s 47 of the Offences Against the Person Act 1861. During the course of the trial, submissions were made on a point of law, but the magistrates ruled against the woman. The solicitor considers that the point of law is pivotal to their case, and that the ruling amounted to a misdirection. The woman is convicted and the solicitor is now considering all options for appeal and is to have a conference with the woman. The woman is anxious about going through the trial process again.

Which of the following best describes the most appropriate advice to give to the woman?

A. The woman should appeal to the Divisional Court of the High Court by way of case stated, as there is a point of law that requires clarification. ☐

B. The woman should appeal to the Crown Court for a complete rehearing as per her right. The point of law can be raised with the judge, who can give a ruling. ☐

C. The woman should appeal to a Divisional Court of the High Court for a complete rehearing as per her right. The point of law can be raised with the judge, who can give a ruling. ☐

D. The woman should appeal to the Crown Court by way of case stated, as there is a point of law that requires clarification. ☐

E. The woman should seek leave to appeal to the Court of Appeal not more than 28 days after the date of conviction. The woman will need to serve a notice to the Registrar. ☐

Q24 of 90 Flag for review

A husband and wife live apart due to the husband working away from the family home on a regular basis. The wife purchases a house in the name of her husband closer to his place of work so that he does not need to use the services of a hotel whilst away from the marital home. At the time of the purchase, the wife wrote a number of letters to her husband whereby she explained that the house was solely for him as a gift from her. Other letters are written that clearly identify the husband as the owner of the house. The husband's son from a different marriage lives with the husband in the house. The wife has now issued divorce proceedings and is claiming that the house belongs to her.

Which of the following best describes the likely interests in the house?

A. The husband alone will have the beneficial interest in the house. ☐
B. The wife alone will have the beneficial interest in the house. ☐
C. The husband and the wife will have a beneficial interest in the house. ☐
D. The son alone will have the beneficial interest in the house. ☐
E. Neither the husband nor the wife has a beneficial interest in the house. ☐

Q25 of 90 Flag for review

A man and woman are the trustees for a small family trust, which consists of land and shares in a private company. The man now wishes to retire from his position. The trust instrument is silent as to the appointment of trustees.

Which of the following best describes the legal position?

A. The man can retire from his position as a trustee so long as his retirement is in writing, and a replacement trustee is appointed orally. ☐
B. The man can retire from his position as a trustee so long as his retirement is in writing; the woman can continue to act as trustee alone. ☐
C. The man can retire from his position as a trustee, which can be done orally, and a replacement trustee is appointed in writing. ☐
D. The man can retire from his position as a trustee, which can be done orally; the woman can continue to act as trustee alone. ☐
E. The man can retire from his position as a trustee so long as his retirement is in writing, and a replacement trustee is appointed in writing. ☐

Q26 of 90 Flag for review

A solicitor wishes to promote her law firm's services to members of the public. The solicitor contacts random individuals on social media to offer her law firm's services; sends marketing emails to current and former clients of the law firm; sets up a booth at a public event to offer free legal advice and discuss the services of her law firm with voluntary attendees; and cold-calls individuals to offer her law firm's services.

Which of the following are likely to be permissible under the Solicitors Regulation Authority Code of Conduct?

A. Sending marketing emails to current and former clients and setting up a booth at a public event. ☐

B. Contacting individuals on social media, sending marketing emails to current and former clients, and setting up a booth at a public event. ☐

C. Contacting individuals on social media and cold-calling individuals. ☐

D. Setting up a booth at a public event and cold-calling individuals. ☐

E. Contacting individuals on social media and sending marketing emails to current and former clients. ☐

Q27 of 90 Flag for review

A solicitor works in a law firm specialising in criminal practice as the firm's Compliance Officer for Legal Practice. The solicitor has become aware of a data breach at their firm that may have resulted in the disclosure of client confidential information.

Which of the following describes the appropriate action that the solicitor should take?

A. The solicitor should ignore the potential data breach unless a client raises a concern. ☐

B. The solicitor need only notify the Information Commissioner's Office of the data breach. ☐

C. The solicitor should immediately inform all affected clients of the data breach and take steps to mitigate the impact of the breach. ☐

D. The solicitor should investigate the matter first before deciding whether to inform the affected clients of the data breach. ☐

E. The solicitor need only notify the Solicitors Regulation Authority of the data breach. ☐

Q28 of 90 Flag for review

A man died, leaving a will in which he gifted his house to his granddaughter. The man's granddaughter predeceased the man. The man did not amend his will prior to his death and there was no substitution clause in the will in respect of the house. The granddaughter was married, and her husband and two children are alive. The granddaughter executed a will prior to her death which left her entire estate to her husband.

Which of the following best describes the legal position?

A. The gift of the house will pass to the next of kin of the man. ☐

B. The gift of the house will pass to the residuary beneficiary of the man's estate. ☐

C. The gift of the house will pass according to the intestacy rules. ☐

D. The gift of the house will pass to the granddaughter's husband. ☐

E. The gift of the house will pass to the children of the granddaughter, shared equally between them. ☐

Q29 of 90 Flag for review

A settlor creates a trust whereby he appoints three trustees for the benefit of his sons. One of the trustees recently secured employment abroad, which requires them to be out of the UK for several months at a time. To date, the trustee was out of the UK for four months, returning for three weeks, out of the UK again for five months, returning for one week, and then out of the UK for a further four months. The trustee has been out of the UK for a total of 13 months and they remain outside the UK to this date. The trustee remains in communication with the co-trustees whilst out of the UK, but the co-trustees now wish to remove the trustee from their position.

Which of the following best describes whether the co-trustees can remove the trustee?

A. The co-trustees can remove the trustee from their position as they have been outside the UK for more than 12 months, without the need to appoint a replacement trustee. The removal must be done in writing. ☐

B. The co-trustees cannot remove the trustee from their position as they have not been out of the UK for a continuous period of 12 months. ☐

C. The co-trustees can remove the trustee from their position as they have been out of the UK for more than 12 months, but will need to appoint a replacement trustee. The removal must be done in writing. ☐

D. The co-trustees cannot remove the trustee from their position as they have been in communication with the co-trustees whilst out of the UK. ☐

E. The co-trustees can remove the trustee from their position as they have been out of the UK for more than 12 months, without the need to appoint a replacement trustee. The removal can be done orally. ☐

Q30 of 90 Flag for review

A man and a woman are married and own a house together. The man had an affair, which the woman later discovered. In anger, the woman threw large bricks through the bedroom window of the house belonging to her and her husband. The man, at the time, was standing by the bedroom window, and glass shattered over him. At the time, the woman thought the man was out of the house, even though the offence was committed at a time during the day where the man was likely to be in the property.

Which of the following statements best describes the relevant law in this case?

A. The woman has committed criminal damage. By throwing the bricks, she intended to damage the property. As the woman owned the property which was damaged, the woman cannot be guilty of aggravated criminal damage.

B. The woman has committed aggravated criminal damage. By throwing the bricks, she intended to damage property and endangered life through recklessness. The fact that she owned the property is irrelevant.

C. The woman has committed aggravated criminal damage. By throwing the bricks, she was reckless in damaging the property, and she intended to endanger the man's life. The fact that she owned the property is irrelevant.

D. The woman has committed criminal damage. By throwing the bricks, she intended to damage the property. As the woman did not intend to endanger life, and the man was not hurt, the woman cannot be guilty of aggravated criminal damage.

E. The woman has committed criminal damage. By throwing the bricks, she intended to damage the property. As the woman only endangered her own life, she cannot be guilty of aggravated criminal damage.

Q31 of 90 Flag for review

A client completed the purchase of a terraced house. A neighbour confronts the client about the external paintwork. The neighbour produces a deed containing a covenant with the previous owner of the terraced house stating that the owner of the terraced house 'agrees to repaint the outside of the property every three years'.

Which of the following best explains whether the client is bound to repaint the property?

A. The client will be obliged to repaint the property, as the covenant is negative and therefore will automatically be binding on successors in title.

B. The client will not be obliged to repaint the property, as the burden of the covenant has not been made to expressly run with the land so will not be binding on successors in title.

C. The client will be obliged to repaint the property, as the burden of the covenant will be implied to automatically run with the land unless expressly excluded.

D. The client will be obliged to repaint the property, as the covenant is positive and therefore automatically binding on successors in title.

E. The client will not be obliged to repaint the property, as the covenant is positive and therefore will not be binding on successors in title.

Q32 of 90 Flag for review

A corporate client is buying a new commercial property, financed by a mortgage. The solicitor is acting for both the client and the lender, and the firm's policy is to operate two separate client ledgers in these circumstances.

How should the firm deal with the mortgage advance when received?

A. The receipt of the mortgage advance will be recorded in the lender's client ledger and then transferred to the buyer's client ledger on the completion date. ☐

B. The receipt of the mortgage advance will be recorded in the buyer's client ledger, but the details column must include the name of the lender and identify the funds as a mortgage advance. ☐

C. The mortgage advance will be paid into the firm's business account on receipt. On completion, it will be transferred into the client account. ☐

D. The mortgage advance will be paid into the firm's client account on receipt. On completion, it will be transferred into the firm's business account. ☐

E. There is no need to record the receipt of the mortgage advance until completion, when it will be credited to the buyer's client ledger. ☐

Q33 of 90 Flag for review

A man is being tried summarily by a lay bench of magistrates for common assault in the magistrates' court. In conference, the man's solicitor discusses the merits and weaknesses of the case and explains what is going to happen during the trial. The man is concerned about the prosecution case and asks the solicitor whether he has to give evidence.

Which of the following best describes the advice the solicitor should give the man?

A. The prosecution bears the burden of proving guilt, and the magistrates will only be able to convict if it is more likely than not that the man is guilty of the offence. The man can be compelled to give evidence. ☐

B. The prosecution bears the burden of proving guilt, and the magistrates will only be able to convict if they are sure that the man is guilty of the offence. The man cannot be compelled to give evidence. ☐

C. The prosecution bears the burden of proving guilt, and the magistrates will only be able to convict if it is more likely than not that the man is guilty of the offence. The man cannot be compelled to give evidence. ☐

D. The defence bears the burden of proving innocence, and the magistrates will only be able to convict if they are sure that the man is guilty of the offence. The man can be compelled to give evidence. ☐

E. The defence bears the burden of proving innocence, and the magistrates will only be able to convict if they are sure that the man is guilty of the offence. The man cannot be compelled to give evidence. ☐

Q34 of 90

Flag for review

A solicitor arrives at the local magistrates' court and is about to have a conference with a man charged with burglary. The solicitor goes through the evidence and notices that the man gave a no comment interview. The man gives the solicitor an exculpatory account of what happened from his perspective, but the solicitor asks him why he did not give this account to the police at interview when asked. The man informs the solicitor that he does not like how the police can twist things, as he has been arrested several times before. The solicitor is about to give the man advice on adverse inferences.

Which of the following best describes the advice that the solicitor should give to the man on pre-charge adverse inferences?

A. If the man gives evidence and offers an alternative version of events, which he relies on at trial, the court may be permitted to draw any inferences that appear proper from the man's refusal to answer questions in interview. ☐

B. If the man gives evidence and offers an alternative version of events, which he relies on at trial, the court must be permitted to draw any inferences that appear proper from the man's refusal to answer questions in interview. ☐

C. If the man gives evidence and offers an alternative version of events, which he relies on at trial, the court will not be permitted to draw any inferences that appear proper from the man's refusal to answer questions in interview. ☐

D. If the man gives evidence and offers an alternative version of events, which he relies on at trial, the court will not be permitted to draw any inferences that appear proper as the man has a good reason for refusing to answer questions in interview. ☐

E. If the man gives evidence and offers an alternative version of events, which he relies on at trial, the court may draw inferences of guilt from the man's refusal to answer questions in interview. ☐

Q35 of 90 Flag for review

A girl, aged 15, is bullied at school by a boy of a similar age. The bullying has been going on for approximately two years. The girl decides to get her revenge and intends to damage the boy's bicycle. The girl follows the boy home one day and makes a note of where he lives. The girl also notices that the boy leaves his bicycle outside in the garden. One night, the girl takes a baseball bat, some petrol, and some matches to the boy's house with the intention to damage and set fire to the bicycle. The girl strikes the bicycle with the bat (which causes most of the damage) and then pours petrol over it. She strikes a match but has second thoughts. Instead, the girl lights a cigarette and just stands next to the bicycle. After taking some deep breaths, she drops the cigarette on the floor, forgetting about the petrol. One of the sparks ignites the petrol and the bicycle is set on fire. The girl is later arrested on suspicion of arson.

Which of the following statements is most accurate?

A. The girl cannot be guilty of arson as there was no intention to damage the bicycle by fire at the time when the fire was started. The girl is, therefore, guilty of aggravated criminal damage. ☐

B. The girl cannot be guilty of arson as she had a lawful excuse to damage the property. Provocation is a defence to aggravated criminal damage and arson, and the defence applies here due to the impact the boy's behaviour has had on the girl. ☐

C. The girl is guilty of arson as she intended to damage the bicycle by fire when she originally set out to commit the offence. The fact that she had second thoughts in the intermittent period is irrelevant. ☐

D. The girl is guilty of arson as she was reckless in damaging the bicycle by fire. Even though the girl had second thoughts after pouring the petrol, she was reckless when smoking a cigarette in the vicinity of the poured petrol. ☐

E. The girl cannot be guilty of arson as the bicycle was predominantly damaged by the strikes with the baseball bat. For the girl to be guilty of arson, the fire must have been a significant contributor to the damage of the property, which is not the case here. ☐

Q36 of 90 Flag for review

A man died without leaving a will. The man was survived by his wife and their two children. The estate is valued at £400,000, excluding personal chattels owned by the man at the time of his death.

Which of the following best describes the entitlement of the wife and the two children under the intestacy rules?

A. The wife and two children would each be entitled to equal shares of the £400,000 and of all personal chattels. ☐

B. The wife would be entitled to £325,000, plus the personal chattels, and the two children would share the remaining £75,000 equally. ☐

C. The wife would be entitled to £335,000, plus the personal chattels, and the two children would share the remaining £65,000 equally. ☐

D. The wife would be entitled to the entire estate, including the personal chattels, as the surviving spouse. ☐

E. The wife would be entitled to £361,000, plus the personal chattels, and the two children would share the remaining £39,000 equally. ☐

Q37 of 90

Flag for review

A client instructs a solicitor to act on their behalf to purchase a leasehold property. The freehold is managed by a management company that is owned by the existing leaseholders. The solicitor has received the management pack including the leasehold property enquiries form, and has noted that the management company is limited by guarantee.

Which of the following documents must be requested by the solicitor before exchange of contracts takes place?

A. A signed stock transfer form.
B. Share certificate.
C. Memorandum and articles of association.
D. A signed transfer of whole.
E. A signed letter from all of the lessees of the management company, confirming their agreement to the purchase.

Q38 of 90

Flag for review

A solicitor is advising a client following their purchase of a property. The client purchased the property with the intention of using the upstairs as accommodation whilst running a physiotherapy studio downstairs. The client has been approached by a neighbour with a complaint about this plan. Both properties were previously owned by the large local landowner. The neighbour produces a deed signed by the landowner and the person the client purchased their property from. It contains a covenant stating: 'The Buyer covenants with the Seller to use the Property only as a private dwelling house.' There is no other documentation relating to the covenant.

Which of the following best explains whether the neighbour is able to enforce the covenant against the client?

A. The neighbour will be able to enforce the covenant because the benefit of the covenant will have automatically passed to the neighbour by statute.
B. The neighbour will not be able to enforce the covenant because the benefit of the covenant has not been expressly assigned to the neighbour.
C. The neighbour will be able to enforce the covenant because the burden of the covenant has passed to the client in law.
D. The neighbour will not be able to enforce the covenant because the benefit of the covenant will only pass under statute if the benefitted land is clearly identifiable.
E. The neighbour will be able to enforce the covenant because the covenant was made by deed and is a legal freehold covenant.

Q39 of 90 Flag for review

During a heated argument in a car park, a man remains seated inside his locked vehicle. He leans out of the driver's side window, raises his clenched fist, and says to another man standing one metre away: 'If you come any closer, I will punch you.'

The second man stops, believing that the man will attack him if he moves. No physical contact occurs.

Which of the following best reflects the man's criminal liability, if any?

A. The man is not criminally liable because words alone cannot amount to an assault. ☐

B. The man may be liable only if the prosecution can prove that the man intended to carry out the threat. ☐

C. The man is not criminally liable because the threat was conditional on the other man moving closer. ☐

D. The man may be liable for common assault because his conduct caused the other man to apprehend immediate unlawful violence. ☐

E. The man is not criminally liable because the prosecution cannot prove the requirement of immediacy for the assault. ☐

Q40 of 90 Flag for review

A solicitor acts for a mother in the sale of her home. On completion, the client asks the solicitor to transfer £18,000 of the net proceeds of sale to be used by her daughter as a deposit on the purchase of her first home. The solicitor is also acting for the daughter in her property purchase.

What accounting entries must be made to record this transaction, and are there any other accounting record requirements?

A. Debit mother's client ledger client account and credit daughter's client ledger client account. A record of the transfer should also be kept in the firm's profit costs ledger. ☐

B. Debit mother's client ledger client account and credit daughter's client ledger client account. A record of the transfer should also be kept in the firm's transfer journal. ☐

C. Credit mother's client ledger client account and debit daughter's client ledger client account. A record of the transfer should also be kept in the respective client files. ☐

D. Credit mother's client ledger client account and debit daughter's client ledger client account. There are no other accounting record requirements. ☐

E. Debit mother's client ledger client account and credit cash sheet client account. Then credit daughter's client ledger client account and debit cash sheet client account. A record of the transfer should also be kept in the respective client files. ☐

Q41 of 90 Flag for review

A solicitor acts for the personal representatives in a probate matter. At the end of the probate period, they bill the clients for £4,000 + VAT (standard rate). The personal representatives approve the estate accounts and the solicitor pays out the remainder of the estate in accordance with the will, retaining sufficient client funds to clear the bill.

What double entries are required to record the transfer of funds to clear the bill?

A. Debit £4,800 client ledger client account and credit £4,800 cash sheet business ledger. ☐

B. Debit £4,800 client ledger client account and credit £4,800 cash sheet client account; credit £4,800 client ledger business account and debit £4,800 cash sheet business account. ☐

C. Credit £4,800 client ledger client account and debit £4,800 cash sheet client account. ☐

D. Credit £4,800 client ledger client account and debit £4,800 cash sheet business account. ☐

E. Debit £4,800 client ledger client account and credit £4,800 profit costs ledger. ☐

Q42 of 90 Flag for review

A man has been charged with causing grievous bodily harm with intent, contrary to s 18 of the Offences Against the Person Act 1861. It is alleged that the man struck the woman significantly with his fists and then broke her arm. The incident was reported to police several hours later after the woman returned home from hospital. The man accepts punching the woman twice but denies breaking her arm. The man cannot explain how the woman came to have a broken arm but insists that something else must have happened before the woman went to hospital. There are no independent witnesses to the event.

Which of the following best describes causation in criminal liability?

A. The prosecution must prove both factual and legal causation. In this case, the prosecution would need to demonstrate that the man's actions were the sole cause of the woman's injuries, and that there was no break in the chain of causation by means of a third party only. ☐

B. The prosecution must prove factual causation only. In this case, the prosecution would need to demonstrate that the man's actions were a substantial cause of the woman's injuries, and that there was no break in the chain of causation by any means. ☐

C. The prosecution must prove legal causation only. In this case, the prosecution would need to demonstrate that the man's actions were a substantial cause of the woman's injuries, and that there was no break in the chain of causation by any means. ☐

D. The prosecution must prove both factual and legal causation. In this case, the prosecution would need to demonstrate that the man's actions were a substantial cause of the woman's injuries, and that there was no break in the chain of causation by any means. ☐

E. The prosecution must prove both factual and legal causation. In this case, the prosecution would need to demonstrate that the man's actions were a substantial cause of the woman's injuries, and that there was no break in the chain of causation by means of a third party only. ☐

Q43 of 90 Flag for review

A solicitor in the magistrates' court is defending a client charged with fraud by false representation. The parties have made their closing submissions and the legal advisor is summarising the law to the lay magistrates. The solicitor notices that the legal adviser has incorrectly advised the lay magistrates on the law. The error is in the favour of the solicitor's client.

Which of the following describes the appropriate action that the solicitor should take?

A. The solicitor should not disclose the error to the legal advisor. ☐
B. The solicitor should draw the court's attention to the procedural irregularity. ☐
C. The solicitor should assume that the legal advisor will discover the error themselves and will properly redirect the lay magistrates on the law when the error is discovered. ☐
D. The solicitor should draw the prosecutor's attention to the procedural irregularity. ☐
E. The solicitor should ask that the bench of lay magistrates be dismissed on the basis of the incorrect legal direction. ☐

Q44 of 90 Flag for review

A client currently owes £100,000 on a mortgage agreement with Bank One. They subsequently granted another mortgage in favour of Bank Two, on which they currently owe £60,000. The client has now granted a further mortgage to Bank Three, on which £10,000 is owed. The client is now unable to pay any of the mortgage agreements. Bank Two commenced possession proceedings and an order to sell the property. The property was subsequently sold for £150,000.

Excluding costs, which of the following best reflects how these mortgages will be repaid?

A. Bank Two will have the entirety of its £60,000 loan repaid to it first because it sought the court order and sold the property. The remaining £90,000 will be split proportionately between Banks One and Three. ☐
B. Bank Two will have the entirety of its £60,000 loan repaid to it first because it sought the court order and sold the property. Bank Two will then repay Bank Three £10,000 and Bank One will receive the remaining £80,000. ☐
C. Bank Two will be required to repay the £100,000 loan to Bank One before paying the remaining £50,000 for its own mortgage. Bank Two can sue in contract for the remaining £10,000. ☐
D. Bank Two will be required to pay £100,000 to Bank One as the first mortgage registered. Bank Two will then pay £10,000 to Bank Three before it can repay £40,000 of its own loan. Bank Two will have to sue under a personal contract to recover its money. ☐
E. Bank Two will be required to pay £10,000 to Bank Three as the most recent mortgage. Bank Two will then repay its own loan as the next most recent. The remaining £80,000 will be used to pay to Bank One. ☐

Q45 of 90 Flag for review

A man and woman were in a romantic relationship and jointly owned a bank account with a balance of £50,000. The man dies without a will. The man and woman were not married, and at the time of his death the man had two children with his ex-wife. The man's ex-wife is still alive.

Which of the following describes what will happen with the £50,000 in the bank account?

A. The £50,000 in the bank account passes under the intestacy rules to the man's children.

B. The £50,000 in the bank account is divided equally between the woman as the surviving joint tenant, and the man's children under the intestacy rules.

C. The £50,000 in the bank account passes under the intestacy rules to the woman.

D. The £50,000 in the bank account passes entirely to the woman as the surviving joint tenant.

E. The £50,000 in the bank account passes under the intestacy rules to the man's ex-wife.

Q46 of 90 Flag for review

A solicitor is advising a client following the sale of a piece of land that they had granted a mortgage over. The mortgagee had taken possession and gained an order for sale. The land was sold at auction for £200,000. The auction details incorrectly stated that the land had planning permission for three properties, whereas in fact the planning permission was for four. The client was also upset as the land was sold during a global financial crisis when property prices were low.

Which of the following best explains whether the client will have any claim against the mortgagee?

A. The client will not have any claim. The mortgagee has the right to sell the land however they wish, and whatever price someone is willing to pay for the land is the true market value.

B. The client will not have any claim. So long as the mortgagee has acted in good faith, they will not be liable even if the land did not achieve true market value.

C. The client will have a claim. The mortgagee has an obligation to accurately advertise the land in order to achieve true market value. The mortgagee will have to repay any loss suffered for the incorrect details. However, they will not be liable for any shortfall from the choice of when to sell the land.

D. The client will have a claim. The mortgagee has an obligation to get the highest price possible. The mortgagee should not have sold the land during a financial crisis.

E. The client will have a claim. The mortgagee had a duty to obtain a true market value of the property, and the property should have been sold by traditional sale as auctions do not obtain the highest price.

Q47 of 90

Flag for review

A client has sought advice over a one-year agreement they recently signed on a one-bedroom flat. The client's long-term partner signed an identical agreement on the same date. The agreement was termed a 'licence agreement' and granted them a 'licence' for one year. The agreement explicitly stated that the client did not have exclusive possession of the property. The agreement stated that the client and their partner were jointly responsible for a licence fee of £1,000 per calendar month, but that the landlord could move in additional licencees with one month's notice.

Which of the following most accurately explains how a solicitor should advise the client as to the nature of the agreement?

A. The client has a legal lease. As the agreement is for under seven years and they have signed an agreement for a permitted duration at a rent, it will be a legal lease despite the lack of deed.

B. The client has a contractual licence. As the agreement states that the client does not have exclusive possession of the property, it cannot be a lease.

C. The client has an equitable lease. Although the client has been granted exclusive possession for a fixed duration, the agreement was not created by deed and so cannot be legal.

D. The client has a legal lease. The agreement grants the client and their partner exclusive possession for a permitted duration and as it is for fewer than three years, it will be legal despite the lack of deed.

E. The client has a contractual licence. The agreement allows the landlord to move in additional licencees and so there cannot be exclusive possession.

Q48 of 90

Flag for review

A settlor created a trust for the benefit of his family and appointed a trustee to manage the trust property. The trust is created for the settlor's wife for her life (aged 60), remainder to his son (aged 40) and grandson (aged 17). All beneficiaries are alive. Seven years ago, the trustee sold £300,000 worth of investments to purchase shares in a private company on behalf of the trust. The trustee took no advice in respect of this purchase and the shares are now worthless. The beneficiaries have only now become aware of this and wish to sue the trustee for breach of trust. The trustee did not deliberately conceal this matter from the beneficiaries.

Which of the following is the most likely advice that would be given to the beneficiaries?

A. The wife is out of time to bring a claim for breach of trust against the trustee; the son and grandson are within time to bring a claim.

B. The wife, son and grandson are within time to bring a claim for breach of trust against the trustee.

C. The wife, son and grandson are out of time to bring a claim for breach of trust against the trustee.

D. The wife and son are out of time to bring a claim for breach of trust against the trustee; the grandson is within time to bring a claim.

E. The wife is within time to bring a claim for breach of trust against the trustee; the son and grandson are out of time to bring a claim.

Q49 of 90 Flag for review

A probate solicitor acts as the firm's Compliance Officer for Finance and Administration. The solicitor is reviewing the types of bank accounts in which client money may be held.

Which of the following statements accurately describes the types of accounts in which client money can be held?

A. Client money must be held in a client bank account. This can either be the firm's general client account or a separate designated deposit client account.

B. Firms can use a third-party managed account as well as their own client accounts.

C. A solicitor can never act as signatory on any bank account other than those operated by the firm.

D. A solicitor can operate a joint bank account, with someone outside the firm, to hold client money in certain circumstances.

E. Client money can only be held in the firm's general client bank account.

Q50 of 90 Flag for review

A client has sought advice from a solicitor following receipt of a rent demand. The client signed a 35-year lease agreement on a property in 1995. In 2015, the client assigned the lease with permission to the current tenant. The current tenant has not paid rent for the previous 12 months. The landlord is now seeking to recover the rent and has served a default notice on the client.

Which of the following explains the current position of the client?

A. The client is bound by privity of contract, and they will be liable for the 12 months of rent under their original contractual obligations.

B. The client will only be bound if the landlord can show that the client signed an Authorised Guarantee Agreement. If so, the client will then be liable for the last 12 months of rent.

C. The client is bound by privity of contract, but will only be liable for any amounts due within the preceding six months.

D. The client has been released from all of the leasehold covenants and so will not be liable for any of the past rent due.

E. The client will be bound by privity of estate, but will only be liable for any amounts due within the preceding six months.

Q51 of 90

Flag for review

A solicitor represents a client charged with theft, contrary to s 1 of the Theft Act 1968 in the magistrates' court. The client has admitted his guilt to the solicitor but wishes to plead not guilty.

What advice should the solicitor give to the client?

A. The solicitor should advise the client to plead guilty. If the client refuses to plead guilty, the solicitor must cease to act for him but must not inform the court of his reasons for doing so. ☐

B. The solicitor should advise the client to plead guilty. If the client refuses to plead guilty, the solicitor should enter a guilty plea on the client's behalf. ☐

C. The solicitor should advise the client to plead guilty. If the client refuses to plead guilty, the solicitor can continue to represent him but can only test the prosecution evidence. ☐

D. The solicitor should advise the client to plead guilty. If the client refuses to plead guilty, the solicitor can continue to represent him as though the client had not admitted his guilt. ☐

E. The solicitor should advise the client to plead guilty. If the client refuses to plead guilty, the solicitor must cease to act for him and must inform the court of his reasons for doing so. ☐

Q52 of 90 Flag for review

A woman executed a will prior to her death. The will is valid and leaves the entirety of her estate to a local charity. The woman's solicitor acts as executor of the will. During her lifetime, the woman attempted to create the following trusts:

- Trust over the woman's grandfather clock for the benefit of the woman's sister. The woman wrote a letter to her sister declaring a trust over the clock for the benefit of her sister, with the woman's friend acting as trustee. The trustee took possession of the clock prior to the woman's death.
- Trust over the woman's house for the benefit of the woman's brother. The woman orally declared a trust over the house for the benefit of her brother, with the woman's friend acting as trustee. The woman delivered the Land Certificate to the trustee, but did not execute a deed of transfer.
- Trust over the woman's shares in a private company for the benefit of the woman's son. The woman orally declared a trust over the shares for the benefit of her son, with the woman's friend acting as trustee. The woman completed a stock transfer form and delivered that to the trustee, along with the share certificate. The trustee failed to send the paperwork to the private company prior to the death of the woman.

Which of the following best describes the legal position?

A. The woman's estate shall pass according to the will to the local charity, except the grandfather clock, which will pass to the woman's sister. ☐

B. The woman's estate shall pass according to the will to the local charity, except the house, which will pass to the woman's brother and the shares in the private company, which will pass to the woman's son. ☐

C. The woman's estate shall pass according to the will to the local charity, except the house, which will pass to the woman's brother. ☐

D. The woman's estate shall pass according to the will to the local charity, except the grandfather clock, which will pass to the woman's sister, and the shares in the private company, which will pass to the woman's son. ☐

E. The woman's estate shall pass according to the will to the local charity, except the shares in the private company, which will pass to the woman's son. ☐

Q53 of 90 Flag for review

A solicitor acts for clients in a residential property sale. The clients ask the solicitor to arrange for a house clearance and cleaning company to prepare the house for sale whilst they are away on holiday for several months. The solicitor receives an invoice from the company for £2,000 + VAT (standard rate) and pays this promptly. The firm's name is on the invoice.

What accounting entry or entries are required in the client ledger to record the payment of the company's invoice?

A. Debit £2,000 client ledger business account. ☐

B. Debit £2,400 (as one entry) client ledger business account. ☐

C. Debit £2,000 and debit £400 (as two separate entries) client ledger business account. ☐

D. Debit £2,400 client ledger client account. ☐

E. Debit £2,000 client ledger client account. ☐

Q54 of 90 Flag for review

A man is charged with fraud by false representation. It is alleged that the man sold a sports car to a woman and orally represented that the car was a special edition model. The car had a special edition badge on the back, but the service history and paperwork identified that the badge was an optional extra and did not reflect the car model accurately. The man, who purported to be an expert in car models, had a suspicion that the car may not be the sports model, but failed to examine the service history and paperwork before selling the car. The man made a profit of over £7,000 on this basis.

Is the man likely to be guilty of fraud by false representation?

A. The man is likely to be guilty of fraud by false representation. The man made an oral representation to the woman, which he knew may have been false or misleading but continued regardless. As a result, the man made a financial gain. ☐

B. The man is likely to be guilty of fraud by false representation. The man made an oral representation to the woman, which, given the fact he purported to be an expert, he ought to have known may have been false or misleading but carried on regardless. As a result, the man made a financial gain. ☐

C. The man is unlikely to be guilty of fraud by false representation. Even though the man made an oral representation that was false or misleading, he did not intend to make a false representation. Even though the man made a financial gain, this was not the intended result. ☐

D. The man is likely to be guilty of fraud by false representation. The man made an oral representation to the woman that was false or misleading. The man should have checked the service history and paperwork, and therefore should have known that the representation may have been false or misleading. The man carried on regardless and made a financial gain as a result. ☐

E. The man is unlikely to be guilty of fraud by false representation. Even though the man made an oral representation to the woman, there is no evidence of reliance on that representation. In order for the man to be guilty of fraud by false representation, the prosecution must establish reliance on, or belief in, the false representation. ☐

Q55 of 90 Flag for review

A man who has a violent history is arrested on suspicion of murder. The man is taken to a police station and booked in by the custody officer. The man is interviewed, and the police are reviewing the information that he provided. The police are now approaching the first 24-hour limit and take the view that the man needs to be detained for a further period.

Which of the following statements best describes the procedure for authorising detention in these circumstances?

A. An officer of at least the rank of superintendent or above is required to authorise this period of further detention. Detention can be authorised for a further 12 hours.

B. An officer of at least the rank of inspector or above is required to authorise this period of further detention. Detention can be authorised for a further 12 hours.

C. An officer of at least the rank of superintendent or above is required to authorise this period of further detention. Detention can be authorised for a further 24 hours.

D. An officer of at least the rank of inspector or above is required to authorise this period of further detention. Detention can be authorised for a further 24 hours.

E. An officer of at least the rank of inspector or above is required to authorise this period of further detention if they are of the view that the detention is necessary to secure further information pertaining to the investigation.

Q56 of 90 Flag for review

A man is the sole trustee for a large family trust for the two grandsons of the settlor, which consists of £250,000 worth of investments. Some of the investments are not performing strongly and the man proposes to reinvest £150,000 into a number of highly speculative schemes. The man contacts the elder grandson (aged 21) and informs him of his plans. The man contacts the elder grandson over the telephone and informs him that the investments are 'likely to be highly profitable' and that it will be a 'superb opportunity for the trust'. The telephone conversation lasts no longer than a minute or two and the elder grandson agrees to the investment. The man also contacts the younger grandson (aged 16) and informs him that the elder grandson has agreed to the investment; the younger grandson also agrees. The man makes the proposed investments, which cause significant losses to the trust fund. The grandsons are considering whether to bring a claim for breach of trust.

Which of the following best describes whether any protection is available for the man for the breach of trust?

A. The man will have a defence to liability as he obtained the consent of the elder grandson; the lack of consent from the younger grandson is irrelevant.

B. The man will not have a defence to liability as he did not obtain the voluntary consent of the elder grandson; the lack of consent from the younger grandson is irrelevant.

C. The man will not have a defence to liability as he did not obtain the informed consent of the elder grandson and the younger grandson did not have the capacity to consent.

D. The man will have a defence to liability as he obtained the consent of both the elder grandson and the younger grandson.

E. The man will not have a defence to liability as he did not obtain the informed consent of the elder grandson; the lack of consent from the younger grandson is irrelevant.

Q57 of 90 Flag for review

In 1990, the freehold owner (landlord) granted a commercial lease by deed to Tenant One for a term of 40 years. The lease contained a repairing obligation on the part of Tenant One and a right of forfeiture. Tenant One's company quickly expanded its business and moved to larger premises, assigning the lease to Tenant Two in 1996. In 2010, the lease was assigned to Tenant Three. Each assignment was completed by deed and with the consent of the freehold owner. The property is in disrepair and Tenant Three does not have the financial resources to undertake the work. The landlord does not wish to bring the lease to an end as it would be difficult to find a new tenant.

Which of the following provides the best advice to the landlord?

A. The landlord should pursue a claim for damages for breach of repair against Tenant Two under privity of contract. ☐

B. The landlord should commence forfeiture proceedings. ☐

C. The landlord should use self-help to enter the property and conduct the repairs. They will then be able to recover the cost from Tenant Three as a debt due. ☐

D. The landlord should pursue a claim in damages for breach of repair against Tenant One under privity of contract. ☐

E. The landlord should pursue a claim in damages for breach of repair against Tenant Three under privity of estate. ☐

Q58 of 90 Flag for review

A woman intends to create a trust for the benefit of the two children of her best friend. The trust consists of shares in a private limited company and £100,000. The woman sends a letter to her best friend, which reads: 'As we discussed over the phone, I am giving you my shares and £100,000 for the benefit of your children. Please hold the property for them until they turn 25. Please give the majority to your eldest child (your daughter) as she needs it the most, but do make sure there is enough left for your son.'

Which of the following most accurately describes the legal position?

A. The woman has created a successful express trust; the best friend holds the shares and money on trust for her two children. ☐

B. The woman has not created a successful express trust as there is a lack of certainty of intention; the best friend will hold the shares and money on resulting trust for the woman. ☐

C. The woman has not created a successful express trust; the best friend is entitled to the shares and money absolutely. ☐

D. The woman has not created a successful express trust as there is a lack of certainty of objects; the best friend will hold the shares and money on resulting trust for the woman. ☐

E. The woman has not created a successful express trust as there is a lack of certainty of subject matter; the best friend will hold the shares and money on resulting trust for the woman. ☐

Q59 of 90 Flag for review

A solicitor acts on behalf of a client who wishes to sell a piece of property. The client has received four offers on the property and has asked the solicitor to submit draft contracts to each party. The client does not wish each individual party to know that contractual documents have been submitted to other parties, however. The solicitor has sought consent from the client to disclose the contract race to the four parties who have made offers. The client has refused to provide such consent.

How should the solicitor act in response to this request from the client?

A. The solicitor can continue to act for the client so long as the client is advised as to the risks associated with submitting draft contractual documents to multiple parties. ☐

B. The solicitor must cease to act immediately and must disclose the reason for ceasing to act to the four prospective buyers. ☐

C. The solicitor can continue to act for the client as it is common for multiple parties to bid on one piece of property. ☐

D. The solicitor must cease to act immediately but must not disclose the reason for ceasing to act to the four prospective buyers. ☐

E. The solicitor can continue to act for the client as the solicitor has an obligation to keep the client's affairs confidential. ☐

Q60 of 90 Flag for review

A divorced woman died leaving an estate valued at £800,000. The woman executed a valid will prior to her death, which stated that the estate was to be distributed to the woman's two children equally. The estate is subject to inheritance tax.

Who is responsible for paying the inheritance tax?

A. The woman's children are collectively responsible for paying the inheritance tax on the estate. ☐

B. The woman's children are individually responsible for paying the inheritance tax on the amount they each receive. ☐

C. The government is responsible for paying the inheritance tax on the estate, given that the estate is valued at less than £1,000,000. ☐

D. The executor of the woman's will is responsible for paying the inheritance tax from the estate before distributing the assets to the woman's children. ☐

E. The creditors of the woman are responsible for paying the inheritance tax on the estate. ☐

Q61 of 90 Flag for review

A client is seeking to assign a 10-year legal lease that they signed in 2020. The original agreement contained a covenant against assignment without the landlord's permission. The client has found an appropriate assignee but the landlord is refusing to grant consent as they have a family feud with the proposed assignee.

Which of the following best explains the client's position?

A. The landlord will have to grant permission. As there is not an absolute covenant against assignment, the landlord cannot withhold their consent for any reason they see fit. ☐

B. The landlord will have to grant permission. As the qualified covenant against assignment is converted to a fully qualified covenant, the landlord must grant consent unless there are reasonable grounds. Family feuds are not reasonable grounds. ☐

C. The landlord will not have to grant permission. As there is a qualified covenant against assignment, the landlord is able to withhold their permission for any reason, including personal reasons. ☐

D. The landlord will not have to grant permission. As there is a fully qualified covenant, the landlord must grant consent unless there are reasonable grounds. Family feuds are reasonable grounds for refusal. ☐

E. The landlord will not have to grant permission. As the qualified covenant against assignment is converted to a fully qualified covenant, the landlord must grant consent unless there are reasonable grounds. Family feuds are reasonable grounds for refusal. ☐

Q62 of 90 Flag for review

A boy (aged 15) is tried and convicted in the youth court for burglary, contrary to s 9 of the Theft Act 1968. The lay bench is about to consider the appropriate sentence and the solicitor is about to make submissions about a referral order.

Which of the following statements best describes a referral order?

A. A referral order is where a youth agrees to abide by a 'contract' of behaviour, which is reviewed by a Youth Offender Panel, and can be made by the youth court, an adult magistrates' court and the Crown Court. ☐

B. A referral order is where a youth agrees to abide by a 'contract' of behaviour, which is reviewed by a Youth Offender Panel, and can be made by the youth court and an adult magistrates' court, but not the Crown Court. ☐

C. A referral order is where a youth agrees to abide by a 'contract' of behaviour, which is reviewed by a Youth Offender Panel, and can be made by the youth court and the Crown Court, but not an adult magistrates' court. ☐

D. A referral order is where a youth agrees to abide by a 'contract' of behaviour, which is reviewed by a Youth Offender Panel. It can be in place for 3–12 months and is considered mandatory only where the youth pleads guilty to an imprisonable offence. ☐

E. A referral order is where a youth agrees to abide by a 'contract' of behaviour, which is reviewed by a Youth Offender Panel. It can be in place for 3–12 months and is considered discretionary in all cases. ☐

Q63 of 90

Flag for review

A solicitor is advising a client in relation to forfeiture proceedings. The client is the tenant under a 10-year lease on a residential premises. The lease contains a repairing covenant and a forfeiture covenant. The tenant has sub-leased part of the co-residential premises with permission. The sub-lease contains the same repairing and forfeiture clauses. The sub-tenant has allowed part of the property to fall into disrepair and the landlord is now seeking to forfeit the client's lease and take possession of the whole property. The client wishes to remain in possession, and is willing to forfeit the sub-lease and carry out the necessary repairs.

Which of the following best explains the position of the client in relation to the lease?

A. The landlord will be required to serve notice on the client to forfeit the lease. However, the client will be able to claim relief from forfeiture and this will likely be successful as the breach is remediable. ☐

B. The landlord will be able to forfeit the lease by peaceable re-entry. The client will not be able to claim any relief as there has been a breach of a leasehold covenant. ☐

C. The landlord will be required to serve notice but can only forfeit the sub-lease as the tenant has not breached any of their covenants. The client will retain the parts of the property they currently occupy. ☐

D. The landlord will not be able to forfeit the lease. Although there is a forfeiture clause, the breach of a repairing covenant is not sufficient and only failure to pay rent will allow the landlord to forfeit the lease. ☐

E. The landlord will be required to serve notice on the client to forfeit the lease. As the client has allowed their sub-tenant to let the property fall into disrepair, they will be responsible and the forfeiture will be successful. ☐

Q64 of 90

Flag for review

A youth is charged with causing grievous bodily harm with intent, contrary to s 18 of the Offences Against the Person Act 1861. This offence is classed as a grave crime, and the lay bench is considering whether to retain jurisdiction or send the case for trial to the Crown Court.

Which of the following statements best describes a grave crime?

A. A grave crime is an offence that can be punished by imprisonment of at least 14 years and is fixed by law for an adult offender over the age of 21. ☐

B. A grave crime is an offence that can be punished by imprisonment of at least 12 years and is not fixed by law for an adult offender over the age of 21. ☐

C. A grave crime is an offence that can be punished by imprisonment of at least 14 years and is not fixed by law for an adult offender over the age of 21. ☐

D. A grave crime is an offence that can be punished by imprisonment of at least 12 years and is not fixed by law for an adult offender over the age of 18. ☐

E. A grave crime is an offence that can be punished by imprisonment of at least 14 years and is fixed by law for an adult offender over the age of 18. ☐

Q65 of 90

Flag for review

A man lived with a woman who was his wife. For over 15 years, the woman subjected the man to abuse, both physical and psychological, which increased in severity as the years went on. The woman would control the bank accounts, burn him with cigarette lighters, physically assault him and emotionally blackmail him using their young children. One day, after reaching breaking point, the man took a baseball bat and struck the woman over the head repeatedly. The woman died as a result, and the man was charged with murder.

Is the defence of loss of control available to the man?

A. The man is likely to be able to rely on the defence of loss of control. The man acted in a way that appears to be out of character and as a result of a qualifying trigger. The question of whether there was a loss of control is one for the jury, and the loss of control does not need to be sudden. ☐

B. The man is unlikely to be able to rely on the defence of loss of control. Although the man acted in a way that appears to be out of character and as a result of a qualifying trigger, the loss of control must be sudden; this is not the case for the man. ☐

C. The man is unlikely to be able to rely on the defence of loss of control. Although the man acted in a way that appears to be out of character, there appears to be no evidence that the man was in fear of the use of violence. ☐

D. The man is likely to be able to rely on the defence of loss of control. The man acted in a way that appears to be out of character. The man could argue that he has been seriously wronged, and the jury must apply an objective test to establish whether the man has been seriously wronged. ☐

E. The man is unlikely to be able to rely on the defence of loss of control. This is because the loss of control does not appear to arise out of a recognised medical condition and cause a substantial impairment. As there is no evidence on the facts of a medical impairment that caused the loss of control, the man cannot run the defence of loss of control. ☐

Q66 of 90 Flag for review

A man died intestate, aged 90. The man lived in a nursing home, the fees being paid for by the local authority. The man has no surviving spouse, and his daughter, an only child, is his only living relative. At the date of death, the man's estate consisted of the following:

- Cash in hand: £114
- Personal bank account: £875
- State pension arrears for the month of death: £164
- Cash in an ISA held with National Savings and Investments (NS&I): £3,632.

The daughter seeks advice as to the proper procedure for dealing with the man's estate.

Which of the following best describes the legal position?

A. The man's daughter must apply for a grant of representation in order to obtain the content of the man's estate as the individual assets owned by the man at the time of his death do not exceed £5,000. ☐

B. The man's daughter is not required to apply for a grant of representation in order to obtain the content of the man's estate as the man's total estate at the time of his death does not exceed £5,000. ☐

C. The man's daughter should contact each relevant institution to ask whether they will release the man's funds without a grant of representation. ☐

D. The man's daughter is not required to apply for a grant of representation in order to obtain the content of the man's estate as the individual assets owned by the man at the time of his death do not exceed £5,000. ☐

E. The man's daughter must apply for a grant of representation in order to obtain the content of the man's estate as the man's total estate at the time of his death does not exceed £5,000. ☐

Q67 of 90

Flag for review

A solicitor is called to the police station to represent two suspects, a woman and a man, accused of robbery of a watch, contrary to s 8 of the Theft Act 1968. The woman is identified by police as the person who pushed the victim and stole the watch whilst the man acted as a lookout.

Which of the following best describes the legal position?

A. A principal offender is an individual who commits the substantive offence and can be considered as the actual perpetrator. In this case, the woman will likely be considered the principal offender.

B. A principal offender is an individual who has jointly committed the substantive offence with another and is considered the actual perpetrator. In this case, both the man and the woman will likely be considered joint principal offenders.

C. A principal offender is an individual who does not commit the substantive offence but has assisted in the commission of the offence in a significant manner. In this case, the man will likely be considered the principal offender.

D. A principal offender is an individual who commits the substantive offence and can be considered as the actual perpetrator. In this case, the man will likely be considered the principal offender.

E. A principal offender is an individual who commits the substantive offence and can be considered as the actual preparator through preparation. A principal offender forms the mens rea for the offence, and takes a leading role in the planning of the execution of the offence when multiple offenders are involved. In this case, the man will likely be considered the principal offender.

Q68 of 90 Flag for review

A man has been charged with murder. It is alleged that the man drove his car onto a railway track and waited for a train to hit him. At the last minute, the man got out of his car and ran away, but the train hit the car, derailed and killed several passengers. To date, the man has been told that he has no defence. A new solicitor attends the man in conference and asks the man more about what happened. The man, who currently has no psychiatric mental illnesses, explains that he intended to kill himself but appreciated that there was a virtual certainty that his actions would cause the death of people on the train. The solicitor is now considering the defence of diminished responsibility.

Which of the following best describes the defence of diminished responsibility and the action that the solicitor should take in light of the conference with the man?

A. The solicitor should advise the man that he has a defence in law. The man has provided evidence of an abnormality of mental functioning that has caused a substantial impairment, providing an explanation for the killing. ☐

B. The solicitor should gain consent from the man to have a psychiatric assessment carried out to determine whether the man has any recognised medical conditions, and to establish whether this caused an abnormality of mental functioning at the material times, which resulted in a substantial impairment. The solicitor should advise that there may be a defence. ☐

C. The solicitor should advise that the man does not have a defence in law. There is no psychiatric evidence to support the man's claim, which shows that the man was suffering an abnormality of mental functioning at the material times. Furthermore, it is not for the solicitor to form a defence from an account offered by the man. ☐

D. The solicitor should gain consent from the man to have a psychiatric assessment carried out to determine whether the man has any recognised medical conditions, and to establish whether this caused an abnormality of the mind at the material times, which resulted in a significant impairment. The solicitor should advise that there may be a defence. ☐

E. The solicitor should advise that the man has a defence in law. The man has provided evidence that he was suffering from an abnormality of the mind, which caused a significant impairment, providing an explanation for the killing. ☐

Q69 of 90 Flag for review

A man is charged with common assault, having pushed a woman over in the street in anger, causing no injury. The man was heavily intoxicated at the time he committed the offence.

Which of the following statements best describes the defence of intoxication?

A. As the man is charged with an offence of basic intent, was voluntarily intoxicated and consumed a dangerous intoxicant, the defence of intoxication can be relied upon. ☐

B. As the man was voluntarily intoxicated, the defence of intoxication can always be relied upon regardless of whether the offence is one of specific or basic intent. ☐

C. As the man is charged with an offence of specific intent, was voluntarily intoxicated and consumed a dangerous intoxicant, the defence of intoxication can be relied upon. ☐

D. As the man is charged with an offence of basic intent, was voluntarily intoxicated and consumed a non-dangerous intoxicant, the defence of intoxication cannot be relied upon. ☐

E. As the man is charged with an offence of basic intent, was voluntarily intoxicated and consumed a dangerous intoxicant, the defence of intoxication cannot be relied upon. ☐

Q70 of 90

Flag for review

A woman has been appointed as the executor of her late father's estate. The woman's father had debts that need to be paid off, but the estate's value is not sufficient to settle all debts as well as the legacies. The woman seeks advice as to the order in which the assets in the estate should be sold to pay off the debts.

Which of the following best describes the order in which assets should be sold to pay off the estate's debts?

A. Property specifically given for the payment of debts; property undisposed of by the will; property charged for the payment of debts; money retained to pay pecuniary legacies; any property gifted in the residue; property over which the woman has a general power; property specifically gifted.

B. Property over which the woman has a general power; property specifically given for the payment of debts; any property gifted in the residue; property undisposed of by the will; money retained to pay pecuniary legacies; property charged for the payment of debts; property specifically gifted.

C. Property undisposed of by the will; any property gifted in the residue; property specifically given for the payment of debts; property charged for the payment of debts; money retained to pay pecuniary legacies; property specifically gifted; property over which the woman has a general power.

D. Property charged for the payment of debts; property over which the woman has a general power; any property gifted in the residue; property specifically given for the payment of debts; property undisposed of by the will; money retained to pay pecuniary legacies; property specifically gifted.

E. Any property gifted in the residue; property undisposed of by the will; property charged for the payment of debts; property specifically given for the payment of debts; property specifically gifted; property over which the woman has a general power; money retained to pay pecuniary legacies.

Q71 of 90

Flag for review

A solicitor is asked to draft a will for a client. The client has retained the solicitor on a number of occasions in respect of his businesses. As a result of their long-standing relationship, the client requests that the solicitor include a legacy in the will that bequeaths £5,000 to the solicitor.

Which of the following best describes how the solicitor should act in these circumstances?

A. The solicitor can draft the will and accept the legacy of £5,000.

B. The solicitor cannot draft the will given the inclusion of the legacy of £5,000 to the solicitor.

C. The solicitor can draft the will but cannot include the legacy of £5,000 in the will.

D. The solicitor cannot draft the will as he has a personal connection to the client which compromises the solicitor's independence.

E. The solicitor can draft the will and can include the legacy of £5,000 in the will so long as the client has taken independent legal advice on that specific legacy.

Q72 of 90 Flag for review

A man arrives at an authorised place of detention under arrest on suspicion of common assault. The man has to wait approximately 30 minutes to be booked into custody. The custody officer records the relevant details and authorises detention. Six hours later, the first review is carried out.

Which of the following statements best describes the review clock?

A. The review clock begins when the man arrives at the authorised place of detention, and a review must be undertaken at periods not less than at 6 hours, 15 hours, and 24 hours into detention.

B. The review clock begins when the man's detention is first authorised by the custody officer, and a review must be undertaken at periods not less than at 6 hours, 15 hours, and 24 hours into detention.

C. The review clock begins when the man's detention is first authorised by the custody officer, and a review must be undertaken at periods not less than at 9 hours, 18 hours, and 24 hours into detention.

D. The review clock begins when the man arrives at the authorised place of detention, and a review must be undertaken at periods not less than at 24 hours, 36 hours, and 72 hours into detention

E. The review clock begins when the man's detention is first authorised by the custody officer, and a review must be undertaken at periods not less than at 24 hours, 36 hours, and 72 hours into detention.

Q73 of 90 Flag for review

A man died intestate, leaving an estate worth £700,000. The following persons intend to submit a claim under the Inheritance (Provision for Family and Dependants) Act 1975 ('the 1975 Act'):

- the man's current girlfriend, with whom he has cohabited for the past six months up to his death
- the man's ex-wife, who has recently remarried
- the man's 21-year-old son
- the man's brother, who was receiving regular payments of large sums of money to him from the man up to the man's death in order to help him pay his bills and debts.

Which of these persons have standing to apply for financial provision under the 1975 Act?

A. Only the man's ex-wife and brother have standing to apply for financial provision.

B. Only the man's current girlfriend and 21-year-old son have standing to apply for financial provision.

C. Only the man's 21-year-old son and brother have standing to apply for financial provision.

D. Only the man's ex-wife, 21-year-old son and brother have standing to apply for financial provision.

E. Only the man's current girlfriend, 21-year-old son and brother have standing to apply for financial provision.

Q74 of 90 Flag for review

A man had an argument with his neighbour because the neighbour kept parking his car on the man's driveway. The argument resulted in the neighbour smashing the man's porch window. The man decided to get his revenge and asked a friend to go with him to threaten the neighbour. It was agreed between the man and his friend that the man only wanted to scare the neighbour. One night, the man and his friend went to visit the neighbour and knocked on the door loudly. The man's friend then started shouting abuse at the neighbour. The neighbour opened the door, and as he did so, the man produced a knife and stabbed the neighbour four times. The neighbour survived, and the man and his friend are jointly charged with attempted murder.

Which of the following statements best describes the law relating to accomplices?

A. For the friend to be convicted as an accomplice, mere presence at the scene is sufficient. The friend must have had knowledge of the essential matters and encouraged the commission of the principal offence. ☐

B. For the friend to be convicted as an accomplice, mere presence at the scene is insufficient. Instead, the friend must have had knowledge of the essential matters and intended to assist or encourage the man to commit murder. ☐

C. For the friend to be convicted as an accomplice, mere presence at the scene is sufficient. Also, the friend must have foreseen that the man was going to commit the more serious offence. ☐

D. For the friend to be convicted as an accomplice, mere presence at the scene is insufficient. The friend must have had knowledge of the essential matters and encouraged the commission of murder. Also, the man must be convicted of attempted murder for the friend to be convicted as well. ☐

E. For the friend to be convicted as an accomplice, mere presence at the scene is sufficient. The friend must have had knowledge of the essential matters and encouraged the commission of murder. If, however, the friend can demonstrate that there was an overwhelming supervening event, he may not be guilty. ☐

Q75 of 90 Flag for review

A man is charged with robbery. The man has one previous conviction for possession of cannabis from 12 years ago, for which he received a financial penalty. There is no evidence of any further offending or any other misconduct. The man gives evidence denying the offence. At trial, the man's solicitor submits that the man should be treated as being of effective good character.

Which of the following best reflects the trial judge's obligations in relation to a good character direction?

A. The judge must refuse to give any good character direction because the man has a previous conviction. ☐

B. The judge may, in the exercise of discretion, give a modified good character direction as necessary to ensure the jury are not misled. ☐

C. The judge must give a full good character direction, including both the credibility and propensity limb, because the conviction is spent. ☐

D. The judge may, in the exercise of discretion, give only a direction on the propensity limb, because the credibility limb applies only if the man had no convictions. ☐

E. The judge must leave the issue of character entirely to the jury without judicial direction. ☐

Q76 of 90 Flag for review

A woman is appointed power of attorney over her aunt's estate. Last year, the woman's aunt was deemed incapable of taking control of her affairs, including finances, and the woman assumed responsibility. Before this, the woman knew that her aunt wanted to invest her money in stocks and shares for her family. After the woman became responsible for her aunt's finances, she started to make small, incremental payments to herself from her aunt's bank account. These payments increased in size and frequency, and the woman referred to them as 'necessary care expenses' for her aunt, but the woman spent this money on herself. The total value was £30,000. The woman is now being prosecuted for fraud.

Which offence is the woman most likely to be charged with?

A. The woman will most likely be charged with fraud by false representation because she made a representation that was misleading by referring to the payments as 'necessary care expenses'. The woman ought to have known that this was false. ☐

B. The woman will most likely be charged with fraud by false representation because she made a false representation of 'necessary care expenses'. The woman knew that this was false, and she made a financial gain from her dishonest conduct. ☐

C. The woman will most likely be charged with fraud by abuse of position because the woman occupied a position of trust and was expected to safeguard her aunt's financial interests. The woman abused this position through dishonesty and made a financial gain. ☐

D. The woman will most likely be charged with fraud by failing to disclose because the woman was under a legal duty to disclose her position to the bank but failed to do so. The woman was dishonest in her conduct, and as a result made a financial gain. ☐

E. The woman will most likely be charged with fraud by abuse of position because the woman occupied a position of trust and was expected to act against the financial interests of her aunt. The woman abused this position dishonestly and made a financial gain. ☐

Q77 of 90 Flag for review

A sole practitioner solicitor acts on behalf of a client in a commercial property transaction. The client has entrusted the solicitor with a substantial amount of money for the purposes of purchasing premises to be used for a commercial enterprise.

Which of the following best describes what the solicitor can do with the money whilst it is entrusted to them?

A. The solicitor can use the money for her own personal expenses so long as she replaces it before the completion of the commercial transaction. ☐

B. The solicitor should hold the client's money in their own personal account as long as the solicitor keeps accurate records of the sum. ☐

C. The solicitor should hold the client's money in their own business account as long as the solicitor keeps accurate records of the sum. ☐

D. The solicitor can use the money to support other clients who require funds, so long as the money is repaid before the completion of the commercial transaction. ☐

E. The solicitor should hold the client's money in a separate client account that is designated as a client account. ☐

Q78 of 90 Flag for review

A woman is the sole owner of her house. The woman purchased the house with use of her own funds, and a loan of £5,000 from her friend. The loan was eventually repaid to the friend. The friend also paid for the conveyancing legal fees, which was not repaid to them. One year ago, the woman invited this friend to live with her. The woman made all mortgage repayments except for a three-month period when the woman was unemployed following redundancy. In this three-month period, the friend made the mortgage repayments. The woman has not paid the friend back for these payments. The friend also paid for the installation of a new kitchen and regularly cared for the woman's children whilst she was at work. The friendship between the woman and the friend has recently broken down and the woman demands the friend leave the house. The friend believes that they have a beneficial entitlement to the house.

Which of the following best describes whether the friend has a claim over the house?

A. The friend will likely have a right to beneficial entitlement because they contributed to the mortgage repayments. ☐

B. The friend will likely have a right to beneficial entitlement because they paid for the installation of a new kitchen. ☐

C. The friend will likely have a right to beneficial entitlement because they contributed to the initial purchase of the house. ☐

D. The friend will likely have a right to beneficial entitlement because they paid for the conveyancing legal fees. ☐

E. The friend will likely have a right to beneficial entitlement because they cared for the woman's children whilst she was at work. ☐

Q79 of 90 Flag for review

A solicitor currently holds client money in the firm's client account to ensure the timely completion of a commercial transaction. The solicitor has sought advice on the circumstances where they are permitted to withdraw money from the client account.

Which of the following best describes when the solicitor can withdraw money from the client account?

A. The solicitor can withdraw any amount of money from the client account so long as they consider that it is in the best interests of the client. ☐

B. The solicitor can withdraw any amount of money from the client account to cover invoices or disbursements related to the matter for which the money is held, or with the client's informed consent. ☐

C. The solicitor can withdraw any amount of money from the client account so long as the money is replaced before the transaction is complete. ☐

D. The solicitor can withdraw any amount of money from the client account if they require the money to pay for the firm's general expenses. ☐

E. The solicitor can withdraw any amount of money from the client account as long as the solicitor notifies the client of this fact before doing so. ☐

Q80 of 90 Flag for review

A client is purchasing a freehold property that has been used as a factory since 1975. The client intends to construct a multi-storey car park in its place. The solicitor acting on behalf of the client has been asked to provide advice in relation to whether the client will need to pay VAT on the purchase.

Which of the following statements provides the best advice to the client?

A. VAT will not be payable as the purchase of the building is zero-rated. ☐
B. VAT will be included in the purchase price if the seller opted to tax prior to completion and the standard conditions are used. ☐
C. VAT will not be payable as the purchase of the building is standard-rated. ☐
D. VAT will be included in the purchase price if the contract excludes the standard commercial property conditions. ☐
E. VAT will not be payable as it will be a transfer of a business as a going concern. ☐

Q81 of 90 Flag for review

A woman died last month. The woman gifted £10,000 to her daughter three years ago and did not make any other lifetime gifts.

Which of the following accurately reflects the legal position regarding lifetime transfers and inheritance tax?

A. The full gift of £10,000 will be subject to inheritance tax. ☐
B. £4,000 of the gift will be subject to inheritance tax. ☐
C. The gift is not subject to any inheritance tax. ☐
D. £7,000 of the gift will be subject to inheritance tax. ☐
E. £3,000 of the gift will be subject to inheritance tax. ☐

Q82 of 90 Flag for review

Three women planned the commission of a burglary of a commercial premises. It was decided that each woman would have a particular role to play. The first woman would drive the getaway car. The second woman would procure the tools to break into the commercial premises and stand guard, but not enter the premises. The third woman would enter the property and take the items.

Which of the following statements best describes the type of offender each of the women would be?

A. The first woman would be an accomplice as she would not be involved in the burglary, whereas the second woman and third woman would be joint principal offenders. ☐

B. The first woman, the second woman and the third woman would all be joint principal offenders as they all shared knowledge of essential matters and knew that a burglary would be committed. ☐

C. The first woman and third woman would be accomplices, and the second woman would be the principal offender, as she procured the tools to commit the substantive offence. ☐

D. The first woman and second woman would be accomplices, and the third woman would be the principal offender. This is because the first woman and the second woman had knowledge of the essential matters, and assisted and encouraged the commission of the substantive offence by the third woman. ☐

E. The first woman would be the principal offender, and the second woman and third woman would be accomplices. This is because the first woman had the intention to assist and encourage the commission of the substantive offence. ☐

Q83 of 90 Flag for review

A solicitor is acting for the buyer of a freehold property with unregistered title. The solicitor has been provided with a series of documents by the seller's solicitor.

Which of the following documents would be sufficient to demonstrate root of good title?

A. A planning permission for the property, dated 15 May 2015. ☐

B. A will devising the property, dated 20 May 1984. ☐

C. A conveyance of the property, dated 21 August 1995. ☐

D. A land charges search certificate, dated 8 March 2000. ☐

E. A deed of trust, dated 3 December 1988. ☐

Q84 of 90 Flag for review

A woman executes a will that includes the following clauses:
'I give £500 to my trustees to care for my dog; I give £1,000 to my church in order to say a private mass in my memory after my death; I give £900 to my trustees for the purposes of providing some useful memorial to myself.'

The woman has only one dog. The woman identifies that the trust shall last no longer than 10 years.

Which of the following gifts (if any) are valid and enforceable?

A. The gift to care for the dog is a valid private purpose trust; the gift to say a private mass and the memorial are not valid as they offend the rules against perpetuity. ☐
B. None of the gifts are valid as there is no ascertainable beneficiary. ☐
C. The gift to care for the dog and the gift in order to say a private mass are valid as private purpose trusts; the gift to provide some useful memorial is not valid as it lacks certainty. ☐
D. None of the gifts are valid as they offend the rules against perpetuity. ☐
E. All of the gifts are valid private purpose trusts. ☐

Q85 of 90 Flag for review

A man has been appointed as the executor of his late father's estate, which includes several rental properties. The man seeks advice as to whether he is personally liable for any Income Tax (IT) or Capital Gains Tax (CGT) that may be due on the estate's income and gains.

Which of the following accurately reflects the liability of a personal representative for IT and CGT?

A. If a personal representative distributes the estate's assets within the tax year of the deceased's death, they are not liable for any IT or CGT. ☐
B. The personal representative is only liable for IT and CGT on the assets that they retain after distributing the estate. ☐
C. A personal representative is personally liable for any IT or CGT due on the estate's income and gains, regardless of whether they distribute the assets. ☐
D. A personal representative's liability for IT and CGT is limited to the value of the estate's assets. ☐
E. The personal representative's liability for IT and CGT depends on whether they are acting as an executor or administrator. ☐

Q86 of 90

Flag for review

A solicitor acts for personal representatives when administering the estate of a client who died intestate. During the administration period, the solicitor instructs an antiques dealer to value certain assets belonging to the estate. The antiques dealer sends the solicitor an invoice for their charges + VAT (standard rate). The firm's name is on the invoice.

Which of the following statements best describes the way in which payment of this invoice should be treated?

A. Payment of the invoice must be made using the principal method. Payment of the charges + VAT must be made from the business account. These can be recouped from the clients when the solicitor sends them a bill.

B. Payment of the invoice must be made using the principal method. Payment can be made from the client account providing there are sufficient funds available to cover the charges + VAT.

C. Payment of the invoice must be made using the principal method. Payment of the charges can be made from the client account providing there are sufficient funds available to cover the bill. However, the VAT element must be paid from the business account.

D. Payment of the invoice must be made using the agency method. Payment can be made from the client account providing there are sufficient funds available to cover the charges + VAT.

E. Payment of the invoice must be made using the agency method. Payment of the charges + VAT must be made from the business account. These can be recouped from the clients when the solicitor sends them a bill.

Q87 of 90

Flag for review

A man has inherited shares in a private company and a piece of land from his late grandfather's estate. The shares were valued at £500,000, and the land was valued at £350,000 at the time of the grandfather's death. The man has now sold the shares for £550,000 and the land for £330,000.

Which of the following accurately reflects the liability of the man for Capital Gains Tax (CGT)?

A. The man is not liable to pay CGT on the shares or the land.

B. The man is liable to pay CGT based on the sale price of the shares and the inheritance price of the land.

C. The man is liable to pay CGT based on the value increase of the shares, and value decrease of the land, since the time of inheritance.

D. The man is liable to pay CGT based on the inheritance price of the shares and the land.

E. The man is liable to pay CGT based on the value increase of the shares since the time of inheritance. The man is not liable to pay CGT on the land.

Q88 of 90 Flag for review

A solicitor acts on behalf of a client purchasing a freehold property in England. A single-storey rear extension was completed two-and-a-half years ago. Planning permission was obtained. The solicitor has received the results of the local authority search, which confirm that planning permission was obtained but building regulation consent was not.

Which of the following statements best represents the advice that should be provided to the client?

A. Proceedings for non-compliance could be brought against the client and therefore insurance should be obtained to protect the client from liability. ☐

B. As planning permission has been granted, this will not be of concern for the client. ☐

C. An enforcement notice requiring alteration or removal cannot be served as the one-year rule has passed. ☐

D. An enforcement option of an injunction will not be served as the one-year rule has passed. ☐

E. The search will not be a concern, providing that the client obtains a full structural survey. ☐

Q89 of 90 Flag for review

A woman is a housekeeper who has lived with a family for much of her life. As part of her duties, the woman cares for a disabled member of the family. The woman was promised the right to stay in the house for as long as she wanted rent-free; in exchange, the woman received no remuneration for the services provided. The woman had numerous opportunities to leave the family and take up another paying job elsewhere but chose not to do so, given the offer to remain in the house rent-free. The disabled member of the family has died, and another member of the household seeks to evict the woman.

Which of the following is the most likely legal position?

A. The woman can prevent her eviction and it is likely that she can exercise a right to occupy the house through proprietary estoppel as she has relied to her detriment on an assurance that she can remain in the house for as long as she wanted. ☐

B. The woman cannot prevent her eviction as she has not acted to her detriment given that she lived in the house rent-free. ☐

C. The woman can prevent her eviction and it is likely that she can claim an interest in the house through proprietary estoppel, as she has relied to her detriment on an assurance that she can remain in the house for as long as she wanted. ☐

D. The woman cannot prevent her eviction as her services are no longer required, given that the disabled member of the family has died. ☐

E. The woman can prevent her eviction and she can automatically exercise a right to occupy the house through proprietary estoppel as she has relied to her detriment on an assurance that she can remain in the house for as long as she wanted. ☐

Q90 of 90

Flag for review

A solicitor acts on behalf of a landlord who has sought advice in relation to a problematic tenant. The tenant has been paying the rent but they have allowed the property to fall into a state of disrepair. The lease was initially granted in 1998 for a period of 125 years. The original tenant assigned the lease to the current tenant three years ago. There is a covenant in the lease that states 'The Tenant covenants with the Landlord ... As often as may be required to repair, renew and maintain the Premises'.

Which of the following statements provides the best advice for the solicitor to give to the client?

A. The landlord should seek a remedy of an injunction for a breach of covenant. ☐

B. The landlord should seek a remedy of pursing the former tenant as they will remain liable for a breach of covenant. ☐

C. The landlord could forfeit the lease immediately for a breach of covenant. ☐

D. The landlord could seek a remedy of damages or specific performance for a breach of covenant. ☐

E. The landlord can only seek a remedy of specific performance for a breach of covenant. ☐

■ REFLECTION

CANDIDATE INSTRUCTIONS

Session 2, and the test, has now ended. In the real SQE1 assessment, once Session 2 has ended you cannot return to this session, nor can you return to Session 1.

In the real assessment, you will see a display screen that reminds you about how to access your results. This information has been summarised on **page 159**. Please also note the timings on the SQE section of the SRA website for the release of results.

PAUSE TO REFLECT

Now that you have completed the *FLK2 Practice Assessments*, reflect on your experience. Be honest with yourself in considering the reflective questions in Table 4.

Table 4: Reflecting on your FLK2 practice assessments

How did it feel to take a closed-book timed assessment?	• Did you feel prepared to sit the simulated SQE-style assessment? • Did you feel confident in your ability to answer the questions without any resources to assist you?
How did you feel about sitting the assessment in general?	• Have you got experience of sitting these types of assessments? • If not, how can you ensure that you are physically and mentally prepared to sit them?
Did you feel under pressure because of the time limit?	• Is there anything you can do to assist in this pressure? • Do you need to review your approach to answering MCQs?
Did you answer the MCQs in the time period permitted?	• If not, do you appreciate that in the real assessment, you will not have the opportunity to revisit any MCQs that you failed to answer? • Do you need to review your style/approach to answering MCQs?
Did you answer the MCQs without using any resources (other than a permitted calculator)?	• If not, do you need to revise the content for FLK2 more thoroughly? • Do you need more time to prepare for the assessment? • What more do you need to do to prepare yourself?

Now, ask yourself one final question: Are you ready for FLK2?

YES ☐ NO ☐

RESULTS AND ANSWERS

You will find the answers to *FLK2 Practice Assessments* overleaf.

Please note that you will not be provided with the answers or your results at the end of your SQE1 assessment. In the real assessment, you will receive your results approximately 5–6 weeks after sitting SQE1. The actual date of your results will be confirmed closer to your assessment and can be found on the SQE Timings website. Details are available on **page 159**.

For this practice assessment, you can use the Answer section as an opportunity to review your knowledge and understanding. Our advice is to review the answer in full and tick the box to record whether or not you chose the correct answer.

Session 1 answers

■ SUMMARY

The following table is a quick reference guide for the answers to Session 1 of *FLK2 Practice Assessments*. Consider using a coloured pen or a highlighter to mark the MCQs that you answered correctly and score yourself 1 mark for each. Add up your total marks, and calculate your percentage for Session 1.

For a summary of the Session 2 answers, see **page 127**.

Question	Answer	Question	Answer	Question	Answer
1	B	31	A	61	B
2	D	32	E	62	C
3	E	33	E	63	D
4	B	34	C	64	E
5	C	35	B	65	B
6	B	36	D	66	B
7	B	37	D	67	E
8	D	38	C	68	B
9	B	39	C	69	E
10	C	40	A	70	D
11	C	41	B	71	C
12	E	42	D	72	D
13	D	43	E	73	A
14	A	44	C	74	A
15	A	45	B	75	A
16	E	46	D	76	B
17	D	47	B	77	C
18	D	48	C	78	D
19	B	49	E	79	C
20	B	50	B	80	D
21	B	51	A	81	C
22	E	52	A	82	A
23	C	53	E	83	D
24	B	54	C	84	E
25	B	55	B	85	E
26	A	56	A	86	A
27	A	57	D	87	B
28	D	58	A	88	C
29	C	59	D	89	E
30	C	60	A	90	B

Your total score for Session 1: ______ **/ 90**

Percentage: ______ **%**

■ DETAILED ANSWERS

A1 of 90 (page 1) **Area of law assessed: Trusts law**

The correct answer was B. This is because the formalities for the creation of an enforceable *inter vivos* trust (ie during the man's lifetime) require that the declaration be manifested and proved by some writing and signed. In this case, the man has has validly declared a lawful trust over land, but as the formalities have not been complied with, the trust is presently unenforceable (option D is therefore incorrect). Options A, C and E are incorrect as an *inter vivos* trust declared by parol (orally) is just as valid as a written declaration, save that it is not enforceable. The consent of a trustee or the order of the court would not make an invalid trust enforceable.

Did you choose the correct answer? YES ☐ NO ☐

See ***Revise SQE: Trusts Law*, Chapter 2** for a discussion of this area of law.

A2 of 90 (page 2) **Area of law assessed: Property practice**

The correct answer was D. This is because the property to be sold/purchased is unregistered title, and therefore the solicitor would need to find out through investigation of title whether there is a statement in the transfer confirming the seller as the sole beneficial owner; if so, the solicitor can assume there was no severance. Severance of a joint tenancy can only take place in equity (therefore option B is incorrect). The equitable title can be held as either a joint tenancy or tenancy in common in equity, and therefore options A and C are incorrect as further investigation would be required in identifying whether there is a statement in the transfer. Option E is incorrect as it refers to the legal title and the focus should be on equitable title (option A is also incorrect for this reason).

Did you choose the correct answer? YES ☐ NO ☐

See ***Revise SQE: Property Practice*, Chapter 2** for a discussion of this area of law.

A3 of 90 (page 2) **Area of law assessed: Solicitors accounts**

The correct answer was E. This is because the accounting entries for a *receipt of client money* are credit *(CR) client ledger and debit (DR) cash sheet*. Both entries must be in the *client account columns* to reflect the fact that the receipt of the deposit is client (rather than business) money. Options A and D are both incorrect because they mention the business account rather than the client account. Further, option D is also incorrect because the credit and debit are the wrong way around. Option B is incorrect because it has two credit entries and therefore is not a valid double entry. Option C is incorrect because the credit and debit are the wrong way around. Answers that do not include a debit and credit, or that mix up client account and business account, will not be valid double entries and can be eliminated as possible choices when deciding which answer is most likely to be correct.

Did you choose the correct answer? YES ☐ NO ☐

See ***Revise SQE: Solicitors Accounts*, Chapter 2** for a discussion of this area of law.

A4 of 90 (page 3) **Area of law assessed: Land law**

The correct answer was B. This is because if the kitchen island is classed as part of the overall design scheme, it will be classed as a fixture. Options A and D are incorrect because both of these refer solely to the degree of annexation. The degree of annexation test is now a secondary consideration in comparison to the purpose of annexation. Option C is incorrect because if the items are included on the sale contract this will be binding; however, this is not conclusive if the items are not included in the sale contract. Option E is also incorrect as it is irrelevant that the seller received incorrect legal advice - the client would still be entitled to claim for the property.

Did you choose the correct answer? YES☐ NO☐

See ***Revise SQE: Land Law,*** **Chapter 1** for a discussion of this area of law.

A5 of 90 (page 3) **Area of law assessed: Property practice**

The correct answer was C. This is because there are now 25 flats, each of whom should share the service charge. Option C provides certainty that the service charges will be apportioned equally between the 25 flats in existence. Whilst options B, D and E would also be reasonable in the lease, they would not provide the level of certainty that the client requires, as the words 'reasonable' and 'fair' are open to interpretation, and having to depend on the square footage means that service charges could be different for each flat; they are not, therefore, the single best answers. Option A would not be appropriate as there are now 25 flats, and this answer would result in an unequal apportionment.

Did you choose the correct answer? YES☐ NO☐

See ***Revise SQE: Property Practice,*** **Chapter 6** for a discussion of this area of law.

A6 of 90 (page 4) **Area of law assessed: Ethics and professional conduct**

The correct answer was B. This is because the SRA Code of Conduct requires solicitors to bring the court's attention to mitigation on part of the defendant where they are unrepresented. If they failed to do so, the solicitor may be treated as abusing their position by taking unfair advantage of an unrepresented defendant. Furthermore, where no reference is made to the mitigation, the solicitor may be misleading the court by their omission. However, the solicitor must not state their personal views on the case. Therefore, options A, C and D are incorrect. Option E is incorrect as withdrawing from the case is not an appropriate course of conduct in the circumstances and would serve to unfairly impact on the defendant.

Did you choose the correct answer? YES☐ NO☐

See ***Revise SQE: Ethics and Professional Conduct,*** **Chapter 5** for a discussion of this area of law.

A7 of 90 (page 4) **Area of law assessed: Criminal law**

The correct answer was B. This is because on the facts the woman has most likely committed a battery, and this reflects the actus reus and mens rea of battery applicable to this scenario most accurately. Options A and C are incorrect because the woman has not committed a technical assault as her actions included applying force to the elderly man. In addition, option A incorrectly implies that injury must result to make out a battery. Option D is incorrect because the woman was not *reckless* in the application of her force; on the facts she *intended* to push him. Option E is incorrect because the apprehension of immediate unlawful violence relates to a technical assault, not a battery.

Did you choose the correct answer? YES☐ NO☐

See ***Revise SQE: Criminal Law,*** **Chapter 6** for a discussion of this area of law.

A8 of 90 (page 5) **Area of law assessed: Land law**

The correct answer was D. This is because the agreement will be binding under the Parol evidence rule as the lease is for under three years, taking effect in possession and at market rent, meaning the lease will be legal even without a deed. Option A is incorrect as there were no witnesses for the signatures and the deed was therefore not validly executed. Option B is incorrect because, despite there not being a valid deed, it will still be legal under the Parol evidence rule. Option C cannot be correct because a lease for under three years, taking effect in possession and at market rent, will be legally binding regardless of a lack of formalities. Option E cannot be correct as if there was only a binding contract; this would be incapable of creating a legal interest.

Did you choose the correct answer? YES ☐ NO ☐

See ***Revise SQE: Land Law*, Chapter 1** for a discussion of this area of law.

A9 of 90 (page 5) **Area of law assessed: Trusts law**

The correct answer was B. This is because there is a personal nexus (ie a connection) between the man and the children who will benefit from the trust. A person linked in such a manner is not a sufficient section of the public capable of satisfying the requirements for a valid charitable trust. Option A is incorrect as the number of employees does not affect the difficulties encountered by the personal nexus test. Whilst the trust may be for a charitable purpose (education), it fails because it is not for a sufficient public benefit (therefore option C is incorrect). Option D is incorrect as the advancement of education is a recognised charitable purpose. Option E is incorrect as there remains a personal nexus between the man and the children, given that their parents are linked to the man as their employer.

Did you choose the correct answer? YES ☐ NO ☐

See ***Revise SQE: Trusts Law*, Chapter 6** for a discussion of this area of law.

A10 of 90 (page 6) **Area of law assessed: Solicitors accounts**

The correct answer was C. This is because both the profit costs and VAT elements of the bill must be recorded on the client ledger in the business account columns (to reflect the fact that the solicitor is charging for her services on behalf of the firm). Option A is incorrect as there must be ledger entries recorded in the client ledger on submission of a bill to show that the client owes money to the firm. Options B and D are both incorrect as the entry must be a debit rather than a credit. Option B is further incorrect as the profit costs and VAT elements of the bill should be recorded separately, whilst option D is further incorrect in that the VAT element is missing and the entry should be in the business account rather than the client account. Option E is incorrect as although it has the correct entry for the profit costs element of the bill, the £100 VAT element is missing.

Did you choose the correct answer? YES ☐ NO ☐

See ***Revise SQE: Solicitors Accounts*, Chapter 5** for a discussion of this area of law.

A11 of 90 (page 6) **Area of law assessed: Land law**

The correct answer was C. This is because the client will have an equitable interest under a constructive trust as a result of an implied common intention when they contributed directly to the purchase price. Option A is incorrect as, despite not being on the legal title, the client will hold part of the equitable title. Option B is incorrect as although there is not an express common intention; one will be implied on the basis of the direct contribution to the purchase price. Option D is incorrect as the client is not listed on the legal title and so cannot hold it; they can only have an equitable interest. Option E is incorrect as, without evidence of a common intention to share the house and the client acting on their detriment in reliance of this, there will not be a constructive trust simply on the basis of their relationship.

Did you choose the correct answer? YES☐ NO☐

See ***Revise SQE: Land Law*, Chapter 1** for a discussion of this area of law.

A12 of 90 (page 7) **Area of law assessed: Land law**

The correct answer was E. This is because in order for an easement to take effect at law, it must be registered. As it has not been registered, it can only take effect at equity and will not be binding. Option A is incorrect as the neighbouring owner bought free from all unregistered interests. Options B and D are incorrect as the easement cannot be legal because it has not been registered. Option C is incorrect as an equitable easement would only be binding if it was protected by a notice on the Charges Register.

Did you choose the correct answer? YES☐ NO☐

See ***Revise SQE: Land Law*, Chapter 6** for a discussion of this area of law.

A13 of 90 (page 7) **Area of law assessed: Criminal practice**

The correct answer was D. This is because a circuit judge (who can be identified from the prefix 'HHJ') is addressed as 'Your honour'. 'Judge' is used to refer to district judges in the magistrates' court (therefore, option A is incorrect). 'Your worship' is the collective term used to refer to a bench of lay magistrates (therefore, option B is incorrect). 'My lord/my lady' is used for High Court judges or senior circuit judges who are the resident judge at that centre (though this depends on the size of the Crown Court centre) (therefore, option D is incorrect). 'Master' is a judge found in the civil courts, and not the criminal courts (therefore, option E is incorrect).

Did you choose the correct answer? YES☐ NO☐

See ***Revise SQE: Criminal Practice*, Chapter 7** for a discussion of this area of law.

A14 of 90 (page 8) **Area of law assessed: Ethics and professional conduct**

The correct answer was A. This is because the SRA Code of Conduct requires solicitors not to abuse their position by taking unfair advantage of clients or others. The decision as to whether the defendant should give evidence is for the defendant alone (option E is therefore incorrect). The solicitor cannot withdraw from the case simply because the defendant refuses to give evidence (therefore, option B is incorrect). The solicitor would also be giving incorrect advice if they told the defendant to change their plea to guilty, or that adverse inference would be automatically drawn (therefore options C and D are incorrect). Option A is the only option that is ethically sound.

Did you choose the correct answer? YES☐ NO☐

See ***Revise SQE: Ethics and Professional Conduct*, Chapter 5** for a discussion of this area of law.

A15 of 90 (page 8) **Area of law assessed: Land law**

The correct answer was A. This is because, as the lease is for more than seven years, it is a registrable disposition and will only take effect in law once it has been validly registered. Option B is incorrect as only leases under three years are automatically overriding. Option C is incorrect as interests in occupation are valid, regardless of the length of the agreement. As a legal lease, the agreement would be a registrable estate and therefore could not be a minor interest (option D is therefore incorrect). Similarly, restrictions are only used to protect interests under a trust and so are not relevant for leases (therefore option E is incorrect).

Did you choose the correct answer? YES ☐ NO ☐

See ***Revise SQE: Land Law*, Chapter 5** for a discussion of this area of law.

A16 of 90 (page 9) **Area of law assessed: Criminal practice**

The correct answer was E. This is because low-value shoplifting concerns offences where the value of the property stolen does not exceed £200. As the watch is valued at £250, the offence remains triable either-way and not a summary offence (therefore options A and C are incorrect). Option B is incorrect because the court will not take the man's plea; rather, the court will ask the man to *indicate* their intended plea. Theft is never triable only on indictment, therefore option D is incorrect. (Note. At the time of updating this edition of the text, the law of low-value shop theft had not yet been abolished. The correct answer remains E both before and after the change in the law in any event.)

Did you choose the correct answer? YES ☐ NO ☐

See ***Revise SQE: Criminal Practice*, Chapter 3** for a discussion of this area of law.

A17 of 90 (page 9) **Area of law assessed: Solicitors accounts**

The correct answer was D. This is because a withdrawal of client money from the client account requires a credit (CR) entry in the cash sheet and a debit (DR) entry in the client ledger. As the transaction involves client money, the entries must be in the client account columns of both ledgers. Option A is incorrect because the profit costs ledger is not relevant to this type of transaction. Option B is incorrect because it shows the accounting entries for a receipt of money into the client account rather than a payment of money out of the client account (the debit and credit are the wrong way around). Option C is incorrect for the same reason as option B, but it is further incorrect because it refers to the business account rather than the client account (the net proceeds of sale are client money so the entries must be in the client account columns). Option E is incorrect because although the cash sheet entry is correct, the client ledger entry refers to the business account rather than the client account. Options that show one entry in the client account columns and one in the business account columns will always be incorrect and can be discounted.

Did you choose the correct answer? YES ☐ NO ☐

See ***Revise SQE: Solicitors Accounts*, Chapter 3** for a discussion of this area of law.

A18 of 90 (page 10) **Area of law assessed: Ethics and professional conduct**

The correct answer was D. This is because the SRA Code of Conduct imposes an obligation not to mislead or attempt to mislead the court. First, the solicitor should try to obtain the consent of the client to disclose the information. This is to ensure that the court is not misled by the client's lies. If the client refuses to do so, the solicitor must withdraw but must not disclose the reasons for said withdrawal. Option A is incorrect because the solicitor can continue to represent the client so long as the client consents to disclosing the lie. Option B is incorrect because the solicitor must obtain the client's consent, otherwise the solicitor will be in breach of confidentiality. Option C is incorrect because the solicitor would be misleading the court by continuing to represent the client and keeping the information confidential. Option E is incorrect because the solicitor must maintain confidentiality.

Did you choose the correct answer? YES☐ NO☐

See ***Revise SQE: Ethics and Professional Conduct*****, Chapter 2** for a discussion of this area of law.

A19 of 90 (page 10) **Area of law assessed: Wills and the administration of estates**

The correct answer was B. This is because a codicil must comply with the same formality requirements as a will; the codicil must be written, signed by the testator and witnessed by two witnesses. As the codicil was not witnessed, it cannot be valid in law. Option A is incorrect as, whilst the man was of sound mind, the codicil does not comply with the necessary formalities. Option C is incorrect because the codicil does not comply with the necessary formalities. Option D is incorrect as it suggests a codicil cannot override a valid will. Option E is incorrect as whilst the codicil may reflect his true intentions, it does not satisfy the necessary formalities for a valid codicil.

Did you choose the correct answer? YES☐ NO☐

See ***Revise SQE: Wills and the Administration of Estates*****, Chapter 1** for a discussion of this area of law.

A20 of 90 (page 11) **Area of law assessed: Ethics and professional conduct**

The correct answer was B. This is because the SRA Code of Conduct imposes an obligation on solicitors to ensure that clients are informed in writing at the time of engagement about their right to complain, how to make a complaint and any right to complain to the legal ombudsman. Once the complaints mechanism in the firm is exhausted, the woman must be advised that she can make a complaint to the legal ombudsman. Option A is incorrect as the correct avenue is the legal ombudsman, not the SRA. Option C is incorrect as the complaint procedure has been exhausted, therefore a senior partner cannot deal with subsequent complaints. Option D is incorrect as the complaint cannot be reconsidered, nor can it be at any cost to the woman; complaint handling must be done free of charge. Option E is incorrect as there is further action that can be taken: making a complaint to the legal ombudsman.

Did you choose the correct answer? YES☐ NO☐

See ***Revise SQE: Ethics and Professional Conduct*****, Chapter 2** for a discussion of this area of law.

A21 of 90 (page 11) **Area of law assessed: Trusts law**

The correct answer was B. This is because the transfer will be recognised in equity as complete where the settlor (the woman) has done everything within her power (everything expected of her) to effect the transfer. The woman has properly executed the correct paperwork and has delivered this paperwork to her brother. The responsibility now lies with the brother to complete the transfer in law. The disposition will thus be recognised in equity (in line with *Re Rose*) without the need for registration (therefore option A is incorrect). In practice, the brother would be required to complete the transfer in law through registration, but this does not affect the validity of the gift. Option C is incorrect because the woman does not have to do *everything necessary*; she must simply do everything within her power. Option D is incorrect because there are no facts to support the conclusion that to resile from the disposition would be unconscionable. Option E is incorrect because, whilst equity will generally not assist a volunteer, equity will also not strive officiously to defeat a gift.

Did you choose the correct answer? YES ☐ NO ☐

See ***Revise SQE: Trusts Law*, Chapter 4** for a discussion of this area of law.

A22 of 90 (page 12) **Area of law assessed: Land law**

The correct answer was E. This is because restrictive covenants are automatically equitable: in the case of unregistered land, they will only be binding if registered as a land charge. Options A and D are incorrect as freehold covenants are not capable of being legal rights. Option B is incorrect as the doctrine of notice does not apply to interests that are capable of being registered as a land charge. Option C is incorrect as, although the freehold covenant is an equitable right, it is capable of being binding as a registered land charge.

Did you choose the correct answer? YES ☐ NO ☐

See ***Revise SQE: Land Law*, Chapter 4** for a discussion of this area of law.

A23 of 90 (page 12) **Area of law assessed: Criminal practice**

The correct answer was C. This is because the only ground that the prosecution could base an objection on would be that, due to her previous record of offending, there are substantial grounds to believe that the woman would commit further offences if released on bail. Given the woman's full-time job, stable residence and plea of self-defence, there is little basis on which the prosecution could realistically argue that there are substantial grounds to believe that the woman would fail to surrender (therefore options A, B and E are incorrect). There is also no evidence of witness intimidation, or a risk of such, therefore the prosecution would be unable to argue that there are substantial grounds to believe that the woman would interfere with witnesses (therefore option D is incorrect). Since 22 March 2026, the objection in option C can only be relied upon where there is a real prospect of immediate imprisonment. As the facts tell you that there is such a real prospect, you know that this objection can be relied upon.

Did you choose the correct answer? YES ☐ NO ☐

See ***Revise SQE: Criminal Practice*, Chapter 2** for a discussion of this area of law.

A24 of 90 (page 13) **Area of law assessed: Property practice**

The correct answer was B. This is because it is an assent of the whole of the registered title by the personal representative and therefore Form AS1 (used for personal representative(s) to assent the whole of a registered title) will need to be submitted alongside an AP1 Form (used to change the register) as it is registered title. A TP1 Form will not be relevant as this relates to a transfer rather than an assent (therefore options A and C are incorrect). Options D and E are incorrect as the lease is already registered and therefore does not need to be sent to HM Land Registry. Option E is further incorrect as the land is already registered, and thus an FR1 Form (used to apply to register land or property for the first time) would not be submitted to HM Land Registry (this is another reason why option C is incorrect). All options correctly identify that an SDLT5 certificate (relating to stamp duty land tax) will also be required.

Did you choose the correct answer? YES ☐ NO ☐

See ***Revise SQE: Property Practice*, Chapter 5** for a discussion of this area of law.

A25 of 90 (page 13) **Area of law assessed: Land law**

The correct answer was B. This is because under the doctrine of overreaching, so long as the purchase price or mortgage monies are paid to two or more trustees (in this case, the son and daughter-in-law), the trust interest will automatically pass from the land to the monies. Option A is incorrect as the land was not owned by a sole owner. Option C is incorrect as overriding interests will be overreached where there are two or more trustees. Option D is incorrect as the requirement of reasonable enquiries is only relevant to rights that are overriding, but these are defeated by overreaching. Option E is incorrect as the doctrine of overreaching means that as the purchase price was paid to two or more trustees, the purchaser/mortgagee will take free from any interests.

Did you choose the correct answer? YES ☐ NO ☐

See ***Revise SQE: Land Law*, Chapter 4** for a discussion of this area of law.

A26 of 90 (page 14) **Area of law assessed: Criminal law**

The correct answer was A. This is because it reflects the wording of the statute most accurately and includes the elements of the offence which are most applicable to this scenario. Option B is incorrect because an offence contrary to s 18 OAPA cannot be committed through recklessness. Option C is incorrect because this answer reflects the wording of a s 20 OAPA offence. Option D is incorrect because s 18 OAPA can only be committed with an intention to cause GBH or with an intention to resist lawful arrest; an intention to wound is not sufficient. Option E is incorrect because, although this accurately reflects conduct that could amount to an offence under s 18 OAPA, it does not apply to the facts of this case.

Did you choose the correct answer? YES ☐ NO ☐

See ***Revise SQE: Criminal Law*, Chapter 6** for a discussion of this area of law.

A27 of 90 (page 14) **Area of law assessed: Criminal practice**

The correct answer was A. This is because in the case of murder, only a Crown Court judge can grant bail (therefore options C and D are incorrect). A Crown Court judge cannot determine the application in the ordinary way (therefore option B is incorrect). Instead, the Crown Court judge must be satisfied that there is no significant risk that the man, if released, would commit an offence that would be likely to cause physical or mental injury to another person. Option E is incorrect because the test of 'exceptional circumstances' does not apply to this case, given that the man does not have any previous convictions. If the man had a previous conviction for murder for example, option E would be correct that bail could only be granted if there were exceptional circumstances justifying it.

Did you choose the correct answer? YES ☐ NO ☐

See ***Revise SQE: Criminal Practice*, Chapter 2** for a discussion of this area of law.

A28 of 90 (page 15) **Area of law assessed: Trusts law**

The correct answer was D. This is because there is uncertainty of subject matter. As the man owns both ordinary and preference shares, he must specify which shares he is referring to. Option A is incorrect as it is irrelevant whether the man only owns shares in one company to this scenario; the issue is that the man owns both ordinary and preference shares. Option B is incorrect because no choice was provided to the son in the trust. Whilst intangible property does not ordinarily require segregation (eg if the man owned only ordinary shares, there would be no issue), because of the difference between ordinary and preference shares, any trust must specify which shares are being referred to (option C is therefore incorrect). Had the man written that the son could choose which shares were to form the 100 shares, a choice may have saved the trust. However, without such choice being provided, the trust is uncertain (therefore option E is incorrect).

Did you choose the correct answer? YES ☐ NO ☐

See ***Revise SQE: Trusts Law*, Chapter 1** for a discussion of this area of law.

A29 of 90 (page 15) Area of law assessed: Ethics and professional conduct

The correct answer was C. This is because the SRA Code of Conduct requires solicitors to make the client aware of all information material to the matter of which they have knowledge. There is no evidence that the exceptions in the SRA Code of Conduct apply in this case, and therefore the information must be disclosed to the client (option A is therefore incorrect). Option B is incorrect as the consent of the senior partner is not required. Option D is incorrect as the information cannot be withheld from the client in these circumstances. Option E is incorrect as disclosing this information to the opposing party would amount to a breach of confidentiality and would not be acting in the client's best interests.

Did you choose the correct answer? YES ☐ NO ☐

See ***Revise SQE: Ethics and Professional Conduct*, Chapter 2** for a discussion of this area of law.

A30 of 90 (page 16) Area of law assessed: Wills and the administration of estates

The correct answer was C. This is because there is evidence that could support the claim of the woman's children that the neighbour has exerted undue influence on the woman. If the woman's children can demonstrate that the neighbour exerted undue influence to benefit herself, then they can challenge the will. Option A is incorrect because the fact that the woman's children suffered injustice is not sufficient grounds to challenge the will. Option B is incorrect as if there is evidence of undue influence, the new will can be challenged. Option D is incorrect as, although evidence is required to prove undue influence, this does not mean that the new will cannot be challenged. Option E is incorrect on the basis that, whilst a lack of testamentary capacity is a ground for challenging a will, that is not the only challenge and not the focus of the challenge in this case, nor is there any evidence of a lack of testamentary capacity.

Did you choose the correct answer? YES ☐ NO ☐

See ***Revise SQE: Wills and the Administration of Estates*, Chapter 1** for a discussion of this area of law.

A31 of 90 (page 16) Area of law assessed: Trusts law

The correct answer was A. This is because the twin sons have an immediate right to the property for the duration of their lives without a condition attached. Their interests are concurrent with each other. The daughter's interest is consecutive in that it is successive of the interests of the brothers (it is in remainder). The daughter's interest is also contingent because a condition is attached to her interest (to reach the age of 25). The sister's interest is in remainder with no conditions attached. All other options are therefore incorrect as they fail to accurately state the beneficial interests of the parties.

Did you choose the correct answer? YES ☐ NO ☐

See ***Revise SQE: Trusts Law*, Chapter 5** for a discussion of this area of law.

A32 of 90 (page 17) **Area of law assessed: Land law**

The correct answer was E. This is because Class D(iii) land charges are related only to equitable easements. Because Class D(iii) entries relate only to equitable easements, all other options are incorrect.

Did you choose the correct answer? YES☐ NO☐

See ***Revise SQE: Land Law*, Chapter 2** for a discussion of this area of law.

A33 of 90 (page 17) **Area of law assessed: Trusts law**

The correct answer was E. This is because the man is liable for breach of trust by misappropriating trust property (this is agreed amongst all options). The wife had no knowledge or suspicion that would make it unconscionable for her to retain receipt of the diamond ring, nor did she dishonestly assist in any way in the breach of trust. The agent is not liable for knowing receipt (also called 'unconscionable receipt') as they have not received the money beneficially (ie for their own use and benefit); they are a mere conduit for the money. However, the agent is liable for dishonest assistance in the breach of trust as they knew the money was misappropriated from the trust (thus demonstrating dishonesty) and they assisted in the breach by forwarding the money to the loans company. The loans company cannot be liable for knowing receipt as it lacks the necessary knowledge that makes it knowing for it to retain receipt of the money; the knowledge of the agent cannot be imputed to the loans company. All other options incorrectly identify the liability of all parties and are thus incorrect.

Did you choose the correct answer? YES☐ NO☐

See ***Revise SQE: Trusts Law*, Chapter 9** for a discussion of this area of law.

A34 of 90 (page 18) **Area of law assessed: Solicitors accounts**

The correct answer was C. This is because the £3,000 is a mixed receipt, incorporating £1,200 business money (to clear the interim bill of £1,000 + £200 VAT) and £1,800 client money on account of future costs and disbursements (£3,000 less £1,200). Mixed receipts must be allocated to the correct bank accounts to ensure that client money is kept separate from business money. Although it is not against the Accounts Rules to pay the full receipt into the business account and then transfer the client money element into the client account, most firms consider it better practice to pay mixed receipts into the client account and then to transfer the business money element into the business account. This is safer as it reduces the risk of client money being left inadvertently in the business account. Options A and B are incorrect because the receipt is neither all client money nor all business money - it is a mixed receipt incorporating elements of both. Option D is incorrect because the split of the mixed receipt is incorrect: the client money element should be £1,800 and the business money element should be £1,200. Also, it would be better practice to pay the mixed receipt into the client account first and then to transfer the business money element into the business account. Option E is incorrect because it does not take account of the submission of the interim bill. Also, it is against the Accounts Rules to transfer money into the business account to cover disbursements that have not yet been paid.

Did you choose the correct answer? YES☐ NO☐

See ***Revise SQE: Solicitors Accounts*, Chapter 6** for a discussion of this area of law.

A35 of 90 (page 18) **Area of law assessed: Trusts law**

The correct answer was B. This is because the woman has been appointed as a director irrespective of her own vote. The woman has obtained 55% of the vote from other shareholders without the need to utilise her own shareholding. As a director can be appointed by a simple majority (51%), the woman has not obtained her directorship by virtue of her position as a trustee, and thus she has not obtained an unauthorised profit and is not in breach of her fiduciary duty (option A is therefore incorrect). Option C is incorrect because it is irrelevant whether the woman voted at all; the focus is on whether the woman would have been appointed irrespective of her vote. Option D is incorrect because the woman is not generally entitled to make any unauthorised profits, given that the role as trustee/fiduciary is generally voluntary. Option E is incorrect as, whilst consent will allow the woman to avoid liability for breach of fiduciary duty, it is not a requirement that consent be obtained (as discussed above, the focus is on whether the woman was appointed by virtue of her position as trustee).

Did you choose the correct answer? YES ☐ NO ☐

See ***Revise SQE: Trusts Law*, Chapter 9** for a discussion of this area of law.

A36 of 90 (page 19) **Area of law assessed: Property practice**

The correct answer was D. This is because it is best practice to obtain an independent witness to the execution of a transfer. Options A and C are incorrect because best practice dictates transfers are to be signed by an independent witness; these options would probably be queried by HM Land Registry at registration of the new legal owners and would not be best practice. Option B is incorrect because the client's solicitors will need a hard copy of the transfer, or a certified copy of it, which a solicitor will not be able to provide without having sight of the original. Option E is incorrect because the transfer has already been signed and therefore the solicitor cannot attest a signature that they have not witnessed (such would also breach the SRA Code of Conduct).

Did you choose the correct answer? YES ☐ NO ☐

See ***Revise SQE: Property Practice*, Chapter 5** for a discussion of this area of law.

A37 of 90 (page 19) **Area of law assessed: Land law**

The correct answer was D. This is because only a bona fide purchaser for value of a legal estate will be 'equity's darling' and is therefore not bound by any equitable interests including a beneficial interest under a trust. Options A and E are incorrect as the purchase must be for value in order to benefit as 'equity's darling'; a volunteer (ie someone who receives the property gratuitously) cannot rely on this doctrine. Option B is incorrect (and option E is further incorrect) as the purchaser of an equitable interest cannot be 'equity's darling'. Option C is incorrect as 'equity's darling' must be a bona fide purchaser.

Did you choose the correct answer? YES ☐ NO ☐

See ***Revise SQE: Land Law*, Chapter 2** for a discussion of this area of law.

A38 of 90 (page 20) **Area of law assessed: Property practice**

The correct answer was C. This is because any restrictive covenants will be covenants imposed by the client (as the seller), which will burden the land being sold (hence 'by' the transferee). Option D is incorrect as it refers to the transferor. Options A and B are incorrect as they relate to rights (ie easements) rather than restrictions (ie restrictive covenants). Option E is incorrect because this is where any required or permitted statements, certificates, applications or agreed declarations are included.

Did you choose the correct answer? YES☐ NO☐

See ***Revise SQE: Property Practice*, Chapter 5** for a discussion of this area of law.

A39 of 90 (page 20) **Area of law assessed: Land law**

The correct answer was C. This is because a legal easement is a registrable disposition, and so to be enforceable must be completed by registration and notice placed on the Charges Register of the burdened land. Option A is incorrect as the Property Register will only contain details of the property, such as the address, and rights that benefit the land. Option B is incorrect as a registered charge is entered on the Charges Register to protect a mortgage over the property. Option D is incorrect as a restriction on the Proprietorship Register restricts the way in which the property is dealt with on registrable disposition, such as when there is a trust of land. Option E is incorrect as this is not a covenant regulating how the land is used.

Did you choose the correct answer? YES☐ NO☐

See ***Revise SQE: Land Law*, Chapter 7** for a discussion of this area of law.

A40 of 90 (page 21) **Area of law assessed: Criminal law**

The correct answer was A. This is because the correct test for recklessness in the context of this offence is: there was a risk of *some* harm in throwing the plant pot, and the woman appreciated this risk but continued to throw the plant pot. Option B is incorrect because there is no requirement (for the mens rea of s 20) for the harm to be *serious*. Options C and D are incorrect because the test is subjective: did the woman personally foresee the risk of some harm? Option E is incorrect because the woman needed to appreciate the risk of some harm herself; the words '*ought to have*' import an objective test (ie the reasonable man).

Did you choose the correct answer? YES☐ NO☐

See ***Revise SQE: Criminal Law*, Chapter 6** for a discussion of this area of law.

A41 of 90 (page 21) **Area of law assessed: Property practice**

The correct answer was B. This is because before taking any of the other steps, such as informing the lender (which is necessary), the client's consent to inform the lender needs to be obtained. Options A and C are incorrect because when acting on behalf of a client and lender, there is a duty to act in their best interests, in addition to a duty of confidentiality. Therefore, a lender cannot be informed of anything without the client's consent. Option D is incorrect as there is not yet a conflict of interests and this would only apply if the client refused to give consent to inform the lender. Option E is incorrect as, provided the lender is made aware, there will be no issue in accepting the incentive, which is common practice with new build developments, and it is the solicitor's duty to act in the best interests of their client. The solicitor must be cautious in all circumstances to comply with the SRA Code of Conduct.

Did you choose the correct answer? YES☐ NO☐

See ***Revise SQE: Property Practice*, Chapter 4** for a discussion of this area of law.

A42 of 90 (page 22) **Area of law assessed: Criminal practice**

The correct answer was D. This is because appeals from the magistrates' court against conviction will be heard in the Crown Court and will be a complete rehearing of the case. Option A is incorrect because appeals by way of case stated (ie appeals on the law) are made to the High Court, not the Crown Court. Option B is incorrect because High Court appeals do not involve rehearings. Option C is incorrect because, whilst the man could appeal to the High Court by way of case stated, he does not challenge the interpretation or application of the law by the magistrates. Option E is incorrect because the man does not seek to challenge the decision-making process (ie judicial review) of the magistrates' court.

Did you choose the correct answer? YES ☐ NO ☐

See ***Revise SQE: Criminal Practice*, Chapter 9** for a discussion of this area of law.

A43 of 90 (page 22) **Area of law assessed: Criminal law**

The correct answer was E. This is because a concussion and bruising is minor injury, not sufficient to found a charge of grievous bodily harm or wounding (therefore options C and D are incorrect). However, suffering a concussion and bruising is more than merely transient or trifling; therefore an assault and a battery are not the appropriate charges (options A and B are therefore incorrect). A s 47 offence (assault occasioning actual bodily harm) is the most likely offence here as the concussion and bruising amounts to any hurt or injury calculated to interfere with the health or comfort of the victim. Had the bottle smashed and caused a cut to the man's head or body, a charge of wounding would be more appropriate. However, there is no such injury on these facts.

Did you choose the correct answer? YES ☐ NO ☐

See ***Revise SQE: Criminal Law*, Chapter 6** for a discussion of this area of law.

A44 of 90 (page 23) **Area of law assessed: Land law**

The correct answer was C. This is because the partner's trust of land would be overriding if they were in actual occupation and the occupation would have been obvious on a reasonably careful inspection of the land. Option A is incorrect as, although the partner's trust of land should have been protected by a restriction, it can also be upgraded to overriding on the basis of an interest in actual occupation. Option B is incorrect as home rights only exist if there is a marriage or civil partnership. Option D is incorrect as a notice cannot be entered on the Charges Register in respect of a trust of land. Option E is incorrect as the partner's interest would be overriding if it was obvious on a reasonably careful inspection.

Did you choose the correct answer? YES ☐ NO ☐

See ***Revise SQE: Land Law*, Chapter 3** for a discussion of this area of law.

A45 of 90 (page 23) **Area of law assessed: Solicitors accounts**

The correct answer was B. This is because you must record the reduction of the bill in the same three ledgers as when you submitted the bill (client, profit costs and HMRC-VAT ledgers). Read the words used in the question carefully – does it say that the bill is reduced *by* £1,200 + VAT or *to* £1,200 + VAT? In this question, the bill was reduced *to* £1,200 + VAT so the ledger entries reflect the reduction in the bill (£300 + VAT). Options A, C and E are all incorrect because they refer to £1,200 (what the bill is reduced to) rather than £300 (what the bill is reduced by). Options A, D and E are all incorrect because they refer to the cash sheet and there are no entries in the cash account for an abatement.

Did you choose the correct answer? YES☐ NO☐

See ***Revise SQE: Solicitors Accounts*, Chapter 5** for a discussion of this area of law.

A46 of 90 (page 24) **Area of law assessed: Trusts law**

The correct answer was D. This is because the law draws a distinction between trustees subject to the ordinary standard (also known as the minimum standard) and those trustees subject to an elevated standard because of their skills/experience or because they are being paid for their role. The first and second trustees do not have experience relevant to the management of a trust, nor are they being paid for their role; therefore, they are subject to the ordinary standard. The third and fourth trustees, however, are subject to the elevated standard because of the skills and experience relevant to managing the trust (the third trustee as a solicitor) or because they are being paid to act as a trustee (the fourth trustee). Therefore, option A is incorrect. Option B is incorrect as it is more accurate to say that the fourth trustee is subject to the elevated standard because they are being paid for their services. Option C is incorrect as the third trustee will likely be subject to an elevated standard due to their skills and experiences as a solicitor. Option E is incorrect as the qualifications of the trustees are not entirely relevant to the determination of the appropriate standard; simply because the first and second trustees possess qualifications in their field does not mean that they have the skills or experience to manage a trust.

Did you choose the correct answer? YES☐ NO☐

See ***Revise SQE: Trusts Law*, Chapter 10** for a discussion of this area of law.

A47 of 90 (page 24) **Area of law assessed: Criminal law**

The correct answer was B. This is because the offence of robbery (contrary to s 8 Theft Act 1968) requires that force must be used or threatened in order to steal at the time or before the stealing takes place. Option A is incorrect because force does not need to actually be applied - the fear of force is sufficient. Option C is incorrect because the defendant has to use force or the fear of force at the time of stealing or before; not after (eg force used or threatened in order to escape is not robbery). Option D is incorrect because the defendant can use actual force or the fear of force, not just the fear of force. Option E is incorrect because even though the timing of the use of force is correct, the defendant can also use the fear of force.

Did you choose the correct answer? YES☐ NO☐

See ***Revise SQE: Criminal Law*, Chapter 7** for a discussion of this area of law.

A48 of 90 (page 25) **Area of law assessed: Criminal law**

The correct answer was C. This is because the man will not, in law, have dishonestly appropriated property to which he had a genuinely held belief he had a legal right, and this can be argued at trial. Option A is incorrect because there is evidence that the man genuinely believed he had a legal claim to the bracelet. Option B is incorrect because the requirement to take all reasonable steps to find the owner applies only to abandoned goods; the man did not consider the goods to be abandoned; he considered the bracelet to be his own. Option D is incorrect because the test is whether the belief was *genuinely* held, not *reasonably* held. Option E is incorrect because if the man believed that the bracelet was his, this may demonstrate that the man lacked dishonesty in his appropriation of the bracelet.

Did you choose the correct answer? YES ☐ NO ☐

See ***Revise SQE: Criminal Law*, Chapter 7** for a discussion of this area of law.

A49 of 90 (page 26) **Area of law assessed: Trusts law**

The correct answer was E. This is because the man has intended to make an immediate *inter vivos* trust over the shares, the man's intention continues to his death, and the wife is appointed as administrator of the estate, having originally been chosen to act as trustee for the *inter vivos* trust. Whilst controversial, the principle in the case of *Strong v Bird* has been extended to apply to administrators as well as executors of estates. As the wife was the original intended trustee for the *inter vivos* trust, the principle in *Strong v Bird* recognises the transfer as complete at the point that she is appointed administrator of the estate. Option A is incorrect because it does not properly explain how the trust is valid; the trust was technically improperly constituted, given that the man did not complete the necessary steps. However, the trust was eventually constituted by the appointment of the wife as administrator. Option B is incorrect because the trust is eventually constituted by the appointment of the wife as administrator. Option C is incorrect because the man did not do everything in his power to complete the transfer; he failed to execute the necessary documents to do so (therefore *Re Rose* cannot be relied upon). Option D is incorrect because the law has extended the rule to cover administrators as well as executors.

Did you choose the correct answer? YES ☐ NO ☐

See ***Revise SQE: Trusts Law*, Chapter 4** for a discussion of this area of law.

A50 of 90 (page 26) **Area of law assessed: Solicitors accounts**

The correct answer was B. This is because the definition of client money in the SRA Accounts Rules includes money held by a solicitor in certain specified roles (this includes a Court of Protection deputy). However, the Rules allow solicitors to withhold money from a client account where there is a conflict with the requirements of their specified role. Here it is appropriate for the money to be held in a separate deputyship account. Option A was incorrect because there is an exception in the Rules that does not require the solicitor to pay the compensation money into the client account. Option C was incorrect because there is no requirement to pay the money into a third-party managed account. Options D and E are both incorrect because the compensation money is deemed to be client money. Option D is further incorrect in that it would be a breach of the Rules (keeping client and business money separate) to pay the money into the business account.

Did you choose the correct answer? YES ☐ NO ☐

See ***Revise SQE: Solicitors Accounts*, Chapter 7** for a discussion of this area of law.

A51 of 90 (page 27) **Area of law assessed: Criminal practice**

The correct answer was A. This is because if the man pleads guilty but there is a significant difference between the prosecution version and the defence version, the court must either accept the defence version of events or hear evidence in a Newton hearing. Options B, C and E are incorrect because the defendant should be sentenced on his version unless there is a significant difference on the facts that would materially affect sentence, in which case a Newton hearing should be held. Option D is incorrect because the guilty plea is correct but the factual basis is significantly different.

Did you choose the correct answer? YES☐ NO☐

See ***Revise SQE: Criminal Practice*****, Chapter 8** for a discussion of this area of law.

A52 of 90 (page 27) **Area of law assessed: Wills and the administration of estates**

The correct answer was A. This is because if one of the named executors renounces their appointment, the other named executors can still act as the executors of the will. As a result, the woman will automatically become the sole executor of the will once the man renounces his appointment as executor. Option B is incorrect as the will remains valid despite the renunciation of the man as the executor. Option C is incorrect because a named executor still remains. If there were no such executor, then an administrator would be appointed, rather than a public trustee. Option D is incorrect as the will remains valid despite the renunciation of the man as the executor and it is not possible to rewrite a will post death for the purposes of altering the appointment of executors. Option E is incorrect because there is no obligation on the woman to renounce her appointment as executor.

Did you choose the correct answer? YES☐ NO☐

See ***Revise SQE: Wills and the Administration of Estates*****, Chapter 2** for a discussion of this area of law.

A53 of 90 (page 28) **Area of law assessed: Criminal practice**

The correct answer was E. This is because the Crown Court can pass any sentence that would have been available to the magistrates' court at the time of sentencing. This means that the Crown Court can increase the sentence imposed by the magistrates' court (therefore option A is incorrect), and may impose a sentence different from that of the magistrates' court (therefore option B is incorrect). Option C is incorrect because the Crown Court cannot pass a sentence greater than the magistrates' court could have passed (ie beyond their powers). Option D is incorrect because there is no such requirement for 'exceptional reasons' in law.

Did you choose the correct answer? YES☐ NO☐

See ***Revise SQE: Criminal Practice*****, Chapter 8** for a discussion of this area of law.

A54 of 90 (page 28) **Area of law assessed: Criminal law**

The correct answer was C. This is because the man went beyond his permissions and knowingly entered the stock room without a member of staff present. The man is likely to be considered a trespasser because permission for one part of a building does not ensure permission for another part of a building. Option A is incorrect because the facts identify that the man is only allowed in the stock room with a member of staff. Option B is incorrect because the man saw the secure stock room door was open and entered regardless, knowing that he was going into the stock room. Option D is incorrect because even though this is factually accurate, the statement does not best reflect the advice that the solicitor should give on the law. Option E is incorrect because, on the facts, the man knew that he needed to be accompanied into the stock room as part of his permissions.

Did you choose the correct answer? YES☐ NO☐

See ***Revise SQE: Criminal Law*****, Chapter 7** for a discussion of this area of law.

A55 of 90 (page 29) **Area of law assessed: Land law**

The correct answer was B. This is because the right of survivorship means that when the property is held as a beneficial joint-tenancy and upon the death of one of the joint-tenants, the interest will pass to the surviving joint-tenants. Option A is incorrect as the four unities are only relevant to establishing whether a joint-tenancy exists and not the passing of property per se. Option C is incorrect as severance of a joint-tenancy must be inter vivos. Option D is incorrect as severance can occur informally without writing. Option E is incorrect as the siblings were expressly beneficial joint-tenants.

Did you choose the correct answer? YES ☐ NO ☐

See ***Revise SQE: Land Law*, Chapter 9** for a discussion of this area of law.

A56 of 90 (page 29) **Area of law assessed: Property practice**

The correct answer was A. This is because the client can claim for contractual compensation (akin to damages) for the delay. The client cannot serve a notice to complete as they are not ready, willing and able to complete (therefore option B is incorrect). Options C, D and E are incorrect because the client can only rescind the contract when time is of the essence (which is not the case here), and they are able to claim for compensation. Option E is also incorrect as the reason for the delay is irrelevant and a notice to complete would need to have been sent before the contract could be rescinded.

Did you choose the correct answer? YES ☐ NO ☐

See ***Revise SQE: Property Practice*, Chapter 5** for a discussion of this area of law.

A57 of 90 (page 30) **Area of law assessed: Solicitors accounts**

The correct answer was D. This is because the solicitor's colleague has breached the SRA Accounts Rules. Client money has not been returned to the client promptly as soon as there is no longer any proper reason to hold those funds (in this case, the money is not being held with respect to any further legal services required by the client). There is also a danger of breaching the Rules by using a client account to provide banking facilities to clients, for example, if the solicitor has paid out or plans to pay out overseas expenses at the client's request that are unrelated to any legal services being delivered to them. In accordance with the Rules, any breach must be corrected promptly upon discovery. This requires the solicitor to pay the balance of all monies in the SDDCA to the client promptly. This will include any interest earned on the account. Options A and B are both incorrect because it would be a continuing breach of the Rules to retain the funds in the SDDCA when there are no ongoing legal services being provided to the client. Option C is incorrect because it would be a breach of Rule 4.1 to pay client money into the business account (as client money and business money must be kept separate). Option E is incorrect because the solicitor must return the money to the client promptly if they still have the details of the client's bank account. As the firm has not heard from the client, the solicitor must make reasonable attempts to trace them. If this is unsuccessful, then after a reasonable lapse of time, they can seek approval from the SRA to withdraw the client money and pay it to a charity. The money should not be transferred to the Law Society.

Did you choose the correct answer? YES ☐ NO ☐

See ***Revise SQE: Solicitors Accounts***, Chapters 3, 6 and 7 for a discussion of this area of law.

A58 of 90 (page 30) **Area of law assessed: Land law**

The correct answer was A. This is because for severance to be deemed to have been delivered, if sent by registered post, it must be shown that it has not been returned to the sender undelivered. Option B is incorrect as, even if the letter is correctly addressed, if it is subsequently returned to the sender, it will not have been deemed to be delivered. Options C and D are incorrect as the letter was neither left at the last known abode, nor read by the sisters. Option E is incorrect as for severance to be effective, it must also be deemed to have been delivered.

Did you choose the correct answer? YES☐ NO☐

See ***Revise SQE: Land Law*, Chapter 9** for a discussion of this area of law.

A59 of 90 (page 31) **Area of law assessed: Property practice**

The correct answer was D. This is because the conversion falls into the category of material change as it is a change of use of a building to a single dwelling house, and therefore enforcement action must be taken within 10 years as it would have taken place on or after 25 April 2024 (option E is therefore incorrect as it refers to four years - this would only apply if substantial completion took place before 25 April 2024). Options A, B and C are incorrect because they relate to the category of operational development (ie the four elements of building, engineering, mining or operations such as demolition), whereas this scenario relates to a material change of use.

Did you choose the correct answer? YES☐ NO☐

See ***Revise SQE: Property Practice*, Chapter 3** for a discussion of this area of law.

A60 of 90 (page 31) **Area of law assessed: Criminal law**

The correct answer was A. This is because a person can be guilty of aggravated burglary if the actus reus and mens rea of burglary are made out, and, at the time, the person has with them an aggravated article. An aggravated article includes a weapon of offence, imitation firearm, firearm or explosive (WIFE). In this case, the woman committed a burglary and, at the time of entry, had in her possession a bladed article, which is a weapon of offence as it is an article made or adapted for use for causing injury to a person, or intended by the person having it with them for such use. Option B is incorrect because there is no requirement to use the weapon during the burglary. Option C is incorrect because there is no requirement to demonstrate an intention to use the weapon. Option D is incorrect because self-defence is irrelevant for these purposes. Option E is incorrect because a bladed article can be classed as a 'weapon of offence' within s 10(1)(b) of the Theft Act 1968.

Did you choose the correct answer? YES☐ NO☐

See ***Revise SQE: Criminal Law*, Chapter 7** for a discussion of this area of law.

A61 of 90 (page 32) **Area of law assessed: Trusts law**

The correct answer was B. This is because a fiduciary has a duty to avoid unauthorised profits. As the trustee has renewed the lease in their own favour, they have obtained profits that they would not have otherwise obtained had they not been a trustee. The profits are linked to their role, and the trustee has thus made an unauthorised profit. Option A is incorrect because it is irrelevant that the landlord would not renew the lease for the infant beneficiary; the trustee should not have renewed the lease in their own favour. Option C is incorrect because the consent of the co-trustee is irrelevant; the focus is on the consent of the beneficiary (which would not be possible as the beneficiary is an infant). Option D is incorrect because there is nothing to suggest that the trustee is acting in bad faith; the trustee may well believe that this is an appropriate course of action and has made profits using the money saved from the ineffectual renewal of the lease for the trust. Option E is incorrect because there is no evidence to suggest that the trust is benefitting in any way from the renewal of the lease. Even if the trust were to benefit, the trustee would still be in breach if they make any profit from the lease.

Did you choose the correct answer? YES ☐ NO ☐

See ***Revise SQE: Trusts Law*, Chapter 9** for a discussion of this area of law.

A62 of 90 (page 32) **Area of law assessed: Criminal practice**

The correct answer was C. This is because where an adult co-accused pleads not guilty and consents to summary trial, if the youth pleads not guilty they must be tried in the adult magistrates' court with their co-accused. Options A and E are incorrect because the client is a youth, since they have not yet attained the age of 18. Option B is incorrect as the client is jointly charged with an adult and therefore falls into one of the exceptions to the general rule that juveniles should be tried in the youth court. Options D and E are incorrect because the magistrates' court have no discretion in this instance.

Did you choose the correct answer? YES ☐ NO ☐

See ***Revise SQE: Criminal Practice*, Chapter 10** for a discussion of this area of law.

A63 of 90 (page 33) **Area of law assessed: Solicitors accounts**

The correct answer was D. This is because by paying out the mortgage redemption monies before the proceeds of sale were received, the solicitor has left the client's ledger with a debit balance on the client account. This is a serious breach of the SRA Accounts Rules because funds in the general client account that belong to other clients have been used to repay the client's lender. This breach must be remedied immediately by transferring sufficient funds from the firm's business account to the client account. Once the proceeds of sale are received, the funds can be transferred back into the business account. Option A is incorrect because it is inappropriate to ask the lender to return the mortgage redemption monies. The firm must use its own business money to make good the deficit in the client ledger. Options B and C are both incorrect because any money improperly withdrawn from the client account must be *immediately* replaced. It is therefore a breach of the Rules to wait until the next day. Option B is also misleading as the buyer's solicitor has not confirmed that the money will be received the next day in any event. Option E is incorrect as although reporting the buyer's solicitor to the SRA is something that the solicitor may choose to do, the *immediate* priority is to replace the funds improperly withdrawn from the client account.

Did you choose the correct answer? YES ☐ NO ☐

See ***Revise SQE: Solicitors Accounts*, Chapter 3** for a discussion of this area of law.

A64 of 90 (page 33) **Area of law assessed: Land law**

The correct answer was E. This is because the starting position is that equity follows the law, unless this presumption can be rebutted by an express declaration of actions of the parties. Unequal contributions alone are not sufficient to rebut this presumption. Option A is incorrect as, whilst the four unities are required for a joint tenancy, they do not determine whether one exists. Option B is incorrect as unequal contributions are not sufficient to demonstrate an intention for tenancy in common. Option C is incorrect as the maxim that equity follows the law is a presumption but it is not always the case that it does so. Option D is incorrect as, whilst an express declaration is conclusive, it is not necessary for there to be a joint tenancy.

Did you choose the correct answer? YES☐ NO☐

See ***Revise SQE: Land Law***, **Chapter 9** for a discussion of this area of law.

A65 of 90 (page 34) **Area of law assessed: Property practice**

The correct answer was B. This is because a deed of variation would protect the client as it is legally binding. Option A is not appropriate as the seller is not the landlord or freeholder, and is therefore not able to renegotiate. Option C would not protect the client in the same way a variation would, as the deed of variation would be registered with the land registry and then take effect in law. Option D would not be appropriate as it is not necessary - provided the variation is approved, the client could continue with the purchase. If they were to withdraw, they may incur fees for the work done to date with their solicitors. Option E is incorrect as although lender approval may be appropriate, there will still need to be a variation of the lease.

Did you choose the correct answer? YES☐ NO☐

See ***Revise SQE: Property Practice***, **Chapter 8** for a discussion of this area of law.

A66 of 90 (page 34) **Area of law assessed: Property practice**

The correct answer was B. This is because CGT principal private dwelling exemption only applies to a seller's only or main residence. Option A is incorrect because the exemption cannot apply to an investment property if it is not the main residence. Option C is incorrect as the exemption only includes grounds of up to 0.5 hectares. Option D is incorrect because the seller's main residence would be eligible. Option E is incorrect as the client would need to have resided in the property as their main residence, and the facts state it is currently being rented out.

Did you choose the correct answer? YES☐ NO☐

See ***Revise SQE: Property Practice***, **Chapter 10** for a discussion of this area of law.

A67 of 90 (page 35) **Area of law assessed: Ethics and professional conduct**

The correct answer was E. This is because the SRA Code of Conduct requires solicitors to keep the affairs of current and former clients confidential unless disclosure is required or permitted by law, or the client consents. In that regard, the solicitor must first seek the client's consent before using the confidential information (even if that information will assist her case). Options A and C are therefore incorrect. Options B and D are incorrect as the newly qualified solicitor must act in the best interests of the client, and whilst they must keep the woman's affairs confidential, they can disclose with their consent. Returning or destroying the notes will not be an act in the best interests of the client. Given that the information is likely to assist the client's case, her consent to disclose should be sought; option E is the best answer.

Did you choose the correct answer? YES☐ NO☐

See ***Revise SQE: Ethics and Professional Conduct***, **Chapter 2** for a discussion of this area of law.

A68 of 90 (page 35) **Area of law assessed: Land law**

The correct answer was B. This is because courts prioritise the interest of secured creditors and will seek to ensure the mortgage is repaid even if it impacts children living at the property (therefore option A is incorrect). Option C is incorrect as the courts will prioritise secured creditors even if there is not a bankruptcy. Options D and E are incorrect as the original intention and purpose of the trust is only considered if there is not a secured creditor.

Did you choose the correct answer? YES ☐ NO ☐

See ***Revise SQE: Land Law*, Chapter 9** for a discussion of this area of law.

A69 of 90 (page 36) **Area of law assessed: Wills and the Administration of Estates**

The correct answer was E. This is because the woman executed a valid will in 2010, a valid codicil in 2015 and a valid will in 2020. The 2020 will being the most recent will, which revoked her previous testamentary dispositions, shall govern the distribution of the woman's estate. Options A and B are incorrect because the 2020 will revokes the 2015 codicil and the 2010 will. Option C is incorrect as the 2020 will included a revocation clause that revoked the 2010 will and 2015 codicil. Until the 2020 will, these were valid documents. Option D is incorrect as there no reason that the 2010 will was not revoked by the 2020 will.

Did you choose the correct answer? YES ☐ NO ☐

See ***Revise SQE: Wills and the Administration of Estates*, Chapter 4** for a discussion of this area of law.

A70 of 90 (page 36) **Area of law assessed: Ethics and professional conduct**

The correct answer was D. This is because under the SRA Code of Conduct a solicitor must only make assertions or put forward statements, representations or submissions to the court or others that are properly arguable. If the solicitor is unsure whether a submission is properly arguable, they must refrain from making it. The solicitor must exercise their professional judgment and competence to assess whether the submission is properly arguable and, if they conclude it cannot be properly argued, they must refrain from making it (option A is therefore incorrect). Options B and C are incorrect because the question of whether a submission is properly arguable is a personal judgment for the solicitor; whilst the court may provide a helpful indication, the responsibility lies with the solicitor. Option E is incorrect because, whilst the prosecutor may provide helpful advice, they are not bound to act in the client's best interests.

Did you choose the correct answer? YES ☐ NO ☐

See ***Revise SQE: Ethics and Professional Conduct*, Chapter 2** for a discussion of this area of law.

A71 of 90 (page 37) **Area of law assessed: Criminal practice**

The correct answer was C. This is because disclosure rules require the woman to give the prosecutor and the court notice indicating whether she intends to call any witnesses at trial and giving details of those witnesses. The obligation applies in relation to cases in both the magistrates' court and the Crown Court. If the woman calls a witness who was not notified, the court and the prosecution may make adverse comment on either the failure to serve a notice or an amended notice, or on the late service of a notice. Option A is incorrect because service of a defence statement is obligatory in the Crown Court and voluntary in the magistrates' court. Option B is incorrect as it fails to state the test fully; the prosecution is under a continuing duty to disclose any material that might reasonably be considered capable of undermining the case for the prosecution against the woman, *or* of assisting the case for the woman. Option D is incorrect as the prosecutor must either be present or have had at least 14 days in which to make representations. Option E is incorrect because the prosecution must satisfy the disclosure test regardless of whether the case is heard in the magistrates' court or the Crown Court.

Did you choose the correct answer? YES☐ NO☐

See ***Revise SQE: Criminal Practice*, Chapter 5** for a discussion of this area of law.

A72 of 90 (page 37) **Area of law assessed: Trusts law**

The correct answer was D. This is because the self-dealing rule prevents a trustee from purchasing property that is entrusted to him. The self-dealing rule is strict; it is irrelevant that the man purchased the beach house above market value (therefore option A is incorrect) and that the beach house was purchased at a public auction (therefore option C is incorrect). Option B is incorrect because the amount of profit made is irrelevant to the question of self-dealing; the man is not permitted to self-deal. Option E is incorrect because the consent of fellow trustees is irrelevant; only beneficial consent will excuse the man from a breach of fiduciary duty.

Did you choose the correct answer? YES☐ NO☐

See ***Revise SQE: Trusts Law*, Chapter 9** for a discussion of this area of law.

A73 of 90 (page 38) **Area of law assessed: Ethics and professional conduct**

The correct answer was A. This is because the solicitor provided an undertaking but was unable to fulfil it within the agreed timescale. As the solicitor has provided an undertaking, they are personally responsible to perform those undertakings. Should the solicitor fail to comply with those undertakings, they bear the liability of any costs incurred. Option B is incorrect as the solicitor must take action given their undertaking. Option C is incorrect as to ignore the undertaking would be a breach of the SRA Code of Conduct. Option D is incorrect as the solicitor is personally liable for any undertakings given. Option E is incorrect as it does not resolve the issue faced by the bank and the client; the solicitor can take proactive steps by offering to compensate the bank to avoid proceedings being brought against the solicitor or client.

Did you choose the correct answer? YES☐ NO☐

See ***Revise SQE: Ethics and Professional Conduct*, Chapter 2** for a discussion of this area of law.

A74 of 90 (page 38) **Area of law assessed: Trusts law**

The correct answer was A. This is because trustees have a power to invest in land so long as it is for the occupation of the beneficiary, for the purpose of investment, or for any other reason. However, the land must be within the UK. Unless the trust instrument permits such investment in land outside the UK, the trustee will be in breach of trust (as we can see, the trust instrument is silent). Option B is incorrect as the relevance of profits does not detract from the fact that the trustee had no authority in law to invest in land outside the UK (though, the beneficiaries may likely consent to such breach in these circumstances). Option C is incorrect as the trust instrument is silent; the prohibition on investing in land outside the UK is a statutory restriction. Option D is incorrect as the consent of fellow trustees is irrelevant to the woman's liability for breach of trust. Option E is incorrect as, whilst the suitability of the villa is relevant to the determination of whether the trustees *should* invest, the issue here is whether the trustees are *permitted* to invest.

Did you choose the correct answer? YES ☐ NO ☐

See ***Revise SQE: Trusts Law*, Chapter 10** for a discussion of this area of law.

A75 of 90 (page 39) **Area of law assessed: Criminal practice**

The correct answer was A. This is because where a defendant is charged with criminal damage (except aggravated criminal damage or arson) and the value of the damage is £5,000 or less, the offence is summary only. As the damage caused is only £4,000, the man must be tried summarily. Criminal damage is otherwise an either-way offence and is not an indictable-only offence (therefore options B and E are incorrect). Option C is incorrect because the man is not entitled to elect trial in the Crown Court (this special rule applies only to low-value shoplifting). Option D is incorrect because the offence is only either-way if the damage caused was over £5,000. Where an offence is triable only on indictment, the defendant is never given the opportunity to elect trial in the magistrates' court (therefore option E is incorrect).

Did you choose the correct answer? YES ☐ NO ☐

See ***Revise SQE: Criminal Practice*, Chapter 3** for a discussion of this area of law.

A76 of 90 (page 39) **Area of law assessed: Ethics and professional conduct**

The correct answer was B. This is because the SRA Code of Conduct requires solicitors to ensure that clients receive the best possible information about how their matter will be priced and, both at the time of engagement and when appropriate as their matter progresses, about the likely overall cost of the matter and any costs incurred. Whilst it is not necessary or appropriate to provide a detailed breakdown of the costs (nor is there any requirement to provide a breakdown of each and every item of expenditure), the solicitor must provide a general estimate of the fees and expenses expected (therefore options A and D are incorrect). Importantly, the duty to keep the client informed of costs is a continuing one, meaning that the solicitor will be expected to update the client as the case progresses (perhaps with more specific details than they would provide at the first engagement). Option C is incorrect as it may not be possible, or appropriate, from the outset to provide detailed estimates of costs due to unexpected costs or occurrences. Explaining that costs are unpredictable and thus a breakdown cannot be provided is not in accordance with the Code (option D is therefore incorrect). Option E is incorrect as, although providing information and advice on funding options is appropriate, the client must still be informed of potential costs.

Did you choose the correct answer? YES ☐ NO ☐

See ***Revise SQE: Ethics and Professional Conduct*, Chapter 2** for a discussion of this area of law.

A77 of 90 (page 40) **Area of law assessed: Trusts law**

The correct answer was C. This is because the trust was created (following the death of the woman) before 1 October 2014. Each child under the will is entitled to £20,000. For trusts created prior to 1 October 2014, the 'presumptive share' (ie the amount that can be advanced to a beneficiary) only extended to one-half of their share. Therefore, the eldest daughter is only entitled to £10,000 to be advanced. Had the trust been created post 1 October 2014, the eldest daughter would be entitled to her full presumptive share (ie £20,000). Option A is therefore incorrect. Option B is incorrect because a beneficiary can be advanced money, although it is a matter of discretion for the trustees. Option D is incorrect because the figure is incorrect. Option E is incorrect because the presence of a contingency does not preclude the power of advancement.

Did you choose the correct answer? YES☐ NO☐

See ***Revise SQE: Trusts Law*****, Chapter 10** for a discussion of this area of law.

A78 of 90 (page 40) **Area of law assessed: Solicitors accounts**

The correct answer was D. This is because the firm must account to the clients for a fair sum of interest on any client money they hold for them (unless there is a written agreement between the firm and the client for a different arrangement). For money held in an SDDCA, the firm should pay the clients all the interest earned on the account. For money held in the general client account, the firm should apply its interest policy to calculate a fair sum in lieu of interest to pay to the clients. Option A is incorrect because it is incorrect to state that there is *never* a requirement to pay a sum in lieu of interest for funds held in the general client account. Option B is incorrect because interest earned on client money held in an SDDCA should be paid to the client. Option C is incorrect because clients are paid a sum in lieu of interest, rather than the actual interest earned, when money is held in the general client account. The firm's interest policy will usually set out the rate of interest applied, and include a de minimis provision. Option E is incorrect because this is not standard practice. It would be a breach of the SRA Accounts Rules for firms to hold substantial sums of client money for protracted periods without accounting to their clients for a fair sum of interest.

Did you choose the correct answer? YES☐ NO☐

See ***Revise SQE: Solicitors Accounts*****, Chapter 4** for a discussion of this area of law.

A79 of 90 (page 41) **Area of law assessed: Wills and the administration of estates**

The correct answer was C. This is because marriage revokes a will unless the will is made in contemplation of marriage. As the will is revoked, the estate shall pass under the intestacy rules. Given that the man had no children, the woman inherits the entire estate. There is no evidence that the will was made in contemplation of marriage, especially since the will was made in 2010, and the marriage was over 10 years later (therefore option E is incorrect). Option A is incorrect as the whole will is revoked by the man's marriage to the woman, and the woman is entitled to the entire estate under the intestacy rules. Option B is incorrect because the revocation of the will on marriage applies to all assets, not just personal property. Option D is incorrect because the marriage has revoked the will.

Did you choose the correct answer? YES☐ NO☐

See ***Revise SQE: Wills and the Administration of Estates*****, Chapter 4** for a discussion of this area of law.

A80 of 90 (page 41) **Area of law assessed: Trusts law**

The correct answer was D. This is because a trust over land is only properly constituted when a deed of transfer (more specifically, a transfer form) has been validly executed and forwarded to HM Land Registry to register the new owner. The title deeds are a mere representation of the title over the property; they cannot be used alone to transfer said title (therefore options A, C and E are incorrect). Option B is incorrect because a deed of conveyance is to be used where the land is unregistered; in this case the land is registered.

Did you choose the correct answer? YES ☐ NO ☐

See ***Revise SQE: Trusts Law*, Chapter 3** for a discussion of this area of law.

A81 of 90 (page 42) **Area of law assessed: Criminal practice**

The correct answer was C. This is because once the issue of admissibility has been raised, it is for the prosecution to prove so that the judge is sure that the confession was not obtained by oppression, or by anything said or done which was likely in the circumstances to render the confession unreliable. Options A, B and D are incorrect in that the burden of proof is on the prosecution, not the woman. Option E is incorrect because the standard of proof required for the prosecution is the criminal standard: so that the judge is 'sure' (also commonly referred to as beyond reasonable doubt). Options B and E are also incorrect because they misstate the test. The test is not whether it would be unfair to rely on the confession; the test is whether the confession was obtained by oppression or is unreliable as a result of the things said or done.

Did you choose the correct answer? YES ☐ NO ☐

See ***Revise SQE: Criminal Practice*, Chapter 6** for a discussion of this area of law.

A82 of 90 (page 42) **Area of law assessed: Criminal practice**

The correct answer was A. This is because where an offence is committed during the operational period of a suspended sentence order, the court is required to activate the suspended term, in whole or in part, unless it would be unjust to do so. Option B is incorrect because the court may decide to activate the sentence unaltered (in full), or in part; it is not restricted to only activating the whole of the sentence. Option C is incorrect because the judge is permitted to impose a more onerous community requirement and there is no 'unjust' test for making such an order. Option D is incorrect because it is irrelevant what kind of offence has been committed during the operational period (other than perhaps being a factor to whether it would be 'unjust' to activate). Option E is incorrect because the length of time into the operational period is irrelevant (other than perhaps being a factor to whether it would be 'unjust' to activate); the defendant must not commit further offences within the entirety of the operational period.

Did you choose the correct answer? YES ☐ NO ☐

See ***Revise SQE: Criminal Practice*, Chapter 8** for a discussion of this area of law.

A83 of 90 (page 43) **Area of law assessed: Land law**

The correct answer was D. This is because for a right to be capable of being an easement, it must be a benefit to any owner of the land; the right to use the forest would only be a benefit to the client and so would not be a valid easement. Option A is incorrect as an easement does not need to be permanent. Option B is incorrect as the right to enter is a recognised category of easements. Option C is incorrect as an easement for the benefit of an individual business would not be valid. Option E is incorrect as the easement would not be valid without being a general benefit to the land.

Did you choose the correct answer? YES ☐ NO ☐

See ***Revise SQE: Land Law*, Chapter 6** for a discussion of this area of law.

A84 of 90 (page 43) **Area of law assessed: Property practice**

The correct answer was E. This is because museums and public libraries both fall under Class F (Local Community and Learning) and therefore the change of use would not require planning permission (option A is incorrect for this reason). Options B and C are incorrect because the class category is not different. Option D is incorrect because there is no mention that the property is a listed building; the simple fact it is a museum is not sufficient to amount to a listed building.

Did you choose the correct answer? YES☐ NO☐

See ***Revise SQE: Property Practice*, Chapter 3** for a discussion of this area of law.

A85 of 90 (page 44) **Area of law assessed: Trusts law**

The correct answer was E. This is because the husband and the son are together absolutely entitled to the estate and, together, can bring the trust to an end. Option A is incorrect as the husband alone cannot terminate the trust, given that the son has an interest in the same. Likewise, option B is incorrect for the same reason, but for the son instead. The consent of the brother is not required as his interest was a substitution of the son's interest in case the son did not meet his contingency. As the son satisfied the condition of reaching the age of 21, the brother has no claim whatsoever to the estate (therefore options C and D are incorrect). Trustee consent is irrelevant to bringing a trust to an end early (another reason why option D is incorrect).

Did you choose the correct answer? YES☐ NO☐

See ***Revise SQE: Trusts Law*, Chapter 5** for a discussion of this area of law.

A86 of 90 (page 44) **Area of law assessed: Land law**

The correct answer was A. This is because there was a common intention for the use of the property that required the client to be able to run water pipes; therefore this right will be implied as an easement. Option B is incorrect as, even though there was no express agreement, an easement could still be implied. Option C is incorrect as the right has not been used for more than 20 years as required for a prescriptive easement. Option D is incorrect as it will not be necessary because the land could still be used for other purposes. Option E is incorrect as the right has been implied into the agreement by implication.

Did you choose the correct answer? YES☐ NO☐

See ***Revise SQE: Land Law*, Chapter 6** for a discussion of this area of law.

A87 of 90 (page 45) **Area of law assessed: Property practice**

The correct answer was B. This is because the local land charges register is provided by the local authority, which is responsible for granting planning permission and building regulations consents. Option A is incorrect as the land charges register relates to unregistered land. Whilst option C may provide some confirmation, it is prudent to confirm with the local authority and not rely solely on the property information form. Option D is incorrect because although the survey would deal with the structural integrity of the property, it will not have all the information in relation to planning permissions. Option E is incorrect because the title deeds relate to the title rather than the property itself, and therefore will not provide any information on planning or building.

Did you choose the correct answer? YES ☐ NO ☐

See ***Revise SQE: Property Practice*, Chapter 3** for a discussion of this area of law.

A88 of 90 (page 45) **Area of law assessed: Criminal practice**

The correct answer was C. This is because the interests of justice test is automatically satisfied for trials to be heard in the Crown Court. However, this does not apply to appeals to the Crown Court against conviction from the magistrates' court. The man does not automatically satisfy the interests of justice test, therefore options B and D are incorrect. As the man earns an adjusted annual income of £24,000 he cannot be passported through the means test (therefore options A and D are incorrect) and does not satisfy the initial means test (the threshold being £12,475 or less). The man must therefore proceed to the full means test (therefore options B and E are incorrect).

Did you choose the correct answer? YES ☐ NO ☐

See ***Revise SQE: Criminal Practice*, Chapter 3** for a discussion of this area of law.

A89 of 90 (page 46) **Area of law assessed: Criminal law**

The correct answer was E. This is because the force used when acting in self-defence must be necessary and proportionate (therefore options B and C are incorrect), and a defendant must have a *genuinely* held belief that it is necessary to use force (therefore option D is incorrect). Self-defence may also apply when protecting another person from such a threat (therefore, option A is incorrect).

Did you choose the correct answer? YES ☐ NO ☐

See ***Revise SQE: Criminal Law*, Chapter 4** for a discussion of this area of law.

A90 of 90 (page 46) **Area of law assessed: Criminal practice**

The correct answer was B. This is because ss 50A and 51B of the Crime and Disorder Act 1998 prescribes that where the prosecution give notice, the magistrates' court must send the case to the Crown Court. Notice is given in circumstances where the fraud is of such seriousness or complexity that it is appropriate that the management of the case should without delay be taken over by the Crown Court. In this case, due to the value of the misappropriated property, the complexity of the fraudulent schemes and the estimated length of trial, it is likely that the prosecution would give such notice. Option A is incorrect because, whilst fraud is an either-way offence, notice is likely to be given in this case. Option C is incorrect because fraud is always an either-way offence, regardless of the value involved. Option D is incorrect because fraud is not an indictable-only offence. Option E is incorrect because the magistrates are only required to send the case to the Crown where notice is given; if no notice is given by the prosecution, the normal rules of allocation apply.

Did you choose the correct answer? YES ☐ NO ☐

See ***Revise SQE: Criminal Practice*, Chapter 4** for a discussion of this area of law.

Session 2 answers

■ SUMMARY

The following table is a quick reference guide for the answers to Session 2 of *FLK2 Practice Assessments*. Consider using a coloured pen or a highlighter to mark the MCQs that you answered correctly, and score yourself 1 mark for each. Add up your total marks, and calculate your percentage for Session 2.

For a summary of the Session 1 answers, see **page 99**.

Question	Answer	Question	Answer	Question	Answer
1	A	31	E	61	B
2	A	32	A	62	B
3	C	33	B	63	A
4	A	34	A	64	C
5	D	35	D	65	A
6	A	36	E	66	C
7	B	37	C	67	A
8	A	38	D	68	B
9	C	39	D	69	E
10	C	40	B	70	C
11	C	41	B	71	E
12	C	42	D	72	B
13	E	43	B	73	C
14	D	44	C	74	B
15	B	45	D	75	B
16	C	46	C	76	C
17	A	47	D	77	E
18	B	48	A	78	A
19	A	49	D	79	B
20	E	50	C	80	B
21	E	51	C	81	B
22	B	52	D	82	D
23	A	53	A	83	C
24	A	54	A	84	C
25	B	55	A	85	C
26	A	56	C	86	A
27	C	57	D	87	E
28	E	58	E	88	A
29	B	59	D	89	A
30	B	60	D	90	D

Your total score for Session 2: ______ **/ 90**

Percentage: ______ **%**

DETAILED ANSWERS

A1 of 90 (page 48) **Area of law assessed: Wills and the administration of estates**

The correct answer was A. This is because a will is to be construed with reference to property as owned at the date of a testator's death unless contrary intention is shown that the testator intends the gift to be of an item owned by them at the date of the will. Contrary intention is usually shown by making specific gifts, identifying an object owned at the date of the will (ie 'my bookcase' - this would be a gift of the bookcase owned at the date of the will). If the specific gift is a generic kind, where the size of the gift is capable of fluctuation between the date of the will and the date of death, the gift will be of all of the specific items of property within that general description at the date of the testator's death (ie 'my entire book collection'). Option E is therefore incorrect. Options B and D are incorrect as this is a specific gift of a generic kind and option B is further incorrect because the gift is of the items matching that description at the date of death, not at the date of the will. Option C is incorrect because the will speaks of 'my entire book collection'; a matter that is to be quantified at the date of death - there is no uncertainty of subject matter in this regard (as opposed to a hypothetical situation where the woman could have said 'some of my books').

Did you choose the correct answer? YES ☐ NO ☐

See ***Revise SQE: Wills and the Administration of Estates*****, Chapter 3** for a discussion of this area of law.

A2 of 90 (page 49) **Area of law assessed: Criminal practice**

The correct answer was A. This is because s 19 MCA 1980 prescribes the approach that must be taken by the magistrates' court when determining allocation. Option A correctly identifies the individual steps that must be taken, and in the correct order. Option B is incorrect as the woman is also permitted to make representations as to whether summary trial or trial on indictment is more suitable, and option D is incorrect as the prosecution must be permitted to make representations. Option C is incorrect because the prosecution must be permitted to present the previous convictions (or lack thereof) of the woman to the court, as the previous convictions will affect whether the magistrates consider their sentencing powers to be adequate. Option E is incorrect because the statutory factors listed in s 19(3) are mandatory (the use of the word 'shall') in s 19(3) and not discretionary (the use of the word 'may' in option E).

Did you choose the correct answer? YES ☐ NO ☐

See ***Revise SQE: Criminal Practice*****, Chapter 4** for a discussion of this area of law.

A3 of 90 (page 50) **Area of law assessed: Solicitors accounts**

The correct answer was C. This is because the agency method of paying disbursements must be used as the invoice is addressed to the clients rather than to the firm. Providing there is a sufficient credit balance on the client account, the firm can pay the invoice using client money. The sum paid should be VAT-inclusive (£500 + VAT (standard rate) = £600). Options A and B are incorrect because the invoice should not be paid from the business account unless there are insufficient funds in the client account. Option A is also incorrect because there are two debits, rather than a debit and a credit, so this is an incorrect double entry. Options B and D are incorrect because they show a VAT-exclusive sum (rather than a VAT-inclusive sum) which is not appropriate for a payment using the agency method. Although in theory the solicitor could send the invoice direct to the personal representatives for payment, it is more usual for the firm to pay the invoice on their behalf, using monies already collected in the administration of the estate. Therefore, option E is incorrect to suggest that the firm *must* send the invoice to the clients.

Did you choose the correct answer? YES☐ NO☐

See ***Revise SQE: Solicitors Accounts*, Chapter 6** for a discussion of this area of law.

A4 of 90 (page 50) **Area of law assessed: Criminal law**

The correct answer was A. This is because when arguing lawful excuse by reason of protecting other property, there is a two-limb test. Objectively, the damage must have been caused to protect property in immediate need of protection, and subjectively, the defendant must have believed that the property was in need of immediate protection. Option B is incorrect because the first limb of the test is objective, not subjective; and the second limb is subjective, not objective. Option C is incorrect as the property that is in need of protection does not need to be owned by the man. Option D is incorrect because the facts identify that the man thought the property (the dog) was in danger of overheating. Option E is incorrect because the law requires a defendant to believe that the property was in *immediate* need of protection.

Did you choose the correct answer? YES☐ NO☐

See ***Revise SQE: Criminal Law*, Chapter 9** for a discussion of this area of law.

A5 of 90 (page 51) **Area of law assessed: Trusts law**

The correct answer was D. This is because the lowest intermediate balance, which reflects the lowest amount that can be traced and claimed by the beneficiaries, is £1,000. By depositing £10,000 of trust money into his account, the man has mixed his own funds with those of the trust (often referred to as 'wrongful mixtures'). As the funds are mixed, the law presumes that the man will withdraw his own money first. By spending £10,000 gambling, the man has dissipated £1,000 of his own money first before then spending £9,000 of the trust's money. This leaves £1,000 in the account, which represents the trust's money, as the lowest intermediate balance. The fact that the man deposited £5,000 of his own money is irrelevant; the beneficiaries cannot claim this amount unless they can prove that the money was intended to be a repayment for the funds spent. Without any evidence of such intention, the only money that is identifiable to the trust is £1,000. All other options are therefore incorrect as they do not proffer the correct figure.

Did you choose the correct answer? YES☐ NO☐

See ***Revise SQE: Trusts Law*, Chapter 12** for a discussion of this area of law.

A6 of 90 (page 51) **Area of law assessed: Criminal law**

The correct answer was A. This is because the circumstances must be such that a reasonable person would have foreseen a *serious* and *obvious* risk of *death*. The risk must also actually exist. Option B is incorrect because the risk needs to be reasonably foreseeable. Option C is incorrect because there needs to be a risk of death, not serious injury (this is why Option E is also incorrect). Option D is incorrect because the risk of death needs to be serious and obvious, not grave and apparent.

Did you choose the correct answer? YES☐ NO☐

See ***Revise SQE: Criminal Law*, Chapter 5** for a discussion of this area of law.

A7 of 90 (page 52) **Area of law assessed: Criminal practice**

The correct answer was B. This is because the treatment from the police may well amount to *something said or done* that is likely to render a confession unreliable. In such circumstances, a confession shall not be admitted. Option A is incorrect because the treatment described in the facts is unlikely to amount to oppression given that this is a very high threshold to reach. Option C is incorrect because, whilst this is a legitimate argument to make for exclusion, it is not the *first* argument that should be made; with confession evidence, s 76 Police and Criminal Evidence Act 1984 arguments should be made first. Options D and E are incorrect because the facts do not detail *why* access to a solicitor was delayed, bearing in mind that access can be delayed in some circumstances.

Did you choose the correct answer? YES ☐ NO ☐

See ***Revise SQE: Criminal Practice*****, Chapter 6** for a discussion of this area of law.

A8 of 90 (page 52) **Area of law assessed: Solicitors accounts**

The correct answer was A. This is because the double entry is the same as for any receipt of client money, so both entries must be in the client account columns and there must be a credit entry on the client ledger and a debit entry on the cash sheet. Because the money is held as stakeholder, the details column must identify the receipt as funds held as stakeholder on behalf of both the buyer and the seller. Option B is incorrect because although the information required in the details column is appropriate, the credit and debit are the wrong way around. Options C, D and E are all incorrect because the details column on the client ledger must identify the funds as a stakeholder deposit held on behalf of both the buyer and the seller. Option D is further incorrect as the double entry is wrongly recorded in the business account rather than the client account. Option E is further incorrect as the double entry mixes one entry in the client account and one in the business account. Any double entry must have two entries in the client account, or two in the business account: they cannot be mixed.

Did you choose the correct answer? YES ☐ NO ☐

See ***Revise SQE: Solicitors Accounts*****, Chapter 7** for a discussion of this area of law.

A9 of 90 (page 53) **Area of law assessed: Property practice**

The correct answer was C. This is because the client will be expected to pay £21,000 (0% on £125,000, 2% on the next £125,000 up to £250,000 (£2,500) and 5% on the remaining £370,000). Option A is incorrect as this is based on SDLT rates between 8 July 2020 and 30 June 2021 (0% on the first £500,000 and 5% on the remaining £120,000). Option B is incorrect as this figure would be payable if the client was a first-time buyer before 31 March 2025 (0% on £425,000 and 5% on £195,000). Option D is incorrect as this figure relates to SDLT rates before 31 March 2025 before they changed (0% on the first £250,000 and 5% on the remaining £370,000 (£18,500)). Option E is incorrect as this figure is based on whether the client was purchasing a second property, which would give rise to higher rates of stamp duty (5% on the first £125,000 (£6,250), 7% on the next £125,000 up to £250,000 (£8,750) and 10% on the remaining £370,000 (£37,000)).

Did you choose the correct answer? YES ☐ NO ☐

See ***Revise SQE: Property Practice*****, Chapter 10** for a discussion of this area of law.

A10 of 90 (page 53) **Area of law assessed: Criminal practice**

The correct answer was C. This is because a judge sitting alone will hear evidence or submissions to determine the facts of the case if the case is being dealt with in the Crown Court. Option A is incorrect because a jury is not involved in Newton hearings. Option B is incorrect because on the facts, this case is not being dealt with in a magistrates' court. Option D is incorrect because the description does not accurately describe a Newton hearing, despite the fact that discussions may take place between both parties to agree a basis of plea. Option E is incorrect because Newton hearings are not sent to the High Court.

Did you choose the correct answer? YES ☐ NO ☐

See ***Revise SQE: Criminal Practice*, Chapter 8** for a discussion of this area of law.

A11 of 90 (page 54) **Area of law assessed: Criminal law**

The correct answer was C. This is because a defendant must commit a base offence first that was unlawful, objectively dangerous, and caused the death of the victim (legal and factual causation principles apply). Option A is incorrect because the base offence must be *objectively* dangerous, not *subjectively* dangerous. Option B is incorrect because, whilst there has been the suggestion that a base offence to found unlawful act manslaughter must be intrinsically criminal, no such phrase is used in law. Option D is incorrect because the act must be *unlawful* as well as objectively dangerous. Option E is incorrect because committing the base offence needs to cause the death of the victim.

Did you choose the correct answer? YES ☐ NO ☐

See ***Revise SQE: Criminal Law*, Chapter 5** for a discussion of this area of law.

A12 of 90 (page 54) **Area of law assessed: Trusts law**

The correct answer was C. This is because the beneficiaries can trace into the car, and any profit (or increase in value) on that property. Whilst the law presumes that the trustee spends their own money first when an account is mixed, this presumption is displaced in circumstances where the wrongdoer may profit from their wrongdoing. Given that the funds have been dissipated, it is not possible for the beneficiaries to recover their funds from the account. In this situation, the law reverses the presumption and treats the first withdrawal as the money for the trust. The money realised in the racehorse is not recoverable as the horse has died (there being no value to now attach to the horse). As such, the only claim that can be made by the beneficiaries is against the car, including the increase in value. All other options are therefore incorrect.

Did you choose the correct answer? YES ☐ NO ☐

See ***Revise SQE: Trusts Law*, Chapter 12** for a discussion of this area of law.

A13 of 90 (page 55) **Area of law assessed: Solicitors accounts**

The correct answer was E. This is because the partners will be specialising in property law, and, therefore, they will be handling client money as part of the legal services they provide, for example, mortgage advance funds, proceeds of sale, purchase monies etc. They will therefore need to operate a client account unless they choose to outsource the management of money belonging to clients and other third parties to a third-party provider who will operate the account on their behalf. Option A is incorrect because it is a breach of the SRA Accounts Rules to keep business money and client money in the same account (there are very limited exceptions to this principle, for example, where the firm specialises in criminal defence work and only acts for legal aid-funded clients). Options B and C are both incorrect because the partners can choose to use a third-party managed account should they wish to do so. There is no prohibition on them making this choice (option B) or requirement to do so (option C). Option D is incorrect because property law transactions require the firm to hold client money as an integral part of the legal services provided.

Did you choose the correct answer? YES ☐ NO ☐

See ***Revise SQE: Solicitors Accounts*****, Chapter 7** for a discussion of this area of law.

A14 of 90 (page 55) **Area of law assessed: Solicitors accounts**

The correct answer was D. This is because bank reconciliation must take place at least every five weeks. Bank statements for all the firm's client accounts must be reconciled with (checked against) the firm's internal accounting records to identify and resolve any discrepancies. It is considered good practice to do the same with the firm's business accounts although this is not specified in the Rules. Options A, B and C are incorrect because there is no requirement for bank reconciliation to take place every week. Option A is also incorrect because it does not mention the firm's client accounts (which are the focus for bank reconciliation requirements in the SRA Accounts Rules). Option C is also incorrect because there is no specified period for reconciling the firm's business accounts. Option E is incorrect because the specified period for reconciling client accounts is five, rather than 10, weeks.

Did you choose the correct answer? YES ☐ NO ☐

See ***Revise SQE: Solicitors Accounts*****, Chapter 8** for a discussion of this area of law.

A15 of 90 (page 56) **Area of law assessed: Criminal law**

The correct answer was B. This is because the focus is on an intention to kill or cause really serious harm, not *who* the intention was directed at. Mistaken identity is irrelevant for these purposes (therefore, Option A was incorrect). Option C is incorrect because the mens rea for murder requires an intention to kill or cause *really serious* harm, not *some* harm. Option D is incorrect because there may well be a virtual certainty of death or really serious harm through driving a car aggressively at someone and at speed, and as mentioned, the identity of the victim is irrelevant providing the requisite intent was present. Option E is incorrect because as the law currently stands in practice, even if a finding of virtual certainty is made, it is a matter of fact for the jury to consider in assessing whether the mens rea is made out; there is no requirement that a jury *must* find intention where there is a virtual certainty.

Did you choose the correct answer? YES ☐ NO ☐

See ***Revise SQE: Criminal Law*****, Chapter 5** for a discussion of this area of law.

A16 of 90 (page 57) **Area of law assessed: Criminal practice**

The correct answer was C. This is because the credibility and reliability issues are likely to mean that a properly directed bench could not convict on the evidence. Option A is incorrect because the submission is to be made after the conclusion of the prosecution case, not after the defendant has given evidence. Option B is incorrect because the prosecution has offered *some* evidence which the defendant could be convicted on. Option D is incorrect for the same reason as Option B, but also because submissions of no case to answer are to be made after the closure of the prosecution's case. Option E is incorrect because this is the incorrect test to be applied.

Did you choose the correct answer? YES ☐ NO ☐

See ***Revise SQE: Criminal Practice*****, Chapter 8** for a discussion of this area of law.

A17 of 90 (page 57) **Area of law assessed: Trusts law**

The correct answer was A. This is because the test for dishonesty is an objective one asking whether the agent is dishonest by the standards of ordinary decent people. There is no requirement for the agent to appreciate that his assistance is dishonest by those standards to be liable (therefore options B, C and E are incorrect). Given that the agent is aware of the trustee's financial difficulties, is surprised that the trustee has been able to find the money, and deliberately turns a blind eye to the source of the money, it is more likely than not that the arbiter of fact will find that the agent is dishonest by the standards of ordinary decent people.

Did you choose the correct answer? YES☐ NO☐

See ***Revise SQE: Trusts Law*****, Chapter 9** for a discussion of this area of law.

A18 of 90 (page 58) **Area of law assessed: Criminal law**

The correct answer was B. This is because voluntary manslaughter is where a person unlawfully kills another and possesses both the actus reus and mens rea for murder, but in the circumstances, a special or partial defence applies. Option A is incorrect because intoxication is not a special or partial defence for these purposes. Option C is incorrect because this is a description of unlawful act manslaughter (which is a form of involuntary manslaughter). Options D and E are incorrect because both the actus reus and mens rea for murder are required to be possessed by the defendant.

Did you choose the correct answer? YES☐ NO☐

See ***Revise SQE: Criminal Law*****, Chapter 5** for a discussion of this area of law.

A19 of 90 (page 58) **Area of law assessed: Solicitors accounts**

The correct answer was A. This is because the SRA Accounts Rules provide that all accounting records must be stored securely and retained for at least six years. As the cupboard contains records that are older than six years, they no longer need to be retained. However, as many of them will contain confidential client information, they should be destroyed as confidential waste. Options C, D and E are incorrect as there is no requirement to retain accounting records for over six years (10 years for options C and D, and indefinitely in option E). Options B and D are incorrect as any accounting records containing confidential client information must be destroyed as confidential waste.

Did you choose the correct answer? YES☐ NO☐

See ***Revise SQE: Solicitors Accounts*****, Chapter 8** for a discussion of this area of law.

A20 of 90 (page 59) **Area of law assessed: Criminal practice**

The correct answer was E. This is because it sets out the requirement for leave to appeal, the correct timeframe to serve the notice, and the correct court which will hear the appeal. Option A is incorrect because leave to appeal is required. Option B is incorrect because an appeal against conviction from the Crown Court will not be heard in the High Court (only appeals from convictions in the magistrates' court can proceed to the High Court). Option C is incorrect because the timeframe in which the appeal notice is to be served starts from the date of conviction. Option D is incorrect because leave is required, and the timeframe is wrong; it starts from the date of conviction.

Did you choose the correct answer? YES☐ NO☐

See ***Revise SQE: Criminal Practice*****, Chapter 9** for a discussion of this area of law.

A21 of 90 (page 59) **Area of law assessed: Ethics and professional conduct**

The correct answer was E. This is because the SRA Code of Conduct requires solicitors to consider and take account of their client's attributes, needs and circumstances. Option E is the best course of action in this situation as it ensures the solicitor considers the options that will best suit the client's needs (eg having a BSL interpreter present, using speech-to-text video technology, having a lipspeaker or a notetaker present). Option A is incorrect as it may not feasible or possible for the client to attend an in-person meeting with a BLS/English interpreter. Option B is incorrect as the solicitor is under a duty to take account of these attributes and needs. Option C is incorrect because it is neither practicable nor reasonable for the solicitor to teach themselves BSL. Option D is incorrect as whilst email and written communications will be an important medium of communication, the facts tell you that the client primarily communicates through BSL - a fact that the solicitor must respect and take account of.

Did you choose the correct answer? YES ☐ NO ☐

See ***Revise SQE: Ethics and Professional Conduct*, Chapter 2** for a discussion of this area of law.

A22 of 90 (page 60) **Area of law assessed: Criminal law**

The correct answer was B. This is because the man's actions, whilst demonstrating an intention to commit the full offence, are unlikely to be regarded as 'more than merely preparatory'. This is because the man must 'embark on the crime proper' (ie be in a position to commit the offence) in order to be liable for an attempt. It is likely to be the case that there are many more steps that must be completed before the offence can be attempted (eg making his way to, or attending at, the address in question). Option A is incorrect because it misstates the law: the man must take steps that are *more than* merely preparatory to be liable for attempted robbery. Option C is incorrect as whilst the man's conduct is preparatory, it is unlikely to be regarded as more than merely preparatory. Option D is incorrect because the offence of robbery is not made out as the man has not committed the offence in full. Option E is incorrect because there is evidence that the man intended the full offence of robbery; the issue is whether his conduct is more than merely preparatory to the commission of the full offence.

Did you choose the correct answer? YES ☐ NO ☐

See ***Revise SQE: Criminal Law*, Chapter 3** for a discussion of this area of law.

A23 of 90 (page 60) **Area of law assessed: Criminal practice**

The correct answer was A. This is because on the facts, the dispute seems to be on a point of law and not an evidential matter. The Divisional Court of the High Court is better placed to deal with such a matter. Option B is incorrect because although it is factually correct, it is not the *best* form of appeal in the circumstances, given the woman is unlikely to want a complete rehearing of the case given her anxieties. Option C is incorrect because a full rehearing would not take place in the Divisional Court of the High Court. Option D is incorrect because the Crown Court does not deal with appeals by way of case stated. Option E is incorrect because despite it being factually accurate for cases from the Crown Court, appeals from the magistrates' courts are never heard in the Court of Appeal.

Did you choose the correct answer? YES ☐ NO ☐

See ***Revise SQE: Criminal Practice*, Chapter 9** for a discussion of this area of law.

A24 of 90 (page 61) **Area of law assessed: Trusts law**

The correct answer was A. This is because, in respect of personalty, a resulting trust would be presumed in favour of the wife as the presumption of advancement does not apply for gifts from wife to husband as they do from husband to wife. However, the property transferred here is land for which the law does not generally presume the existence of a resulting trust unless there is some additional evidence that would point to an intention on the part of the person giving the gift (the wife in this case) to retain the beneficial interest. Therefore, the wife cannot rely on the fact that the law presumes a resulting trust (unlike if the property concerned was personalty). In addition, the letters from the wife are sufficient to demonstrate an intention to gift the property to the husband. In this case, a resulting trust would not be found in her favour; the house belongs to the husband alone. The son has no interest in the house at all. As such, all other options are incorrect.

Did you choose the correct answer? YES☐ NO☐

See ***Revise SQE: Trusts Law*, Chapter 7** for a discussion of this area of law.

A25 of 90 (page 61) **Area of law assessed: Trusts law**

The correct answer was B. This is because there is no minimum number of trustees that must be in place for a trust over land. Retirement of a trustee must be done in writing; it cannot be done orally. Therefore, so long as the man retires in writing, the woman can continue to act as the sole trustee (though this is often inadvisable). Therefore, all other options are incorrect.

Did you choose the correct answer? YES☐ NO☐

See ***Revise SQE: Trusts Law*, Chapter 10** for a discussion of this area of law.

A26 of 90 (page 62) **Area of law assessed: Ethics and professional conduct**

The correct answer was A. This is because the SRA Code of Conduct requires solicitors not to make unsolicited approaches to members of the public, with the exception of current or former clients, in order to advertise legal services provided by them, or their business or employer. Solicitors are permitted to advertise their services to the public so long as this is done in a non-intrusive and non-targeted way. This means that solicitors cannot make direct or specifically targeted 'approaches' to members of the public in person, by phone or via other means that target them individually. The only activities that are permissible in this case, therefore, are the sending of marketing materials to current and former clients (which is expressly permitted under the Code), and setting up a booth at a public event (which does not involve a targeted or instructive approach). Contacting random people on social media will be considered intrusive (even though it is random), as will cold-calling. Option A is the only answer with the correct combination of permissible activities; all other options are therefore incorrect.

Did you choose the correct answer? YES☐ NO☐

See ***Revise SQE: Ethics and Professional Conduct*, Chapter 2** for a discussion of this area of law.

A27 of 90 (page 62) **Area of law assessed: Ethics and professional conduct**

The correct answer was C. This is because the SRA Code of Conduct requires solicitors to be honest and open with clients if things go wrong, and if a client suffers loss or harm as a result, they put matters right (if possible) and explain fully and promptly what has happened and the likely impact. The solicitor is under a positive obligation, therefore, to be open and honest with clients affected by the data breach, and take steps to mitigate matters/put them right. Option A is incorrect because waiting for clients to raise concerns or ignoring the issue altogether is not a sufficient response to a data breach, as it could harm clients and erode their trust towards the firm and the legal profession. Option D is incorrect as, although the solicitor must investigate the breach, they must notify the affected clients. Whilst both the SRA and the ICO should be notified of the breach, the solicitor must still inform the affected clients (therefore options B and E are incorrect).

Did you choose the correct answer? YES☐ NO☐

See ***Revise SQE: Ethics and Professional Conduct*****, Chapter 2** for a discussion of this area of law.

A28 of 90 (page 63) **Area of law assessed: Wills and the administration of estates**

The correct answer was E. This is because an exception to the doctrine of lapse is where the legatee under a will is a child or remoter descendant of the testator, and whilst they predecease the testator, the legatee leaves children. In this case, the children of the legatee will benefit from the gift. In this case, therefore, the children of the granddaughter will receive the house shared equally between them (per stirpes). Option A is incorrect because the next of kin is not relevant to this circumstance. Option B is incorrect because of the exception to the doctrine of lapse involving children or the remoter descendants of the testator. Option C is incorrect because, even if the exception to the doctrine of lapse did not apply, the will remains valid and the gift would pass via the residue. Option D is incorrect because the doctrine of lapse does not operate to pass property according to the will of the intended beneficiary.

Did you choose the correct answer? YES☐ NO☐

See ***Revise SQE: Wills and the Administration of Estates*****, Chapter 3** for a discussion of this area of law.

A29 of 90 (page 63) **Area of law assessed: Trusts law**

The correct answer was B. This is because the absence from the UK must be for a continuous period of 12 months or more. As the trustee returned to the UK on two occasions of varying length, she has not been out of the UK for a continuous period of 12 months and cannot be removed by the trustees. The trustee may be removed by other means, but the MCQ specifically asks about the power of the trustees and not, for example, of the court or the beneficiaries. Option A is incorrect because if the trustee had been out of the UK for a continuous period of 12 months, the co-trustees would still have to appoint a replacement trustee. Option C is incorrect because the 12-month period must be continuous (otherwise, it would be correct). Option D is incorrect because it is irrelevant whether the trustee kept in contact with the co-trustees; the focus is on the continuous period of absence from the UK. Option E is incorrect because there would be a need to appoint a replacement trustee, and the removal must be done in writing.

Did you choose the correct answer? YES☐ NO☐

See ***Revise SQE: Trusts Law*****, Chapter 10** for a discussion of this area of law.

A30 of 90 (page 64) **Area of law assessed: Criminal law**

The correct answer was B. This is because on these facts, the woman is likely to have committed aggravated criminal damage. There was an intention to damage the house through throwing bricks at the window, and the woman was reckless as to endangering life in doing so. A person may still be guilty of aggravated criminal damage even if they damage their own property (therefore

Option A is incorrect). Option C is incorrect because, on the facts, there appeared to be no *intention* to endanger life. Option D is incorrect because the focus is on intention or recklessness. The fact that the man was not actually hurt is irrelevant. Option E is incorrect because there is nothing in the facts to suggest that the woman's life was endangered.

Did you choose the correct answer? YES ☐ NO ☐

See ***Revise SQE: Criminal Law*, Chapter 9** for a discussion of this area of law.

A31 of 90 (page 64) **Area of law assessed: Land law**

The correct answer was E. This is because positive covenants cannot run with the land and will not be binding without an express assignment. Option A is incorrect as the covenant to repaint is not a negative covenant. Option B is incorrect as the burden of a positive covenant can never run. Option C is incorrect as the burden of a positive covenant can never run with the land. Option D is incorrect as a positive covenant cannot run with the land and therefore will not bind successors in title.

Did you choose the correct answer? YES ☐ NO ☐

See ***Revise SQE: Land Law*, Chapter 7** for a discussion of this area of law.

A32 of 90 (page 65) **Area of law assessed: Solicitors accounts**

The correct answer was A. This is because the firm's policy is to operate two separate client ledgers (one for the buyer and one for the lender). In this circumstance, it is appropriate for the receipt to be credited to the lender's client ledger. This reflects the fact that the money belongs to the lender until completion. At completion, the money is transferred from the lender's client ledger to the buyer's client ledger so that it can be used to finance the purchase of the new property. Option B is incorrect: although it is a valid way of dealing with the receipt of a mortgage advance, it is not appropriate here as the firm's policy is to record such receipts in separate client ledgers (rather than just in the buyer's client ledger). Options C and D are incorrect as the mortgage advance is client money and therefore cannot be paid into a business account at any point (either on receipt or completion) without breaching the SRA Accounts Rules. Option E is incorrect as the mortgage advance is client money. As such, it must be recorded in the firm's ledgers as soon as it is received.

Did you choose the correct answer? YES ☐ NO ☐

See ***Revise SQE: Solicitors Accounts*, Chapter 7** for a discussion of this area of law.

A33 of 90 (page 65) **Area of law assessed: Criminal practice**

The correct answer was B. This is because this answer accurately reflects the burden and standard of proof, and that the man cannot be compelled to give evidence. Option A is incorrect because guilt cannot be proven on the balance of probabilities (the civil test also referred to as 'more likely than not'). Option C is incorrect as the standard of proof is the criminal standard, not the civil standard. Option D is incorrect because the defence does not bear the burden of proof in this case, and a defendant cannot be compelled to give evidence. Option E is incorrect as the defence does not bear the burden of proof in this case.

Did you choose the correct answer? YES ☐ NO ☐

See ***Revise SQE: Criminal Practice*, Chapter 6** for a discussion of this area of law.

A34 of 90 (page 66) **Area of law assessed: Criminal practice**

The correct answer was A. This is because the man had an opportunity to offer his account (which he intends to rely on now) at interview, and without good cause, refused to. In these circumstances, any inferences that a court deems proper may be drawn. Option B is incorrect because the court is not compelled to draw inferences. Option C is incorrect because a court is entitled to draw inferences in certain circumstances. Option D is incorrect as the reason given by the man as to why he refused to answer questions is unlikely to be reasonable. Option E is incorrect because the court does not draw inferences of guilt; it can draw inferences that *appear proper.*

Did you choose the correct answer? YES ☐ NO ☐

See ***Revise SQE: Criminal Practice*****, Chapter 6** for a discussion of this area of law.

A35 of 90 (page 67) **Area of law assessed: Criminal law**

The correct answer was D. This is because the girl was reckless in damaging the bicycle by fire. Even though the girl intended to set fire to the bicycle when she initially set out to commit the offence, she had second thoughts at the scene and did not intentionally start the fire. However, she was reckless in smoking after pouring the petrol. Option A is incorrect because the fire that caused the damage can be started intentionally or recklessly. Option B is incorrect because provocation is not a lawful excuse. Option C is incorrect because at the material time the girl did not *intentionally* start the fire. Option E is incorrect because there is no requirement in law that fire itself has to cause a particular degree of damage.

Did you choose the correct answer? YES ☐ NO ☐

See ***Revise SQE: Criminal Law*****, Chapter 9** for a discussion of this area of law.

A36 of 90 (page 67) **Area of law assessed: Wills and the administration of estates**

The correct answer was E. This is because the intestacy rules prescribe three elements of entitlement for a surviving spouse where the intestate is also survived by issue (children). First, the spouse is entitled to the statutory legacy of £322,000 (which has been the figure from 26 July 2023 to the present day). The spouse is also entitled to all personal chattels owned by the intestate at the time of death (subject to some exceptions not relevant here). Finally, where the intestate is survived by children, the surviving spouse will inherit half of the residue estate (here that would be £39,000 as half of £78,000 remaining from deducting the statutory legacy of £322,000 from the estate value of £400,000). The total amount for the spouse would therefore be £361,000. The surviving children would then be entitled to the other half of the residue (a share of £39,000 equally between them). All other options are incorrect as the figures are wrong: option C represents the statutory legacy figure from 6 February 2020 to 25 July 2023 and the distribution of the residue (£270,000 statutory legacy plus one-half of £130,000 representing the residue) and option B represents the figure from 1 October 2014 to 5 February 2020 and the distribution of the residue (£250,000 statutory legacy plus one-half of £150,000 representing the residue).

Did you choose the correct answer? YES ☐ NO ☐

See ***Revise SQE: Wills and the Administration of Estates*****, Chapter 5** for a discussion of this area of law.

A37 of 90 (page 68) **Area of law assessed: Property practice**

The correct answer was C. This is because there may be restrictions in the articles of association that could affect the marketability of the property, and therefore this should be reviewed before the client has exchanged contracts. A stock transfer form and share certificate are not applicable because the company is limited by guarantee, therefore options A and B are incorrect. Option D is incorrect as a signed transfer would be provided by the seller's solicitors on completion (signed by the seller) to transfer ownership to the client with HM Land Registry. Option E is incorrect as a signed letter would not be sufficient to make the client aware of any restrictions (as per option C).

Did you choose the correct answer? YES☐ NO☐

See ***Revise SQE: Property Practice*, Chapter 7** for a discussion of this area of law.

A38 of 90 (page 68) **Area of law assessed: Land law**

The correct answer was D. This is because as the benefit of a covenant has not been expressly annexed to the land, it will only run with the land through statutory annexation. In order for this to apply, the benefitted land must be identifiable from the deed or other documents. As the original covenantor was a large landowner, the benefitted land will not be identifiable without further documentation. Option A is incorrect as the benefitted land must be identifiable. Option B is incorrect as, although it has not been expressly assigned, it could still have been annexed to the land. Option C is incorrect as the burden of a covenant can never run at the common law. Option E is incorrect as freehold covenants can never be legal rights.

Did you choose the correct answer? YES☐ NO☐

See ***Revise SQE: Land Law*, Chapter 7** for a discussion of this area of law.

A39 of 90 (page 69) **Area of law assessed: Criminal law**

The correct answer was D. This is because the man commits an assault where he does an act (which may include words or gestures), which causes the victim to apprehend immediate unlawful violence, intending or being reckless as to causing that apprehension. A conditional threat can still amount to an assault where the condition does not negate immediacy. Here, the threat is that violence will occur immediately if the victim takes one small step. That is sufficient to create immediate apprehension. Immediacy does not require instantaneous violence, but violence that could occur within moments. Being seated in a car does not prevent immediacy where the victim reasonably believes the violence could follow immediately upon movement. Option A is incorrect because words alone can constitute an assault, particularly when supported by context or gestures. Option B is incorrect because conditional threats do not automatically prevent liability if immediacy remains. Option C is incorrect because physical barriers do not negate immediacy if violence could still imminently follow. Option E is incorrect because common assault does not require intention to carry out the threat, only intention or recklessness as to causing apprehension.

Did you choose the correct answer? YES☐ NO☐

See ***Revise SQE: Criminal Law*, Chapter 6** for a discussion of this area of law.

A40 of 90 (page 69) **Area of law assessed: Solicitors accounts**

The correct answer was B. This is because an inter-ledger transfer requires double entries in the client columns, with a debit (DR) entry in the client ledger from which the sum is transferred (here the mother's client ledger) and a credit (CR) entry in the client ledger into which the sum is transferred (here the daughter's client ledger). All inter-ledger records should be recorded in the firm's transfer journal. Option B is the only option that includes this accounting record requirement accurately. Option A was incorrect because although the double entries were correct, the transfer is unrelated to client billing so no entries should be made in the firm's profit costs ledger. Options C and D are both incorrect because the debits and credits are the wrong way around (showing a transfer from the daughter to the mother instead). Options C and E identify good practice in keeping records on the client files. However, this is not an *accounting record* requirement. Option E is incorrect because the double entries reflect a cash transfer rather than an inter-ledger transfer.

Did you choose the correct answer? YES ☐ NO ☐

See ***Revise SQE: Solicitors Accounts*****, Chapter 6** for a discussion of this area of law.

A41 of 90 (page 70) **Area of law assessed: Solicitors accounts**

The correct answer was B. This is because a cash transfer from the client account to the business account is required to clear the bill. £4,800 must be transferred out of the client account (requiring a debit entry in the client ledger and a credit entry in the cash sheet); and then into the business account (requiring a credit entry in the client ledger and a debit entry in the cash sheet). Option A is incorrect because it only describes the first part of the transfer (ie transferring £4,800 out of the client account). Option C is incorrect because the credit and debit are the wrong way around, and it does not contain any reference to the money being received into the business account. Option D is incorrect because one entry is in the client account and one entry is in the business account. All double entries like this will always be incorrect. Double entries must either be both in the client account, or both in the business account. Option E is incorrect because when a bill is paid, there is no entry in the profit costs account. Payment of a bill will involve entries in both the client ledger and the cash sheet.

Did you choose the correct answer? YES ☐ NO ☐

See ***Revise SQE: Solicitors Accounts*****, Chapter 6** for a discussion of this area of law.

A42 of 90 (page 70) **Area of law assessed: Criminal law**

The correct answer was D. This is because the prosecution must prove that the man's actions were a substantial cause of the woman's injuries and that there was no break in the chain of causation by any means raised. Both legal and factual causation must be established and proved. Option A is incorrect because the man's actions do not need to be the *sole* cause of the woman's injuries, and the chain of causation can be broken by other means; not just through the acts of a third party. Option B and C are incorrect because both factual *and* legal causation must be established. Option E is incorrect because the chain of causation can be broken by the acts of a third party, an act of God (a natural and unforeseeable event), or by an act of the victim themselves.

Did you choose the correct answer? YES ☐ NO ☐

See ***Revise SQE: Criminal Law*****, Chapter 1** for a discussion of this area of law.

A43 of 90 (page 71) **Area of law assessed: Ethics and professional conduct**

The correct answer was B. This is because the SRA Code of Conduct requires solicitors to draw the court's attention to relevant cases and statutory provisions, or procedural irregularities of which they are aware, and that are likely to have a material effect on the outcome of the proceedings. In this case, an incorrect statement of the law that is favourable to the client's case may have a material effect on the outcome of proceedings. Therefore, the procedural irregularity must be brought to the court's attention (options A and C are therefore incorrect). Option D is incorrect because the obligation under the Code is a personal one: merely directing the prosecutor's attention to the irregularity, for them to then inform the court, is not sufficient to discharge the duty. Option E is incorrect because there is no requirement that the lay bench be dismissed due to the incorrect legal direction; the lay magistrates can simply be redirected on the correct law.

Did you choose the correct answer? YES ☐ NO ☐

See ***Revise SQE: Ethics and Professional Conduct*, Chapter 2** for a discussion of this area of law.

A44 of 90 (page 71) **Area of law assessed: Land law**

The correct answer was C. This is because the power of sale specifies that all mortgages must be repaid in the order in which they were registered. As Bank One was the first interest registered, their whole loan will have to be repaid before Bank Two can recover any money. Options A and B must be incorrect as Bank Two will not be repaid first. Option D is incorrect as after Bank One, Bank Two was the next registered charge. Option E is incorrect as Bank Three is the most recently registered charge, so will be repaid last.

Did you choose the correct answer? YES ☐ NO ☐

See ***Revise SQE: Land Law*, Chapter 8** for a discussion of this area of law.

A45 of 90 (page 72) **Area of law assessed: Wills and the administration of estates**

The correct answer was D. This is because the rule of survivorship applies to joint tenants; meaning that the woman becomes the sole owner of the account upon the death of the man. The joint account balance will not be included in the man's estate and therefore will not be distributed according to the intestacy rules (therefore Option A is incorrect). Option B is incorrect because the bank account was owned as a joint tenancy and not a tenancy in common and so does not form part of his estate. Option C is incorrect because the property does not pass under the intestacy rules and, even if it did, the woman would not be entitled as she was not the spouse of the man. Option E is incorrect because the ex-wife would not be entitled to any property under the intestacy rules.

Did you choose the correct answer? YES ☐ NO ☐

See ***Revise SQE: Wills and the Administration of Estates*, Chapter 6** for a discussion of this area of law.

A46 of 90 (page 72) **Area of law assessed: Land law**

The correct answer was C. This is because a mortgagee is under a duty to obtain the true market value at the time of sale, including accurately advertising the land. The mortgagee, however, has the choice of when and how to sell the land. Option A is incorrect as the incorrect advertising price prevented the land from achieving the true market value. Option B is incorrect as, although the mortgagee acted in good faith, they were negligent in the incorrect advertising. Option D is incorrect as the mortgagee can choose when to sell the property. Option E is incorrect as the mortgagee has the choice as to the method of selling, so long as it exposes the property to the market.

Did you choose the correct answer? YES ☐ NO ☐

See ***Revise SQE: Land Law*, Chapter 8** for a discussion of this area of law.

A47 of 90 (page 73) **Area of law assessed: Land law**

The correct answer was D. This is because, although the agreement states that there is no exclusive possession and the landlord can move in additional licencees, the court will look at the practical substance of the agreement. In this case, the client and her partner's agreements will be read together to grant exclusive possession. Furthermore, as the agreement is for fewer than three years, there are no formalities required for it to be legal. Option A is incorrect as there is no mention of exclusive possession that is required for a valid lease. Options B and E are incorrect as the nature of the agreement is determinative, rather than the wording and those clauses will be ignored. Option C is incorrect as, although there is not a deed, this is not necessary for leases under three years.

Did you choose the correct answer? YES ☐ NO ☐

See ***Revise SQE: Land Law*, Chapter 5** for a discussion of this area of law.

A48 of 90 (page 73) **Area of law assessed: Trusts law**

The correct answer was A. This is because a six-year limitation period applies to breaches of trust. There is no evidence in this case to suggest dishonesty on part of the trustee to prove fraud, nor is there any deliberate concealment by the trustee of the breach of trust (meaning that the limitation period cannot be delayed). As such, the wife's claim is time-barred as the cause of action accrued seven years ago. On the other hand, time does not begin to run against a remainder person until their interest has vested in possession, nor does it run against an infant until they reach the age of majority. For those reasons, the claim of the son and grandson is not time-barred. All other options are therefore incorrect.

Did you choose the correct answer? YES ☐ NO ☐

See ***Revise SQE: Trusts Law*, Chapter 11** for a discussion of this area of law.

A49 of 90 (page 74) **Area of law assessed: Solicitors accounts**

The correct answer was D. This is because the SRA Accounts Rules permit a solicitor to operate a joint account in certain circumstances. For example, this will be appropriate where the solicitor is appointed as an executor of a will alongside one or more other executors who are not employed by the firm. Options A and E are incorrect because client money can be held in a range of accounts beyond just the general client account (option E) or including separate designated deposit client accounts (option A). For example, a solicitor may act as a signatory on a client's own account or operate a joint account in certain circumstances (so option C is also incorrect). A firm can also outsource the management of client money to a third-party managed account. Option B is incorrect because the Rules state that a firm can only use a third-party managed account where it does not operate any of its own client accounts. Money held in a third-party managed account is not client money because it is not under the control of the firm.

Did you choose the correct answer? YES ☐ NO ☐

See ***Revise SQE: Solicitors Accounts*, Chapter 7** for a discussion of this area of law.

A50 of 90 (page 74) **Area of law assessed: Land law**

The correct answer was C. This is because, as a pre-1996 lease, the client will remain bound as the original tenant through privity of contract. However, the tenant will only be liable for any fixed charges, including rent, that became due within the six months prior to a default notice being served. Option A is incorrect as the client will not be liable for the rent from more than six months before the default notice was served. Options B and D are incorrect as the use of Authorised Guarantee Agreements and the release of previous tenants from leasehold covenants are only relevant in post-1996 leases. Option E is incorrect as only the current tenant is bound by privity of estate.

Did you choose the correct answer? YES ☐ NO ☐

See ***Revise SQE: Land Law*, Chapter 5** for a discussion of this area of law.

A51 of 90 (page 75) **Area of law assessed: Ethics and professional conduct**

The correct answer was C. The is because the SRA Code of Conduct requires a solicitor not to mislead or attempt to mislead the court or others, either by their own acts or omissions or allowing or being complicit in the acts or omissions of others (including their client). Should a defendant admit their guilt to their solicitor, the solicitor can continue to represent them but is not permitted to put forward a positive defence case (ie they may only test the prosecution's case). Option A is incorrect because the solicitor is not obliged to withdraw, but is correct in that, should the solicitor withdraw, they must not inform the court of the reasons for withdrawing (which is why Option E is entirely incorrect). Option B is incorrect because any plea must be of the defendant's choosing; the solicitor cannot choose the defendant's plea. Option D is incorrect because the solicitor would be prevented from putting forward a positive defence case.

Did you choose the correct answer? YES ☐ NO ☐

See ***Revise SQE: Ethics and Professional Conduct*****, Chapter 2** for a discussion of this area of law.

A52 of 90 (page 76) **Area of law assessed: Wills and the administration of estates**

The correct answer was D. This is because the grandfather clock and shares in a private company have been disposed of by way of an *inter vivos* trust. All other property in the estate will pass according to the will. Taking each property in turn: The grandfather clock was delivered to the trustee, evidenced by the fact that the trustee has possession of the clock (in addition to an intention to transfer by the woman) prior to the woman's death. This is sufficient to constitute the trust. The house will not pass to the woman's brother as the woman did not execute a valid deed of transfer over the land. Without a deed of transfer, the trust over land cannot be constituted. Furthermore, the formalities for a valid trust over land were not complied with as the declaration was oral, and not evidenced by some writing and signed. The shares in a private company will pass to the woman's son as the woman has made every effort (or has done everything within her power) to constitute the trust by sending the stock transfer form to the trustee. The fault for the lack of registration lies with the trustee; the court will treat the trust as valid in equity. All other options are therefore incorrect as they do not properly identify how the property will be disposed of.

Did you choose the correct answer? YES ☐ NO ☐

See ***Revise SQE: Wills and the Administration of Estates*****, Chapter 6** for a discussion of this area of law.

A53 of 90 (page 76) **Area of law assessed: Solicitors accounts**

The correct answer was A. This is because this disbursement is recorded using the principal method because the firm's name is on the invoice. A VAT-exclusive payment is made from the business account as the firm is liable for the invoice as principal. When the firm bills the client in due course, they will pass on the charge for both the £2,000 fee + £400 VAT, and the accounting records will be updated to record this. Options B and C are incorrect because the entries are for a VAT-inclusive amount (option B) or for the original sum + VAT (option C). The entry on the client ledger should be VAT-exclusive instead. Options D and E are incorrect because payment of disbursements using the principal method must always be from the business account, rather than the client account. Option D is further incorrect as it includes a VAT-inclusive payment.

Did you choose the correct answer? YES ☐ NO ☐

See ***Revise SQE: Solicitors Accounts*****, Chapter 6** for a discussion of this area of law.

A54 of 90 (page 77) **Area of law assessed: Criminal law**

The correct answer was A. This is because this option correctly focuses on the subjective nature of the law relating to fraud by false representation. The man knew that the representation may have been false or misleading but continued regardless. Options B and D are incorrect because the law is not concerned with what the man *should* or *ought* to have known; more so with what that man *actually* knew. Option C is incorrect because there does not need to be a strict intention per se to make the false representation. Option E is incorrect because fraud offences are conduct offences and do not require the prosecution to prove that there was a belief or reliance on the false representation; the focus is on the making of the representation.

Did you choose the correct answer? YES ☐ NO ☐

See ***Revise SQE: Criminal Law*, Chapter 8** for a discussion of this area of law.

A55 of 90 (page 78) **Area of law assessed: Criminal practice**

The correct answer was A. This is because at the first review, an officer of the rank of superintendent or above is required to authorise a further 12 hours of detention (this is also the maximum period of extension at this stage). Option B is incorrect because an inspector is junior to a superintendent. Option C is incorrect because the maximum period of further detention at this stage is 12 hours, not 24 hours. Option D is incorrect because the rank of officer and extension limits are incorrect. Option E is incorrect because, whilst detention can be authorised for the reason given, it must be a superintendent that authorises the further detention.

Did you choose the correct answer? YES ☐ NO ☐

See ***Revise SQE: Criminal Practice*, Chapter 1** for a discussion of this area of law.

A56 of 90 (page 78) **Area of law assessed: Trusts law**

The correct answer was C. This is because in order to give effective consent, there are three elements that must be proved: first, the beneficiary must have the capacity to consent (meaning that they are over the age of 18 and do not suffer from any mental impairment); second, the consent must be freely given (ie without undue pressure or duress); third, the consent must be informed (meaning that the beneficiary has sufficient information about the proposal to give consent). In this scenario, the elder grandson cannot be said to have given informed consent as he is told very little about the proposal (eg he is not informed about the risks involved), and the younger grandson does not have the capacity to give consent due to his age. The man will therefore be liable for breach of trust to both grandsons. All other options are incorrect as they fail to identify an accurate statement of the consent of the grandsons.

Did you choose the correct answer? YES ☐ NO ☐

See ***Revise SQE: Trusts Law*, Chapter 11** for a discussion of this area of law.

A57 of 90 (page 79) **Area of law assessed: Land law**

The correct answer was D. As the lease was created pre-1996, Tenant One is liable under privity of contract and as their business has expanded, Tenant One seems the most financially stable target to recover the cost of repair. Option A is incorrect as Tenant Two is not bound by privity of contract; they were only bound by privity of estate whilst they were tenants. Option B is incorrect as the landlord does not wish to end the lease, therefore forfeiture is not a good option. Options

C and E are incorrect as Tenant Three does not have the resources to pay for the repairs so it is not sensible to pursue it either via either privity of estate or self-help.

Did you choose the correct answer? YES☐ NO☐

See ***Revise SQE: Land Law*****, Chapter 5** for a discussion of this area of law.

A58 of 90 (page 79) **Area of law assessed: Trusts law**

The correct answer was E. This is because there is a lack of certainty as to the beneficial shares of the beneficiaries (the two children). Dictating that the 'majority' should be given to the daughter is uncertain and the trust cannot take effect. An automatic resulting trust will thus take effect in favour of the woman, or her estate (therefore option A is incorrect). Option B is incorrect because there is sufficient certainty as to the intention of the woman; the issue is subject matter. There is no intention to gift the property to the best friend; therefore, it would be unconscionable to allow the friend to keep the shares and money absolutely for themselves (therefore option C is incorrect). Option D is incorrect because the objects of the intended trust are certain (the two children); the issue is subject matter.

Did you choose the correct answer? YES☐ NO☐

See ***Revise SQE: Trusts Law*****, Chapter 7** for a discussion of this area of law.

A59 of 90 (page 80) **Area of law assessed: Ethics and professional conduct**

The correct answer was D. This is because the SRA Code of Conduct requires a solicitor not to abuse their position by taking unfair advantage of clients or others, and must not mislead or attempt to mislead others. By requesting the solicitor to submit multiple contracts to bidders, the seller is engaging in a contract race. To ensure compliance with the Code (which does not explicitly deal with contract races), the solicitor must obtain the consent of the seller to disclose the presence of a race to the potential buyers. If such consent is not forthcoming, the solicitor must cease to act, but must not disclose the reason for ceasing to act (in order to maintain their client's confidentiality). The other options do not represent the proper course of conduct that should be taken in contract races.

Did you choose the correct answer? YES☐ NO☐

See ***Revise SQE: Ethics and Professional Conduct*****, Chapter 7** for a discussion of this area of law.

A60 of 90 (page 80) **Area of law assessed: Wills and the administration of estates**

The correct answer was D. This is because inheritance tax is levied on the estate of the woman and it is the responsibility of the executor of the will to pay the tax from the assets of the estate before distributing them to the beneficiaries (ie the two children). The woman's estate is valued at £800,000 and is subject to inheritance tax. The executor of the will is responsible for calculating the amount of inheritance tax due and paying it to HMRC before distributing the remaining assets to the children per the will. Options A and B are therefore incorrect. Option C is incorrect as the government is not responsible for paying inheritance tax. Likewise, the woman's creditors are not responsible for inheritance tax (therefore option E is incorrect).

Did you choose the correct answer? YES☐ NO☐

See ***Revise SQE: Wills and the Administration of Estates*****, Chapter 10** for a discussion of this area of law.

A61 of 90 (page 81) **Area of law assessed: Land law**

The correct answer was B. This is because, although the original covenant is only a qualified covenant, this is converted to a fully qualified covenant by statute. Therefore, the landlord can only refuse consent if they have reasonable grounds. As family feuds do not relate to their ability to fulfil their obligations as a landlord or tenant, these will not be reasonable. Option A is incorrect as the landlord can refuse consent reasonably. Options C and E are incorrect as the landlord is not able to refuse permission for personal reasons, including family feuds. Option D is incorrect as there is not a fully qualified covenant.

Did you choose the correct answer? YES ☐ NO ☐

See ***Revise SQE: Land Law*, Chapter 5** for a discussion of this area of law.

A62 of 90 (page 81) **Area of law assessed: Criminal practice**

The correct answer was B. This is because a referral order is where the youth agrees to be bound by a contract of behaviour that aims to address the cause of offending, and can only be imposed by a youth court or adult magistrates' court; the Crown Court cannot impose a referral order. This is why Options A and C are incorrect. Option D is incorrect because, whilst referral orders are considered mandatory where a youth pleads guilty to an imprisonable offence, there are additional criteria to meet. Option E is incorrect because there are some instances where referral orders are mandatory.

Did you choose the correct answer? YES ☐ NO ☐

See ***Revise SQE: Criminal Practice*, Chapter 10** for a discussion of this area of law.

A63 of 90 (page 82) **Area of law assessed: Land law**

The correct answer was A. This is because the landlord must serve notice in order to be able to forfeit an occupied property; the tenant will be able to claim relief and the court will consider whether it is fit to do so. As the client is prepared to remedy the breach and is capable of doing so, the court will likely see it as equitable to grant relief. Option B is incorrect as this is a residential property and the tenant is in occupation, so peaceable re-entry is not permitted. Option C is incorrect as the landlord is not able to deal directly with the sub-tenant; their only remedy is against the client. Option D is incorrect as a landlord is able to forfeit a lease for breach of a repairing covenant so long as it is fair to do so. Option E is incorrect as the tenant is willing to carry out the repairs, so it will be deemed equitable to grant relief from forfeiture.

Did you choose the correct answer? YES ☐ NO ☐

See ***Revise SQE: Land Law*, Chapter 5** for a discussion of this area of law.

A64 of 90 (page 82) **Area of law assessed: Criminal practice**

The correct answer was C. This is because a grave crime is considered one that does not have a term of imprisonment fixed by law, but one that can be punished by imprisonment for at least 14 years for an adult offender over the age of 21. Option A is incorrect because the punishment is not fixed by law. Option B is incorrect because the term of imprisonment must be at least 14 years. Option D is incorrect because the relevant period of imprisonment must apply to an adult offender over the age of 21 – not 18. Option E is also incorrect for this reason, and because the punishment cannot be fixed by law.

Did you choose the correct answer? YES☐ NO☐

See ***Revise SQE: Criminal Practice*****, Chapter 10** for a discussion of this area of law.

A65 of 90 (page 83) **Area of law assessed: Criminal law**

The correct answer was A. This is because the defence of loss of control is open to the man in these circumstances, as the man seemed to act in response to things said or done by the woman (often referred to as the 'anger trigger'). It will be a question of fact for the jury, but the loss of control does not need to be sudden. Option B is incorrect because there is no requirement for the loss of control to be sudden. Option C is incorrect because the 'fear trigger' is not the only trigger to cause a loss of control. This option ignores the 'anger trigger'. Option D is incorrect because the question of being 'seriously wronged' for these purposes is *subjective*, not objective. Option E is incorrect because this answer relates to the defence of diminished responsibility, not loss of control.

Did you choose the correct answer? YES☐ NO☐

See ***Revise SQE: Criminal Law*****, Chapter 5** for a discussion of this area of law.

A66 of 90 (page 84) **Area of law assessed: Wills and the administration of estates**

The correct answer was C. This is because the small estates procedure appears to apply in the instant case. The small estates procedure permits payment by the relevant organisations (ie the bank, Department of Work and Pensions and NS&I) to be made without the grant of representation where the value of the asset does not exceed £5,000. This procedure permits payment without a grant; it does not oblige the organisations to make payment without a grant. As such, it is wrong to suggest that the man's daughter *must* apply for the grant of representation (therefore options A and E are incorrect). Options B and D are incorrect for the same reason: the man's daughter cannot be advised that she will not have to apply for the grant of representation; her conduct is determined by the relevant organisations.

Did you choose the correct answer? YES☐ NO☐

See ***Revise SQE: Wills and the Administration of Estates*****, Chapter 7** for a discussion of this area of law.

A67 of 90 (page 85) **Area of law assessed: Criminal law**

The correct answer was A. This is because a principal offender is the offender who commits both the actus reus and mens rea of the substantive offence, and may well be considered as the offender who actually commits the offence. The woman will be the principal offender whilst the man will be an accessory (therefore option D is incorrect). Option B is incorrect because this is a definition of a joint principal offender and only the woman would be a principal offender. Option C is incorrect because this is an inaccurate description of a principal offender; this is a description of an accessory. Option E is incorrect because a principal offender commits both the actus reus and mens rea of the substantive offence.

Did you choose the correct answer? YES☐ NO☐

See ***Revise SQE: Criminal Law*****, Chapter 2** for a discussion of this area of law.

A68 of 90 (page 86) **Area of law assessed: Criminal law**

The correct answer was B. This is because the solicitor has a duty to act in the man's best interests and has been provided with information that may give rise to a defence. The solicitor should identify that elements of the diminished responsibility defence are present. Option A is incorrect because the man does not have a definitive defence of diminished responsibility at this stage. Option C is incorrect because the man *may* have a defence of diminished responsibility, and the solicitor would not be forming a defence from the facts, merely investigating whether the defence is open. Options D and E are incorrect because *significant impairment* and *abnormality of the mind* are inaccurate terms to describe the elements of the diminished responsibility defence.

Did you choose the correct answer? YES ☐ NO ☐

See ***Revise SQE: Criminal Law*, Chapter 5** for a discussion of this area of law.

A69 of 90 (page 86) **Area of law assessed: Criminal law**

The correct answer was E. This is because in cases where the defendant was voluntarily intoxicated when an offence of basic intent was committed (in this case, likely a battery), the defence of intoxication cannot be relied upon (unless the intoxicant is non-dangerous and the defendant is not reckless in taking the intoxicant) (therefore option D is incorrect). Option A is incorrect because the intoxication defence does not apply where the offence is one of basic intent. Option B is incorrect because the voluntary intoxication defence may only be relied upon where the offence is one of specific intent. Option C is incorrect because battery is a basic intent offence (therefore intoxication is not a defence).

Did you choose the correct answer? YES ☐ NO ☐

See ***Revise SQE: Criminal Law*, Chapter 4** for a discussion of this area of law.

A70 of 90 (page 87) **Area of law assessed: Wills and the administration of estates**

The correct answer was C. This is because the statutory order must be followed unless there is a direction in the will to the contrary. Option C is the only option that correctly identifies the correct order by which assets in the estate will be used to satisfy debts. Naturally, if there are no assets of that description, or not enough to satisfy the debts, the next asset in the list will then be considered.

Did you choose the correct answer? YES ☐ NO ☐

See ***Revise SQE: Wills and the Administration of Estates*, Chapter 8** for a discussion of this area of law.

A71 of 90 (page 87) **Area of law assessed: Ethics and professional conduct**

The correct answer was E. This is because the SRA Code of Conduct requires a solicitor not to abuse their position by taking unfair advantage of clients and must act in the client's best interests. There is nothing preventing the solicitor from benefitting under the will that they draft, but the client must obtain independent legal advice before any such clause can be drafted. All other options are therefore incorrect.

Did you choose the correct answer? YES ☐ NO ☐

See ***Revise SQE: Ethics and Professional Conduct*, Chapter 6** for a discussion of this area of law.

A72 of 90 (page 88) **Area of law assessed: Criminal practice**

The correct answer is B. This is because the review clock begins when the man's detention is first authorised by the custody officer, and a detention review must be undertaken in three stages: the first review must be undertaken no later than 6 hours after the man's detention is first authorised; the second review no later than 9 hours after the first; and any subsequent reviews at intervals not more than 9 hours. In practice, this means that a review must be undertaken (at the latest) at the 6-hour mark, the 15-hour mark, and the 24-hour mark. Option A is incorrect because the *detention clock* begins when the man first arrives at an authorised place of detention, not the *review* clock. Option C is incorrect because the timeframes are incorrect. Options D and E are incorrect because the timeframes given are detention time limits - not review timeframes.

Did you choose the correct answer? YES☐ NO☐

See ***Revise SQE: Criminal Practice*****, Chapter 1** for a discussion of this area of law.

A73 of 90 (page 88) **Area of law assessed: Wills and the administration of estates**

The correct answer was C. This is because the 1975 Act clearly establishes which persons have standing to make a claim for financial provision. Taking each person in turn: the man's current girlfriend does not have standing as she has not been living in the same household as the man for the whole of the period of two years ending immediately before the date when the man died (she has only been living with him for six months). The man's ex-wife does not have standing as she has remarried, and is thus prevented from making a claim; had she not remarried, the ex-wife would have standing subject to the wording in the divorce settlement. The man's 21-year-old son has standing as the child of the deceased; the age of the son does not affect his standing. The man's brother has standing on account that he was being wholly or partly maintained by the man immediately prior to his death. The man was making a substantial contribution in money towards the reasonable needs of the brother (ie payment of bills and debts). Option C is the only option that identifies the correct persons with standing.

Did you choose the correct answer? YES☐ NO☐

See ***Revise SQE: Wills and the Administration of Estates*****, Chapter 9** for a discussion of this area of law.

A74 of 90 (page 89) **Area of law assessed: Criminal law**

The correct answer was B. This is because mere presence at the scene of an offence is insufficient to convict through accessorial liability. The friend would have needed knowledge of the essential matters, and the friend would have needed to intend to assist or encourage the man to commit murder with knowledge of the man's intent. Option A is incorrect because mere presence at the scene is *not* sufficient, unless such presence encourages the commission of the offence. Option C is incorrect because this is a misstatement of the law. Option D is incorrect because there is no need for the man to be convicted of the more serious offence for the friend to be convicted as well. Option E is incorrect because again, mere presence at the scene is not sufficient.

Did you choose the correct answer? YES☐ NO☐

See ***Revise SQE: Criminal Law*****, Chapter 2** for a discussion of this area of law.

A75 of 90 (page 89) **Area of law assessed: Criminal practice**

The correct answer was B. This is because a defendant who is not of absolute good character may nevertheless be treated as being of effective good character where a previous conviction is old, minor, and of limited relevance to the present offence charged. In such cases, the trial judge has a discretion as to whether, and how, to give a good character direction. The judge may modify the direction to reflect the nature and age of the conviction, give either or both limbs (credibility and propensity), if fair and appropriate and should explain the relevance of the defendant's largely good character whilst acknowledging the conviction. Option A is incorrect because a previous conviction does not automatically prevent a good character direction. Option C is incorrect because the judge is not required to give a full direction; the matter is discretionary and may be modified. Option D is incorrect because both limbs may still be relevant for a defendant of effective good character. Option E is incorrect because the judge must provide appropriate legal directions to the jury where character evidence is in play; the judge cannot leave the jury to speculate.

Did you choose the correct answer? YES ☐ NO ☐

See ***Revise SQE: Criminal Practice*****, Chapter 7** for a discussion of this area of law.

A76 of 90 (page 90) **Area of law assessed: Criminal law**

The correct answer was C. This is because a charge of committing fraud by abuse of position is most suitable to the facts of this case. The woman was in a position that is arguably akin to one with a fiduciary duty: there was an expectation to safeguard her aunt's financial interests and she conducted herself dishonestly, resulting in a financial gain. Options A and B are incorrect because the facts are more akin to fraud by abuse of position. Option D is incorrect because there is nothing to suggest that the woman was under a legal duty to disclose any information in the facts. Option E is incorrect because the woman was not expected to act *against* the financial interests of her aunt.

Did you choose the correct answer? YES ☐ NO ☐

See ***Revise SQE: Criminal Law*****, Chapter 8** for a discussion of this area of law.

A77 of 90 (page 90) **Area of law assessed: Ethics and professional conduct**

The correct answer was E. This is because the SRA Code of Conduct requires a solicitor to safeguard money and assets entrusted to them by clients and others. By holding money in a separate client account, the solicitor is complying with this obligation. The solicitor would be in breach of the Code and the SRA Accounts Rules by using client money for their own personal expenses or for use by other clients (even if they intended to repay the money). Therefore, options A and D are incorrect. Options B and C are incorrect because the solicitor must not hold client money in their own personal or business account, given the risk of the solicitor's own insolvency and the need to protect client money.

Did you choose the correct answer? YES ☐ NO ☐

See ***Revise SQE: Ethics and Professional Conduct*****, Chapter 8** for a discussion of this area of law.

A78 of 90 (page 91) **Area of law assessed: Trusts law**

The correct answer was A. This is because the friend will likely be able to assert a beneficial interest in the house by way of a common intention constructive trust. Whilst there is no express common intention to share the property, the court may find there to be an implied common intention. In order for there to be an implied common intention, the courts would have to look at the conduct of the parties, specifically at the financial contributions of the parties. Generally, only direct contributions towards the purchase price of a house can be used to find a common intention; such contributions may be to the initial payment, or payment towards mortgage instalments. Option A is the only option involving a contribution to the purchase price of the house over the three-month period. Option B is incorrect because the installation of a new kitchen, whilst it may increase the capital of the house, does not contribute to the purchase price. It has been suggested in *obiter* that making improvements that added significant value to the property should be sufficient to generate an interest. However, the best answer remains a direct contribution to the purchase price. Option C is incorrect because, whilst the friend did contribute to the initial purchase of the house, this money was a loan and cannot be regarded as a financial contribution. Option D is incorrect as ancillary contributions (such as the conveyancing fees) are not financial contributions to the purchase price. Option E is incorrect as the contribution must be of a financial nature to the purchase price; caring for the woman's children is not sufficient to find a common intention constructive trust.

Did you choose the correct answer? YES ☐ NO ☐

See ***Revise SQE: Trusts Law*, Chapter 8** for a discussion of this area of law.

A79 of 90 (page 91) **Area of law assessed: Ethics and professional conduct**

The correct answer was B. This is because the SRA Code of Conduct requires a solicitor to safeguard money and assets entrusted to them by clients and others. Equally, the SRA Accounts Rules state that solicitors can only withdraw client money from a client account for the purpose for which it is being held, following receipt of instructions from the client, or on the SRA's prior written authorisation. In this case, the money is held in the client account for the purposes of completing a commercial transaction. In essence, the solicitor cannot withdraw client money from a client account for any purpose other than that for which it was intended, and a client account must be separated from the firm's general account, a solicitor's personal account or another client's account. All other options are therefore incorrect.

Did you choose the correct answer? YES ☐ NO ☐

See ***Revise SQE: Ethics and Professional Conduct*, Chapter 7** for a discussion of this area of law.

A80 of 90 (page 92) **Area of law assessed: Property practice**

The correct answer was B. This is because the standard conditions state that the purchase price is inclusive of VAT if the seller opted to tax prior to completion. Option A is incorrect because the property is an old commercial building and not therefore zero-rated, and whether VAT is payable depends on whether the seller opted to tax prior to completion (a fact that option A does not account for). Option C is incorrect as it has been used as a factory since 1975; it would only be standard-rated if it was a new freehold commercial building. Option D is incorrect as the standard commercial property conditions state that VAT is payable if it is required by the seller. Option E is incorrect as the purchase is not a transfer of a business as a going concern but is being changed from a factory to a multi-storey car park. If it was a transfer of a business as a going concern, VAT would not be chargeable on the transaction.

Did you choose the correct answer? YES ☐ NO ☐

See ***Revise SQE: Property Practice*, Chapter 10** for a discussion of this area of law.

A81 of 90 (page 92) **Area of law assessed: Wills and the administration of estates**

The correct answer was B. This is because a lifetime transfer will be immediately chargeable for inheritance tax if it exceeds the annual exemption limit (£3,000) and if the gift was made within seven years of the donor's death. However, the annual gift exemption of £3,000 can used to reduce the inheritance tax burden, and can be rolled forward from a previous year if unused. Therefore, the woman can use the exemption from four years ago (£3,000) and the exemption from three years ago (£3,000) to reduce the inheritance tax burden by £6,000. This means that the remaining £4,000 of the gift is now subject to inheritance tax. Lifetime transfers are gifts made by the donor during their lifetime to the donee. Depending on the specific conditions of the transfer, they can either be immediately chargeable, meaning that they are immediately subject to inheritance tax, or potentially exempt, meaning that they may become subject to inheritance tax in the future. All other options are therefore incorrect.

Did you choose the correct answer? YES ☐ NO ☐

See ***Revise SQE: Wills and the Administration of Estates*, Chapter 10** for a discussion of this area of law.

A82 of 90 (page 93) **Area of law assessed: Criminal law**

The correct answer was D. This is because the third woman is the principal offender as she actually committed the substantive offence. The first woman and the second woman assisted and encouraged the commission of the substantive offence. Option A is incorrect because the second woman did not, herself, commit the actual burglary; she never entered the property. Option B is incorrect because the third woman was the only woman who committed the burglary. Option C is incorrect because procuring the tools to commit burglary, and not going on to commit the substantive offence, does not make the second woman a principal offender. In addition, the third woman is the principal offender. Option E is incorrect because this is not an accurate definition of a principal offender.

Did you choose the correct answer? YES ☐ NO ☐

See ***Revise SQE: Criminal Law*, Chapter 2** for a discussion of this area of law.

A83 of 90 (page 93) **Area of law assessed: Land law**

The correct answer was C. This is because the root of good title is the most recent document that is more than 15 years old and deals with or shows ownership of the whole legal and equitable interest in the land. Option C is therefore the most recent document that fulfils this criterion. Options A and D are incorrect as they do not deal with the ownership of the property. Options B and E are incorrect as they both predate the conveyance.

Did you choose the correct answer? YES ☐ NO ☐

See ***Revise SQE: Land Law*, Chapter 2** for a discussion of this area of law.

A84 of 90 (page 94) **Area of law assessed: Trusts law**

The correct answer was C. This is because there are three anomalous exceptions to the beneficiary principle: gifts for the care of single-named animals; gifts for the erection and maintenance of tombs and monuments; and gifts for the saying of private masses. All three exceptions must comply with the rules against perpetuities (21 years given that no life is being specified). The perpetuity period must be for no longer than a specified life plus 21 years, or in the absence of a specified life, simply 21 years. As the woman has specified that the trust is to last no longer than 10 years, this will not offend the perpetuity rules. However, the gifts must still satisfy the requirement of certainty (ie certainty as to what the purpose of the trust is). The clause that reads 'providing some useful memorial to myself' is not sufficiently clear; what constitutes a 'useful memorial'? As such, the gift to look after the dog and to say a private mass are valid, but the gift for a memorial is not valid. For these reasons, all other options are incorrect.

Did you choose the correct answer? YES ☐ NO ☐

See ***Revise SQE: Trusts Law*, Chapter 6** for a discussion of this area of law.

A85 of 90 (page 94) **Area of law assessed: Wills and the administration of estates**

The correct answer was C. This is because a personal representative has a duty to ensure that any inheritance tax (IT) or capital gains tax (CGT) due on the estate's income and gains is correctly calculated and paid to HMRC. The personal representative can be held personally liable for any unpaid tax, interest and penalties due on the estate's income and gains. In this case, the man has a duty to ensure that any IT or CGT due on the rental income or gains made from selling the properties is correctly calculated and paid to HMRC. It is his personal responsibility to ensure that this is done, regardless of whether he distributes the assets (options A and B are therefore incorrect). Option D is incorrect because the personal representative can be held personally liable for any unpaid tax, interest and penalties due on the estate's income and gains, regardless of the estate's value. Option E is incorrect because both executors and administrators have the same duty to ensure that any IT or CGT due on the estate's income is correctly calculated and paid to HMRC.

Did you choose the correct answer? YES ☐ NO ☐

See ***Revise SQE: Wills and the Administration of Estates*, Chapter 10** for a discussion of this area of law.

A86 of 90 (page 95) **Area of law assessed: Solicitors accounts**

The correct answer was A. This is because the principal method must be used to pay the invoice because it is in the firm's name. The firm must therefore pay the invoice (including VAT) from the business account as the valuation service has been provided to them as principal. The solicitor can then pass on these charges (including VAT) when they deliver their bill to the clients. Option B is incorrect because the principal method requires payment to be made from the business account. It cannot be made from the client account as the invoice is not in the names of the clients. Option C is incorrect because both the charges and the VAT must be paid from the business account when using the principal method. Options D and E are incorrect in that they state the payment must be made by the agency method (although option E goes on to correctly describe payment by the principal method). Option D is further incorrect as it states that payment can be made from the client account. This is never correct for a disbursement being paid using the principal method.

Did you choose the correct answer? YES ☐ NO ☐

See ***Revise SQE: Solicitors Accounts*, Chapter 6** for a discussion of this area of law.

A87 of 90 (page 95) **Area of law assessed: Wills and the administration of estates**

The correct answer was E. This is because capital gains tax (CGT) is levied on the increase in the capital value of an item, measured from the price at acquisition to the sale price. The shares have appreciated in value by £50,000; it is this amount that will be subject to CGT (the difference between the acquisition price and the sale price). CGT is not payable on capital losses; therefore, the man is not liable for CGT on the land. All other options are therefore incorrect.

Did you choose the correct answer? YES ☐ NO ☐

See ***Revise SQE: Wills and the Administration of Estates*, Chapter 10** for a discussion of this area of law.

A88 of 90 (page 96) **Area of law assessed: Property practice**

The correct answer was A. This is because there is no longer a time limit for prosecuting in respect of a breach of building regulations control, and an enforcement notice requiring work to be altered or removed can be served within 10 years of completion of the works. Option B is incorrect because planning and building regulation regimes are independent of each other, and therefore it is pertinent to check that both have been complied with. Option C is incorrect: because the works were completed after 1 October 2023 and therefore as the work was completed two-and-a-half years ago, an enforcement notice requiring work to be altered or removed can still be served within the next seven-and-a-half years. This is because enforcement proceedings can now be brought within 10 years from completion of the work under the Building Safety Act 2022. Option D is incorrect because enforcement options such as injunctions can be used after the one-year enforcement period if the works are unsafe (Building Act 1984, s 36(6)). Option E is incorrect because although a full structural survey may identify the property as structurally sound, there is still a risk of enforcement action.

Did you choose the correct answer? YES ☐ NO ☐

See ***Revise SQE: Property Practice*, Chapter 3** for a discussion of this area of law.

A89 of 90 (page 96) **Area of law assessed: Trusts law**

The correct answer was A. This is because the woman has a strong claim of proprietary estoppel. An assurance has been made to the woman that she can live in the house rent-free for as long as she wants, and that assurance has been detrimentally relied on by the woman (who could have taken another job elsewhere). The assurance was that she can remain in the house (ie a right to occupancy), as opposed to having an interest in the house (therefore, option C is incorrect). Option B is incorrect as the woman has acted to her detriment in remaining with the family. Option D is incorrect as it is irrelevant that the disabled family member has died; the focus is on the assurance given and the detrimental reliance of the woman. Option E is incorrect because the remedy available is discretionary and not automatic.

Did you choose the correct answer? YES ☐ NO ☐

See ***Revise SQE: Trusts Law*, Chapter 8** for a discussion of this area of law.

A90 of 90 (page 97) **Area of law assessed: Property practice**

The correct answer was D. This is because the landlord has the choice of remedies between damages and specific performance, the latter requiring the tenant to do something. Option A is incorrect because an injunction would not force the tenant to do something; this is relevant in relation to breaches of negative covenants. Option B is incorrect because the lease was granted after 1996, so former tenants would not be liable unless they entered into an authorised guarantee agreement. If the agreement had been entered into before 1 January 1996, the basic principle would be that the original tenant remains bound by the covenants in the lease. Option C is incorrect because the breach is not related to non-payment of rent and therefore the landlord would need to serve notice prior to attempting to forfeit the lease. Option E is incorrect because whilst the landlord may be able to seek specific performance, it is not the only remedy available to the landlord.

Did you choose the correct answer? YES ☐ NO ☐

See ***Revise SQE: Property Practice*, Chapter 8** for a discussion of this area of law.

Your results

Now add your scores for Session 1 and Session 2 together, and award yourself an overall mark out of 180.

Your total score for Session 1: ______ **/ 90**
Your total score for Session 2: ______ **/ 90**
Your total raw score for FLK2: ______ **/ 180**

■ PASS MARK

In September 2023, the SRA amended the manner in which candidates are scored for the FLK1/2 assessments, following the introduction of week-long assessment windows. The SQE now features 'scaled scoring', which is designed to eradicate any unfairness between candidates of the same ability sitting FLK1/2 across different papers in the same assessment window.

Candidates sitting FLK1/2 will therefore be provided with two scores:

- Raw score: this is a mark out of 180 to reflect how many questions the candidate answered correctly.
- Scaled score: this is a mark out of 500 to reflect the candidate's relative performance according to the difficulty of their paper, compared to a paper another candidate will have taken. The relative difficulty of the paper will be assessed by the SRA and a formula will be designed to create the scaled score.

There is no pass mark for the raw score on FLK2. However, the pass mark for the scaled score will always be 300 (ie 60%). In order to pass SQE1, you must therefore score at least 300.

According to the SRA Marking and Standard Setting Policy, the pass mark is determined by the SRA Assessment Board through the Modified Angoff method. This method involves a panel of qualified solicitors familiar with Day One competence, which reviews each question and predicts how many out of 10 just-competent Day One solicitors would answer the question correctly. A summary and average of the rating for each question by each member of the panel produces a cut score.

Further statistical processing based on the actual performance of the candidates and to correct for measurement errors is then carried out to arrive at a final pass mark for the assessment. Whilst the pass mark for the scaled mark will remain 300 for every sitting, it is not possible to state the number of questions a candidate must answer correctly (ie the raw score) in order to pass the assessment. Furthermore, the formula used to create the scaled score will be relative for each assessment sitting and cannot simply be recreated for our purposes.

For this reason, it is not possible to prescribe a pass or fail result based upon your performance in *FLK2 Practice Assessments*. The SRA has provided information based upon previous sittings of SQE1 to assist your understanding of the likely pass mark, contained in Table 5.

Table 5: Pass mark and rate of FLK2

Date of SQE1 assessment	FLK2 pass mark	FLK2 pass rate
November 2021	56% (101 correct answers)	54% (out of 1078 candidates)
July 2022	55% (99 correct answers)	55% (out of 1981 candidates)
January 2023	56% (101 correct answers)	56% (out of 3253 candidates)
July 2023	53% (96 correct answers)	66% (out of 3647 candidates)
January 2024	300 (scaled score)	61% (out of 6476 candidates)
July 2024	300 (scaled score)	50% (out of 5519 candidates)
January 2025	300 (scaled score)	61% (out of 7230 candidates)
July 2025	300 (scaled score)	48% (out of 6442 candidates)
January 2026	300 (scaled score)	57% (out of 8461 candidates)

You can access the statistical breakdown for subsequent assessments on the SRA (sqe.sra.org.uk) and Revise SQE (revise4law.co.uk) websites.

Remember:

- Only **you** can decide when, and if, you feel adequately prepared to sit SQE1.
- Only **you** can decide when is the appropriate time to sit SQE1.
- Do not be complacent, and remember to ensure that you are fully prepared by using all resources available to you.

You can use the companion volume, *FLK1 Practice Assessments, Mock Exam No.1*, to test your knowledge in preparation for the first SQE1 assessment.

Final words and FAQs

We hope that you found *FLK2 Practice Assessments* to be beneficial in your preparation for the real SQE1 assessments.

■ FINAL WORDS

Whilst reflecting on your performance in this practice assessment, we advise the following:

- Review your answers to the practice questions carefully. If there are any MCQs that you answered incorrectly, consider whether you need to return to one of our *Revise SQE* guides to consolidate your understanding and knowledge. If you answered an MCQ correctly, do not become complacent; stay on top of your knowledge and understanding.
- Review your approach to answering MCQ-style questions. Use the guidance at the start of every *Revise SQE* guide, and the advice in the Introduction of this book to assist you.
- Review your preparation for sitting a closed-book timed assessment. Consider how you best retain large amounts of information, and whether you need to consider a different approach to retaining information. If nerves got the better of you, what could you do to mitigate this in the future?

The team at *Revise SQE* wish you the best of luck in your SQE1 assessments.

■ FREQUENTLY ASKED QUESTIONS

Below are a number of FAQs that you may have about SQE1. If you have a question not considered below, please get in touch with the team via our social media channels, where we will endeavour to answer your questions.

1 **Do I need a degree to sit SQE1?**

Whilst you do not need to have a degree (law or otherwise) to sit the SQE1 assessments, you cannot be admitted as a solicitor without a degree or an equivalent qualification.

2 **Do I have to undertake an SQE-preparation course?**

You are not required to undertake an SQE-preparation course in order to undertake the SQE1 assessments. However, if you wish to consider an SQE-preparation course, visit the Revise SQE website at revise4law.co.uk for a list of providers.

3 **When do the SQE1 assessments take place?**

In January 2024, the SQE1 sittings moved to week-long (Monday to Friday) assessment windows for each component, with FLK1 assessments in week 1 and FLK2 assessments in week 2. Subject to availability, you will be able to pick whichever day in each week you prefer. For example, you might choose to sit FLK1 on Monday in week 1 and FLK2 on Friday in week 2. Dates will be published 12 months before the relevant assessment window.

4 **What are the SRA rules on verifying my ID?**

When you register for the SQE, you have to provide a valid, official photo identification. You will need to upload an image of your ID when you register, to allow the SRA to authenticate it and verify your identity. Suitable ID includes a passport or photocard driving licence. The SRA recommends using a passport.

5 **What ID is required on the day of my SQE1 assessment?**

You must bring two forms of ID with you to both of your SQE1 assessments - a 'primary' and 'secondary' form of ID:

- The primary form of ID must include a photograph of you (eg a photocard driving licence or passport).
- The secondary form of ID must contain your full name and signature (eg a signed debit or credit card).

The SRA warns that if you fail to present the correct forms of identification, you will be denied entry to the examination and forfeit your examination fee. Furthermore, the name on your ID must exactly match the name you provided when you registered with the SQE.

6 **Are reasonable adjustments available for SQE1?**

Under the Equality Act 2010, the SRA has an obligation to make reasonable adjustments for any person who has a disability. Whilst all candidates must be assessed against the Statement of Solicitor Competence and the Statement of Legal Knowledge, and must reach the Threshold Standard to qualify, reasonable adjustments will be made to ensure that candidates with disabilities are not disadvantaged.

It is the responsibility of the candidate to identify that they require reasonable adjustments when they register for the SQE1 assessments, and supporting evidence is required. Reasonable adjustments are determined and afforded on a case-by-case basis, but can include additional time and breaks, a separate room, a reader and many more. The SRA has a dedicated page on reasonable adjustments for SQE on its website (sqe.sra.org.uk).

7 **Is there a dress code for sitting SQE1?**

There is no dress code for SQE1. You can wear what you feel comfortable in, but you may be asked to remove bulky external clothing during security checks. You are advised to wear sufficient layers of clothing to ensure you are comfortable, depending on the room temperature at the test centre.

8 **What if something happens during the assessment?**

Following the SQE1 assessment, if you feel something has happened that could affect your performance during the assessment, you can submit a claim for 'mitigating circumstances'. These include:

- a mistake or irregularity in the administration or conduct of the assessment
- evidence of bias in the conduct of the assessment
- subject to the Fit to Sit Policy and SQE Assessment Regulations, a candidate's illness or other personal circumstances beyond their reasonable control which have materially and adversely affected their marks or performance in the assessment, or are likely to.

Disagreement with the academic judgment of the assessors cannot amount to mitigating circumstances.

9 When do I find out about my results in the real SQE1 assessment?

You will get your results approximately 5-6 weeks after the final sitting in the assessment window of FLK2 for SQE1. In most cases, results will be released while the booking window for the next SQE2 booking window is still open. Alongside the assessment dates, the SRA also publishes the results day on their website. The SRA will send you an email notifying you that the results are available in your SQE account. Results will only be posted within your account on the SQE website and will not be sent out to you. You will be able to save them as a PDF.

10 What do I get when I receive my results for the real SQE1 assessment?

For each FLK assessment, you will receive information about the date of the assessment, the date of the transcript, the attempt number of that sitting, the deadline to pass SQE and the pass mark expressed as a scaled score (always 300). For each FLK assessment, you will also receive two scores as part of your results: a raw score (out of 180) and a scaled score (out of 500). You will also receive a breakdown of results by practice area (out of 500) to allow you to see which practice areas you have performed well in, and which areas you might need to work on. Finally, you will be provided with your quintile score (ie where you are placed in your assessment, in comparison to everyone else who took the assessment with you) and your result (ie whether or not you have passed - for which you must score 300 or above on the scaled approach).

11 What is a quintile score in SQE1?

Candidates are afforded a quintile score as part of their results for SQE1. Your quintile score tells you how you were placed in comparison to other candidates sitting the SQE. This score is likely to be relevant to employers. There are five categories:

- 1st (top) quintile candidates - the top 20% of performers
- 2nd quintile - the next 21–40%
- 3rd quintile - the next 41–60%
- 4th quintile - the next 61–80%
- 5th quintile - the final 81–100%.

12 When can I book SQE2 assessments?

Unless you have an exemption from sitting SQE1, you cannot book SQE2 until you have received your results for SQE1. Similarly, you cannot book to resit an SQE1 assessment until you have received the results for your previous attempt at that assessment.

13 How many attempts do I get at SQE1?

You will only be allowed three attempts at both FLK1 and FLK2. These have to be taken within six years from the first attempt of an SQE assessment. The clock starts from the first day of the first assessment you sit. If you fail FLK1 and/or FLK2 three times during this six-year period, you must wait until that six-year period expires before reapplying, and previous passes will not be carried forward.

14 Can I retake an assessment I have passed?

You cannot resit an assessment you have passed to improve your marks, under any circumstances.

15 Do I have to pass both FLK1 and FLK2?

In order to pass the SQE, you must pass both SQE1 and SQE2. SQE1 consists of two exams, FLK1 and FLK2, and you must achieve the necessary mark in both to pass SQE1 as a whole. If you fail either FLK1 or FLK2, you are only required to resit the assessment that you failed. You must also pass both SQE1 and SQE2 in order to apply to become a solicitor.

16 If I fail an assessment, do I have to pay a resit fee?

Yes, a fee is required if you have to resit either FLK1 or FLK2. The full SQE fee is required if a candidate has to resit both FLK1 and FLK2. The current resit fees are available on the SRA website.

17 Can I appeal if I fail SQE1?

Yes, there is a process for appealing against the decision of the Assessment Board. Any appeal must be made on one of the recognised grounds, and must be made in writing via the Appeals Form, which is available in your candidate account. A fee is required to be paid to submit an appeal; this fee is refundable if your appeal is upheld. The SRA has published an Appeals Policy, available on its website.